Gary Morecamssful career as a
publicist for a full-time writer
in 1982 and h m biography to
fiction. After l has now settled
in Wiltshire with his wife Tracey and their three sons, Jack, Henry
and Arthur.

Martin Sterling was born in Manchester in 1962. A freelance
writer and broadcaster, he has extensive experience in journalism
and has written plays and television scripts. This is his second book.
He now lives in Norfolk and his special interests include theatre,
film, literature and current affairs.

This book is dedicated to all those who find themselves mentioned somewhere between its covers: in some way, big or small, you are all part of the story of Morecambe and Wise.

Acknowledgements

The authors would like to extend a huge personal thank you to all those who have helped us write this biography. Without them, this would have been a very thin book.

We are particularly indebted to Rowan Atkinson, Bill Cotton, Ben Elton, Bryan Forbes, Michael Grade, Glenda Jackson, Philip Jones, Penelope Keith, Jan Kennedy of Billy Marsh Associates, Ernest Maxin, Warren Mitchell, Des O'Connor, Angela Rippon, Sir Harry Secombe, Jimmy Tarbuck, Baroness Thatcher and John Thaw.

For their support and practical help, we would also like to thank Tracey Bartholomew, David Coupe, Jennifer Luithlen and Dorothy Twist; and also Louise Dixon, Jeremy Robson and everyone at Robson Books who has helped make the publication of this book such an easy and enjoyable process.

We would also like to thank Catherine Hurley and Pan Books for ensuring this paperback version was equally easy and enjoyable.

And we would like to say a big thank you to Joan Morecambe and Ernie Wise, without whom this book would have been an impossibility.

Morecambe and Wise

Behind the Sunshine

Gary Morecambe & Martin Sterling

PAN BOOKS

First published 1994 by Robson Books Ltd

This edition published 1995 with an epilogue by Pan Books
an imprint of Macmillan General Books
Cavaye Place London SW10 9PG
and Basingstoke

Associated companies throughout the world

ISBN 0 330 34140 5

9 8 7 6 5 4 3 2 1

A CIP catalogue record for this book is available from the British Library

Phototypeset in North Wales by Derek Doyle & Associates, Mold, Clwyd.
Printed and bound in Great Britain by Cox & Wyman Ltd, Reading, Berkshire

Introduction

Behind the Sunshine strives to analyse the relationship between Eric Morecambe and Ernie Wise, while studying the background and people so relevant to making this comedy duo equipped to sustain nearly five decades of laughter-making.

From childhood hopefuls they became acknowledged legends but, in spite of Eric claiming that 'showbusiness is all fun', the journey was at no time as easy as they portrayed it.

Though a biographical book, this is also a documentary. It offers a glimpse into the world and fluctuating fortunes of early- to mid-twentieth-century British entertainment; a lavish and unpredictable era of board-treading artistes, lack-lustre theatrical agents, variety treadmills and landladies of varying temperament and ability.

Above all else it is a serious attempt to deliver the full history of Morecambe and Wise while examining the style and method of their work, which endured not just the arrival of other comedy acts, but also the constantly changing face of society.

This year, 1994, marks the tenth anniversary of Eric Morecambe's sudden death, and the pages of this book have proved an opportune time and place for friends and colleagues alike to discuss Morecambe and Wise in a surprisingly uninhibited way. With their comments and judgements, and comparisons to other double acts such as their inspiration, Laurel and Hardy, as well as our own analysis and assessment, this book tries to understand how the right foundations for Morecambe and Wise were put in place, and how the combination of these two personalities was unique to British light entertainment.

For me, as Eric Morecambe's son, it has at times been difficult to write with total objectivity. I have, however, been fortunate to have a co-author in Martin Sterling who, being unrelated to Morecambe or Wise, has remained totally unbiased in his probing search for hard truth and knowledge. Where I have found myself on occasion tending towards familiar clichés and platitudes as a means of easy escape, Martin has intercepted with honest critical opinion and observation.

Inevitably this book is a miscellany, and it is at times deliberately discursive. Not inappropriate, really, as Morecambe and Wise were formed of so many intriguing components that went beyond the basic comic-feed relationship of their numerous predecessors, and whose trademark was fast cross-talk and controlled confusion.

What both Morecambe and Wise wanted from their comedy was only the same as Laurel and Hardy, Abbott and Costello, and scores of other comics before and after them, wanted. Indeed, it is probably what every comedian has always wanted but not always achieved. To make people laugh.

It is surely the apparently simple nature of much of their humour that makes it so enduring and so instantly recognisable as Morecambe and Wise. As Eric himself once wrote, 'I know what makes me laugh and I know that I can make others laugh with it.'

ERNIE: Any telephone calls for me while I was out?
ERIC: A director rang from Hollywood. Alfred somebody.
ERNIE: Hitchcock?
ERIC: He might have, I didn't ask.

That a new generation can enjoy Morecambe and Wise in full flow is the true testament to their genius.

GM, 1994

1

*'Dealing with Morecambe and Wise was
like dealing with one life-form.'*

Billy Marsh

For many people in Britain in May 1984, hearing of Eric
Morecambe's death was like hearing of the death of a member of
their own family. That reaction transcended the simple fact that
Eric was a popular comedian: Tommy Cooper had died just
months earlier and, although he is still keenly missed, his death
didn't generate the same outpouring of national mourning as
Eric's. Just as people old enough were able to recall where they
were and what they were doing when they heard Kennedy had
been assassinated, so many Britons will always recall their
circumstances when hearing of Eric Morecambe's final, fatal heart
attack.

Put simply, the Morecambe and Wise partnership, which began
when two teenagers put together a few jokes to do a double act in
1941 and developed into the most celebrated comedy team in
Britain, was part of our national psyche.

Throughout the 1970s, half the nation would routinely sit down on Christmas Day to watch their TV special. The day after any Morecambe and Wise show had been transmitted it would be the main topic of conversation in offices and factories across the country.

Suddenly, it was over. Morecambe was gone. Wise was left without a partner. And a little bit of us all had died with Eric.

Fortunately, a decade after Eric's death, the act lives on in the immortality of videotape. It preserves them at their peak and allows us to relive their inspired lunacy, often imitated but never equalled.

Slip in a tape, and Eric and Ernie are at once incompetent stage hands putting the boot into Shirley Bassey. Here they are with André Previn who is exasperated with Eric's attempts to play Grieg's Piano Concerto. And here's the classic take-off of *Singin' in the Rain*, which dared to be more memorable than the original; so much so that Gene Kelly felt compelled to offer his own praise when viewing it on a visit to London. Routines that are now twenty years old, but as fresh and funny as ever.

TV producers still search in vain for the 'new' Morecambe and Wise. Many have aspired to duplicate their success and national acclaim but it has eluded them all. The 'Eric and Ernie' tag alone is proof of that. Everyone knows who is being referred to when 'Eric and Ernie' are mentioned.

In a sense, the traditional double act all but died with Eric since the most successful double acts to succeed them – The Two Ronnies, French and Saunders, Smith and Jones, Fry and Laurie – are not, strictly speaking, double acts. They are pairings of two performers who quite often work successfully apart (in the same manner as Hope and Crosby, and Martin and Lewis across the Atlantic). We also have the Hale and Pace type of double act: very professional but targeted at adult audiences, as shown by the late hour their shows are screened. And it is surely no coincidence that the annual TV comedy treat for recent Christmases has been a sit-com: *Only Fools and Horses*. Morecambe and Wise have not been replaced because they are simply irreplaceable.

But why were they so popular? Crucially, Morecambe and Wise cut across all social classes and appealed to every age group. Innuendo was acceptable; blue material was not. That was a constant rule. Ernie describes their humour as 'Naughty schoolboy humour'.

They never offended and had no political axe to grind. Deliberately choosing to deprive themselves of these safety devices so often used by other acts, Morecambe and Wise were still sharper than any of them with Eric, in particular, acknowledged by the critic Kenneth Tynan as possessing the most devastatingly incisive brain in comedy.

The result was immense popular appeal, the breadth of which astonished even Eric and Ernie themselves.

'Broad is usually the term for bawdy, basic humour, which theirs certainly wasn't,' says Rowan Atkinson, 'but they had broad appeal. It's difficult to find that these days: something which all the family, from the age of six to sixty, can enjoy and identify with. There wasn't anything going over the heads of children, or very little, and generally middle-aged and older people liked it as well. Everyone had genuine enthusiasm for them.'

It was this sheer love for Morecambe and Wise which brought their shows a guest list comprising the very top names from politics and theatre. Glenda Jackson, Vanessa Redgrave, Elton John, Cliff Richard, Dame Flora Robson, Nanette Newman, Dame Judi Dench, Peter Cushing, Keith Michell, Frank Finlay, Lord (Harold) Wilson, Lord (Laurence) Olivier, Sir Ralph Richardson, Sir Robin Day, Sir John Mills are but a few of those who appeared on the show.

Politicians felt especially safe in their hands because Eric and Ernie were never partisan. When former Labour Prime Minister, Harold Wilson, appeared on their Christmas show in 1978, the set was decked out in 'Vote Conservative' stickers; and Baroness Thatcher, who knew Eric from the late 1950s onwards, told the authors in August 1993, that she was a great fan of the Morecambe and Wise show.

The Royal Family were longtime devotees of the act, and the Queen Mother even once asked them how Eric did his little trick with the paper bag and imaginary ball.

'Eric always told me that the reason we were so successful was that we stayed together,' says Ernie. 'A simple enough statement, but also very profound. We were together from the early 1940s, and from that moment on we sweated at it. We were good rehearsers and hard workers who were determined to persevere.'

They also benefited from the sheer diversity of their showbusiness experience, succeeding, though not always immediately, in each new medium embarked upon. They were there as a musical hall/variety act in the 1940s and 1950s. They saw that medium die, so moved into radio, then television, always returning to traditional variety until that, itself, died.

By the time Morecambe and Wise were at their peak, most of the other acts they had struggled with and worked with were gone. But Morecambe and Wise were still there, joking about Ernie's wig and insulting their famous guest stars. They had stayed the course – or stayed together, as Eric rightly said – and emerged triumphant.

Performing together, Eric and Ernie were as one. Anyone standing in the wings of a theatre just moments before the curtain went up on a Morecambe and Wise show, was astonished by one curious thing: the absence of visible tension. It was presumably there – probably buckets of it – and had been, no doubt, for several hours before the curtain went up. But it was totally suppressed by a far greater emotion: the genuine delight Eric and Ernie got from performing in front of a theatre audience. They viewed it almost as an indulgence: something to feel slightly guilty about when the cheque came in. Eric even said in later years that the theatre shows had become so easy. He wasn't being complacent. What he meant was that it was something they had done all their lives and theatre audiences, who had originally been their bread and butter, were still the foundation of their viewing public.

Television studio audiences were receptive, too, but the whole concept and process of television is very different from a stage appearance. Though the final product was much the same as if Morecambe and Wise had been filmed in a theatre – the cross-talk, the music hall tabs, the guest stars, the song and dance – TV diluted the pace. Theatre is immediate and personal whereas studios are metallic, alien places; a high-tech environment where everything stutters along in a mass of separate sections, gelled during and after by producer and editor watching it all as it happens on hidden monitors.

Some acts found it impossible to make the transition and, in the same way that many silent movie stars' careers were destroyed by the coming of sound, so too were many variety performers' by television.

Despite a disastrous first outing with their own show, when Eric and Ernie listened to others instead of their instincts, Morecambe and Wise adapted to it brilliantly – ironically because they didn't noticeably alter their variety act to suit the medium. But it shouldn't, by rights, have been the natural medium in which they could display their comic talent.

'I've never worked alone!' quipped Eric in one of their TV shows when he'd driven an irate Ernie from the stage. And that's how the audience wanted it to stay. Not for Eric and Ernie the departure to a sit-com. Morecambe and Wise were the act, period. They didn't work separately because, put bluntly, the public wouldn't let them. And by the 1970s, when they were the biggest comedy draw around with no serious pretenders to their throne, that public also wanted them to stay just as they were.

More than a decade before Eric died, both Eric and Ernie were making public noises about wanting a change from their successful and universally popular format. But deep down, both men knew that a radical change was out of the question. Having been together since 1941, they now found themselves the nation's premier clowns, which – while a great honour and achievement – gave them the added pressure to produce shows that were at least as good as the last.

By 1983, Eric hinted he was tiring of comedy and was finding a new direction in life: writing books. He found it increasingly tiresome to attempt to produce humour; to go through the gruelling ritual of writing, rehearsing and recording shows to meet such high expectations. He also said that he no longer enjoyed being funny; that he would rather try a straight role in something completely divorced from Morecambe and Wise.

Whether he would have changed his mind and they would have gone straight back into another series or Christmas show, one can only speculate. But assuming Eric was genuinely prepared to finish the partnership, the reason why one of our greatest British clowns should even have contemplated such a thing at the relatively young age of fifty-six is arguably the most fascinating and hitherto unexplored area of the whole Morecambe and Wise story.

Eric Morecambe's status as a comic legend will for ever be recognised. But while he was alive, the downside of this was that Ernie's role was usually eclipsed by his partner's. This is a customary professional hazard for the straight man. Lest anyone be in any doubt of Ernie's value to the partnership, those who knew and worked with the duo point out that Eric's genius needed the best partner in the business, and in Ernie Wise he got it.

Despite being a double act of the traditional school, it is misleading to label Morecambe and Wise purely as funny man and feed. For another fascinating aspect of their story is the way they subtly evolved over their forty-three years together. Their standard double act roles became so blurred that at their peak it became increasingly hard to define which one was what in relation to their act.

Their timing was – still is – a joy to behold, and it enabled them to scale comic heights with even the slightest material. But it was another sort of timing which was to play a crucial part in their success story.

Had they been ten years older or younger, it is entirely possible they might not have enjoyed success at the level they finally did. Not only did television emerge as a force more or less simultaneously with Morecambe and Wise arriving fresh-faced but reasonably experienced on the scene but, as Glenda Jackson has pointed out, success in show business has less to do with where a performer is at any given time than with where the audience is.

For the first two decades of their careers, Morecambe and Wise were clearly ahead of their audiences. In the 1960s and 1970s their audiences caught up with them, and they achieved astonishing ratings with successive shows. This neatly coincided with them being within what they both considered the essential twenty-year peak of a comic's career. Morecambe and Wise believed true comic creativity was at its height between the ages of thirty and fifty. Comics younger than that ran the risk of seeming too inexperienced: older ones ran the even greater risk of tragedy, with audiences recalling them in their heyday. Both men had seen the problems declining years created; in the 1950s they witnessed their inspirational heroes, Stan Laurel and Oliver Hardy, mumbling to half-filled British theatres in the tragic nadir of their careers.

After Eric Morecambe's death, increasing competition from video, satellite and cable began to fragment TV audiences. This means that ratings figures of twenty-eight million are now all but unattainable for any programme. The shared common culture of mass television watching no longer exists as it did in the 1970s.

Timing was also important in bringing the two performers together at a young age. Because they worked together from their early teens, their most formative years were spent developing the shared trust which would later lift their act above that of any of their rivals. By the time they reached thirty, they'd already worked as a double act for fifteen years and had endured the downs of showbusiness together, just as they would go on to enjoy increasing popularity and eventual stardom.

And there had been some terrible downs. The Eric and Ernie who were watched by an audience of twenty-eight million viewers on Christmas Day 1977 were the same Eric and Ernie who had walked on to the stage of the Glasgow Empire in the 1950s to the sound of their own footsteps, and walked off to the same sound. They were the same Eric and Ernie who had been sacked after a week at Vivian Van Damm's glorified strip-joint, the Windmill, in 1949, because another double act was deemed funnier. And they were the same Eric and Ernie who, in 1954, found their first TV series rubbished so severely by every television critic in the land that they thought themselves finished, with Eric vowing never again to make another television series.

One final, happy timing in their lives was that they benefited from having been born at a time when Hollywood was really beginning to exert its global influence; and at a time when variety, although already starting to display the first signs of terminal illness, would stagger on long enough to give them the opportunity to hone their craft in front of live audiences.

The embryonic double act would watch the films of Laurel and Hardy, and of Abbott and Costello, and absorb the essence of their popularity. Exposed to the whole seductive glamour of Hollywood's musicals – of sequined ball-gowns, top hats and tails, of the exquisite movements of Astaire and Kelly down endless sweeping staircases – they would store those memories through the decades until they finally unleashed some glorious pastiches on television audiences.

Coming in at the tail end of variety, they still found themselves sharing bills with some of the biggest names in showbusiness, like Max Miller or Adelaide Hall, who passed on useful advice to the budding stars.

Although they were both married and spent little time together when not performing, Eric and Ernie were inseparable in the mind of the public from 1941 to 1984. Theirs was a professional association stretching through five decades, and built on the solid foundations of mutual trust and respect – what 1990s psychologists would doubtless dub 'Male Bonding'.

A criticism of Ernie in any small way in front of Eric would bring Eric down on you like a ton of bricks. Criticise Eric in front of Ernie, and it was the same story. In interviews, Eric would say something and Ernie would finish it, or vice versa. Small wonder their longtime agent, Billy Marsh, likened working with Eric and Ernie to dealing with one life-form.

When Eric Morecambe died, Morecambe and Wise ended for good. But the act will never be forgotten, and their incomparable comic legacy will remain as long as a TV screen exists. As the late Dickie Henderson once remarked, 'Whenever you think of Eric you smile. And the entire nation feels that way. That's a tremendous legacy to leave.'

Theirs is a complete and inspiring story of two working-class Northern lads who worked and struggled to prove they were good. Against all odds, they achieved the seemingly impossible when they captured the love and imagination of the viewing public.

It is a story, too, of a very determined lady called Sadie Bartholomew, who was to ensure it all happened.

2

'... The three of us were inseparable.'

Ernie Wise

Without Sadie Bartholomew, there wouldn't have been, couldn't have been, Morecambe and Wise.

From the first moment when she suggested they team up as a double act, she elected herself as the driving force that took them to their first successes, and the chaperone to protect them against the harshest realities of the professional variety circuit.

While they struggled to put together and then sustain their double act, she began thinking up new routines for them. And when inspiration eluded her, she did not blanche at stealing other comics' material to incorporate into their act – though, as she probably justified it to herself, the pirating of jokes was a common enough practice among comedians in variety at that time.

And yet, unlike the fictitious Mrs Worthington, whom Noël Coward lyrically implored not to push her daughter on to the boards, Sadie was not the archetypal showbusiness mother in any recognised sense. Coward's superbly-crafted tirade was accurately aimed at the mother whose showbusiness aspirations blind her to any limitations in her child's talent: limitations that are more than apparent to the rest of us. Sadie Bartholomew was no Mrs Worthington. She wasn't a fool with fanciful dreams. She knew her son, John Eric Bartholomew, had talent. And when she saw Ernie Wise for the first time, she knew he had talent, too. Although she was, naturally enough, the first to spot it in Eric, she was by no means the first to recognise Ernie's talent since, by the time of their first meeting, he was already established as a child star with a West End show and several radio broadcasts behind him.

With remarkable perception, however, she was the first to recognise that a fusion of these complementary talents in a double act would more than double the sum of its parts. Once she had recognised this herself, she was dedicated to the task of making sure that others did too.

Joan Morecambe, Eric's widow, who grew exceptionally close to Sadie over the years, accepts that it's all too easy to dismiss Sadie as just another stage mum, but claims this perception is profoundly flawed.

'It always hurts me when she's described that way because she wasn't like that all. There were lots of stage mothers around at that time and, believe me, they were hard women. That had a lot to do with the harsh environment many of them lived in. They had stars in their eyes and, yes, wanted the best for their children. But, basically, they saw a way that fame and fortune could come to them through their children.

'Sadie, though, was both too intelligent and too fair for that to be her motive. She was shrewd, she was tough – criticising Eric when she felt he warranted it – but also extremely fair. And the bottom line was she was just going to do the very best she could for Eric – and, later, for Eric and Ernie.'

In later years, when Eric and Ernie were established major stars, and journalists questioned Sadie's motives in pushing them forward in the beginning, Eric quashed any suggestion of selfishness on her part. 'Her motives? They were the highest,' he said. 'I was her only child and she had ambitions for me beyond the average run-of-the-mill working-class man.' Which meant in Sadie's own expression, she didn't him want him tied to a whistle as his father had always been.

Sadie was not interested in, or fuelled by, any thoughts of self gain. She was not desperately materialistic and was a likeable, confident and practical person who had little space in her life for personal glory.

In those later years, when she would occasionally be pointed out as 'Eric Morecambe's mother' she would allow herself the luxury of enjoying the reflected glory, but always in a modest, understated manner. A compliment or two at the market place in Lancaster was enough. And it was the best reward she could have wished for.

That's not to say she had never had ambitions of her own. Sadie loved showbusiness and she'd have liked a career on the stage. But in the early years of the twentieth century the theatre was still deemed an unsuitable working environment for 'proper' girls. In fact in conservative Lancashire, where she spent virtually her whole life, a career of any kind wasn't really on the agenda.

Marriage. The rearing of children. These were the only real expectations for women of Sadie's class and generation. So any thoughts of the stage were surrendered from the beginning. Perhaps she could have succeeded in another field.

'She could have been a writer,' says Joan. 'She really did have a rare gift for words, and when you consider the little education she'd had, she was a very bright lady indeed who read enormously. She was also a great talker: in fact, you had difficulty getting away from her sometimes because she just wanted to talk and talk about anything and everything.'

That ability with words was coupled with the sharpest of minds which meant that Sadie could relate a story, fact or fiction, with great lucidity.

She was also prodigiously decisive; a trait which was ably demonstrated when, on meeting George Bartholomew, she decided instantaneously that he was the man she would marry.

Their marriage surprised everyone, not least, it seems, George, and not only for the bold manner in which Sadie had entrapped him. On the surface they appeared to family and friends alike to be complete opposites. She was short, forceful, bright, determined and confident. He was tall, happy-go-lucky with a gentle disposition and generous nature, always wholly content with his lot.

'I envied my dad his quiet dignity and philosophy,' said Eric in the 1970s, 'and his delight in simple pleasures such as watching the sunset over Morecambe Bay. He truly believed that sunset to be the most magnificent in the world.'

But although Eric loved his father, it was with his mother he could more easily identify. Essentially, Sadie believed that anything was possible in life if you worked for it. She doughtily faced the world head-on – however vulnerable she herself felt at times – believing you should stretch yourself without letting limitations stop you from going for your chosen goal.

The Bartholomews, though, came from intrinsically conservative stock which regarded any kind of celebrity with the deepest suspicion and doubted the capacity of any 'flash-in-the-pan' success to provide lasting security.

These two opposites, Sadie and George, respected each other's basic philosophies for the rest of their lives together and neither changed the other, nor tried to. If being the mother of Eric Morecambe occasionally allowed Sadie to bask modestly in her son's fame, being his father altered George's life not one jot. Indeed, long after Eric had achieved fame and fortune, George continued to work resolutely on with the Morecambe Corporation until his natural retirement. By that time he'd worked there for forty-five years, two years longer than Eric's partnership would last with Ernie.

George and Sadie were married in Morecambe and made their home at 48 Buxton Street. On 14 May, 1926, they had what was to be their only child: a boy whom they christened John Eric Bartholomew, but who would be remembered as Eric Morecambe.

Six months earlier, on 27 November, 1925, Ernest Wiseman, with whom Eric was destined to be forever linked, was born in Yorkshire.

One of five children, Ernie was brought up in East Ardsley, which is between Wakefield and Leeds. Harry, his father, was a railway porter who had won a medal for bravery during the First World War when he'd saved a sergeant's life – an experience he rarely talked about.

Just as the marriage between George and Sadie Bartholomew had been the attraction of opposites, so was that of Ernie's parents.

Ernie's mother, Connie, came from a respectable and comparatively well-to-do family who, when she married Harry, thought she'd married far beneath her.

Her father felt this so strongly that he tried everything in his power to prevent the wedding: when his persuasion and blackmail failed, he cut her out of his will for going against his wishes.

'All she left home with was the piano she had saved so hard for as a young woman,' says Ernie.

Unlike Eric, who naturally gravitated towards his mother's influence, Ernie feels he inherited opposing characteristics from his parents: the performing show-off qualities of Harry, and the shyer, introverted nature of Connie.

Though Eric's upbringing was far from affluent, by comparison the Wiseman household was positively deprived in the material, though not emotional, sense.

Money was the single burning issue which divided Harry and Connie. Connie was careful with money, and with seven mouths to feed she had good reason to be. As he became older and witnessed her constant battle with meagre financial resources, Ernie's own attitudes to money were moulded. Though his later comic persona of being parsimonious was largely exaggerated by scriptwriters, Connie's horror of debt would be shared by her son for the rest of his life.

Where Connie was careful, Harry was far more laid-back about money. 'Although he always tipped up his wages at the end of the week and kept only a small portion back for a smoke and a drink,' says Ernie, 'he had a reckless way with money which my mother was at a loss to understand.'

The result of the Wisemans' differing attitudes to financial matters meant that while Connie struggled to feed the family, Harry was sending away to the newspaper for a home movie projector which he would crank by hand to project on to the pantry wall.

Not surprisingly, to his children, Harry was a source of wonderful sunny memories, full of optimism and energy. Harry's own father had toured Northern working men's clubs as a singer and Harry had followed him, being a well-established amateur performer on the circuit by the time Ernie was born.

'Money was the reason he did it,' says Ernie. 'I suppose there could've been some desire to be on the stage, but the real reason was to supplement the family income. He performed out of a sense of duty and habit rather than from the pleasure of performing.'

Within a few years of Ernie's birth, Harry sensed that this child, more than the others, had inherited the Wiseman performing characteristics, and he began teaching him to tap-dance.

When Ernie displayed a natural aptitude for dancing, his father decided they should tour the working men's clubs as a double act which finally ended up being called 'Bert Carson and His Little Wonder'. The act formed a bond between father and son which has always remained with Ernie.

Launching themselves on to the amateur club circuit, 'Bert Carson and his Little Wonder' soon earned for themselves a reputation which led to a solid date-book of good bookings. They also created worries for themselves. At the age of seven, Ernie was far below the legal age permitted for performing: the result was that when he accepted bookings for their act, Harry always had to keep one eye out for the local education authorities.

Not that Ernie's education suffered. Education was something he endured rather than enjoyed: an attitude he was unwittingly sharing with his future partner.

Eric Bartholomew – the John had been discarded almost at once in favour of his second name – was also no scholar. For both Eric and the school, his attendance at Lancaster Road Council School was a non-event. 'I spent most of my time in the school lavatory smoking anything I could ignite,' he confessed many years later.

Eric's indifference to school could not be shaken even by pushing from Sadie, who was frequently disappointed by his reports. But for Ernie, his own indifference was compounded by the horrendous treatment meted out to him by the education establishment.

Describing himself as being 'just plain dumb', Ernie often found he was the target for physical and mental abuse from the cruel teachers he encountered at the depressing Victorian edifice called East Ardsley Secondary School. One teacher, in particular, who knew of Ernie's increasing reputation as a performer out of school, seemed to delight in regularly humiliating him in front of his classmates. The result was that Ernie was ill at ease in school, and his thoughts often turned to performing: a world where he was appreciated and applauded. Fortunately, Ernie did not have to suffer the abuse of his school for long. National fame was to be his by the time he was thirteen.

For some years the Bradford *Telegraph and Argus* had staged an annual charity show called 'The Nignog Revue'. Featuring children, it was staged at the Alhambra Theatre in Bradford. Ernie joined the Nignogs in 1936, and appeared in three of their revues over the next couple of years.

In 1938, the impresario Bryan Michie was touring the north of England looking for juvenile talent for a revue. Following his success with 'The Nignog Revue', Ernie auditioned for Michie, but heard nothing for several months. Then, out of the blue, he was contacted by the impresario and bandleader, Jack Hylton, who'd been tipped off about Ernie by Michie. In a turn of events straight out of a Hollywood wish-fulfilment fantasy, Hylton invited Ernie to London to audition for his show, *Bandwagon*, which was playing at the Prince's Theatre (now the Shaftesbury).

Ernie auditioned for Hylton in his office above the theatre on the morning of 7 January, 1939. Hylton was so impressed that he put Ernie into the show that same evening. An unknown thirteen year old sharing the stage with Arthur Askey, the star of *Bandwagon*! 'Even now,' says Ernie, 'that wonderful succession of events has a fairy-tale quality.'

Immediately the railway porter's son from Leeds became a media sensation and he made front-page news in many papers being described variously as a 'thirteen-year-old Max Miller' and 'a great discovery'.

Hylton signed him to a three-year contract, and changed his name from Ernest Wiseman to Ernie Wise.

But if the railway porter's son was a sensation, there was no place for the railway porter himself. Hylton did offer Harry a contract but, because of his responsibilities at home, he felt he couldn't possibly accept. Pausing just long enough to determine that Ernie was in safe hands, Harry returned alone to Leeds. He was just thirteen years old, but Ernie would never live at home again. Although Ernie would not be aware of it until years later, Harry never really got over this separation from his son.

While Ernie was on his remarkably brief journey from West Yorkshire unknown to West End star, his future partner was grudgingly enduring dance lessons paid for by Sadie's taking on extra work as a waitress.

Eric did not enjoy the lessons and was unaware of just how important a part they would ultimately play in his future, when song and dance would be so important a part of the Morecambe and Wise shows. Sadie, though, was determined he should have the lessons, and her determination to see him do something useful with himself – especially in view of his increasingly dire school results – was her motivation.

In later years, when with Ernie he was steadily climbing the variety bills, Eric would frequently express the opinion that Sadie had been hard on him in those early years, but also fair. Indeed, he would often take great pleasure from making gentle gibes at her, as though exacting revenge for what she'd made him achieve.

The truth though, as they both knew it, was that he would have achieved much less in his life without her constant support. Since this was perfectly well understood between them, the gibes were a ritualistic repartee of their relationship, good-naturedly accepted by both of them.

A vague-minded child, Eric had been in need of Sadie's alert focusing: even throughout his teens and early twenties, Sadie felt it impossible to slacken her grip on him. It was precisely this determined pushing of Eric which was to prove so vital to his future success. And the dancing lessons were a perfect example of this.

'I didn't want to do them; simple as that,' said Eric. 'I never liked the lessons and I'd have much preferred to have spent my time kicking a ball around with my mates.'

But Sadie's insistence paid off. Slowly, Eric not only became adept at dancing but also began to put together a little act which included take-offs of Flanagan and Allen and Fred Astaire.

Gradually, Eric Bartholomew became more assured and as his self-confidence grew, so he began entering and then winning a succession of local amateur talent contests in cinemas and ballrooms.

One of these competitions was held in Hoylake in 1939, and he won. The win, as reported in *Melody Maker*, led to one of his first reviews:

> There were a hundred competitors in the area and the ten finalists appeared at the Kingsway Cinema, Hoylake, a week ago. Eric Bartholomew put over a brilliant comedy act which caused the audience to roar with laughter. In an interview, he said, 'My ambition is to become a comedian. My hero is George Formby.'

Though Eric's most influential role models would later be Laurel and Hardy, and Abbott and Costello, Formby was his first comedy hero – mainly because Formby, like himself, came from Lancashire. (Eric's admiration for Formby led to an amusing mix-up when he met Hollywood star Cary Grant many years later. Grant told Eric that he, too, was a George Formby fan. Only after they had talked 'Formby' for several minutes did it dawn on Eric that Grant was in fact talking about Formby's father, who had pre-empted his son as a stage act a generation before.)

Eric's prize as winner of the Hoylake competition was an audition before Jack Hylton. It was also destined to be his first meeting with Ernie Wise.

To say Eric was less than enthusiastic about his prize is an understatement: he hated auditions and the cap-in-hand uncertainty of the young artiste. Indeed, despite Sadie's opinion to the contrary, Eric did not actually much care for performing at all. In fact, he found it a chore and years later admitted that he'd never enjoyed performing until he and Ernie had become 'names' and started making a good living from it. So, as well as doing it because he was untrained to do little else, he was doing it for Sadie.

She genuinely believed he adored performing, and was unaware of his real feelings – and didn't choose to take them on board when he spelt them out in future years. Had Eric displayed abject misery, then she would not have pushed at all, and comedy would have been deprived of one of its greatest clowns.

The part of his routine Eric loathed most was when he sang the old Ella Shields number *I'm Not All There*, dressed in a cut-down tail-coat, short trousers, red socks and a flat beret. The idiotic image was rounded off with his sucking of an enormous wooden lollipop. Eric kept that prop in his attic until the day he died, as a constant reminder of where he'd come from.

However much Eric privately had misgivings about performing, both he and Sadie knew that the opportunity to audition in front of Hylton was too good to miss.

By this time Hylton and Michie were touring the country with a 'child discoveries' show. By its very nature, the show required a constant stream of new discoveries and Sadie, in particular, appreciated that being taken on by Hylton at this time would be a marvellous kick-start to a career in showbusiness.

In 1939, most people were preoccupied with the political situation which was inexorably drawing Britain into war. But Sadie was concerned only with Eric's future as they travelled from Morecambe to Manchester. 'She drummed into me all the way from Morecambe that this just might be the most important day of my life,' said Eric. 'And she was right, of course.'

The audition was held in a cinema in the centre of Manchester, and Jack Hylton was not the only person present: sitting next to him was his thirteen-year-old protégé, Ernie Wise. This was, however, to be no great meeting between the two future giants of British comedy. On their first encounter they exchanged nothing more than one or two meaningful stares. Ernie was impressed by Eric, and until that moment had felt virtually unassailable. The excited ripples caused by his overnight stardom had scarcely died away and Jack Hylton had clearly selected him as the star of the future he wanted to promote. In Eric, Ernie at once sensed a young and talented challenger to his position, and he readily admits that for the first time he felt threatened.

Eric, himself, was unaware how well he'd done at the audition, a feeling reinforced by Hylton's noncommittal response when Sadie tentatively broached the matter.

Hylton's response of, 'Your boy's talented, Mrs Bartholomew. Maybe we can use him. We'll let you know,' gave her little to cling to on the journey home.

As the weeks passed and there was no subsequent word from Hylton's office, both Sadie and Eric came to the conclusion that

Hylton's words, roughly translated, had been the old showbiz put-down, 'Don't call us, we'll call you.' Having accepted that, it was all the more surprising and joyous when, three months after the audition, Sadie received a telegram from Hylton.

'It asked if I could appear at the Nottingham Empire as one of Bryan Michie's discoveries in the touring show, "Youth Takes a Bow",' said Eric. 'My mother was expected to join me as chaperone on the tour, and my salary was to be five pounds a week plus travelling expenses for the two of us.' It was obviously an offer they couldn't refuse, and mother and son set out on the road to Nottingham.

Two months into the run with 'Youth Takes a Bow', Eric heard a rumour circulating through the cast that Ernie Wise was joining them at Swansea. Though still only thirteen, Ernie was most definitely a star to the rest of the young cast. Not only had he co-starred with Askey in *Bandwagon*, but as a direct result of this he had made several radio broadcasts for the BBC. For Ernie it was the archetypal Hollywood dream: discovery and instant stardom.

'Even before I'd won that contest at Hoylake, I knew who Ernie Wise was,' said Eric. 'I can remember listening to him and a girl called Mary Naylor on the radio with Arthur Askey and "Stinker" Murdoch.

'Ernie was taller than me in those days. And he was in long trousers. He joined the train at Crewe, but I didn't meet him until somebody's mother introduced him to my mother while I was there. He said, "Hi!" in a breezy fashion and bounced off. I used to watch him on stage, and he was good. He could do a good tap-dance and he looked so assured. But I thought he was a big-head.'

What no one realised was that Ernie's cockiness hid a desperate sense of homesickness after the initial euphoria of *Bandwagon* had worn off – no one, that is, apart from Sadie, who sensitively picked up at once what Ernie's problem was and took him under her wing. In turn, Ernie took to Sadie instantly, and despite Eric's initial doubts regarding his future partner, once they began talking there was an immediate spark between them.

Their friendship wasn't the only one they would form among fellow 'discoveries'. Another face who would later be a regular feature on the BBC Morecambe and Wise shows came into their lives at that time: Arthur Tolcher, the harmonica player. He would be used in their 'live' dates as well as their TV shows as a running gag. At the most inappropriate moment, Tolcher would run on with his harmonica to play a few bars only to be told by Eric and/or Ernie, 'Not now, Arthur!'

The importance of the 'Youth' tour at the very start of their careers cannot be over emphasised. It was excellent grounding for performers, like Eric and Ernie, who were aiming to make a living from professional variety because it not only gave them the invaluable experience of working in front of 'live' audiences – a luxury not enjoyed by many acts starting out in the 1990s – but it also exposed them to older, experienced performers. Michie's show devoted the second half to the 'discoveries', but the first half comprised traditional, professional, variety acts. So while they were learning their trade, they had the opportunity to work alongside established acts such as Adelaide Hall and Tessie O'Shea. More important from Eric and Ernie's standpoint were the comedians they were exposed to. In the case of 'Youth Takes a Bow', the regulars included Archie Glen and a double act, Moon and Bentley.

At this time, of course, there was no suggestion of Eric and Ernie performing a double act together, and it was merely their casual friendship which developed in the first few months of their tour. For one thing, Ernie was developing his persona as a sophisticated young song and dance man: for another, they had been taken on to perform their separate, individual acts within the show.

In Oxford, however, both fate and war brought them closer together in a move which would fuse their personal friendship and lead to the inevitability of them pooling their respective talents into an act which would eventually blossom into the most popular British double act of all time. And, as usual, chance, played its part.

During 'Youth', Ernie's fellow young 'discoveries' felt envious of him not only because he was already established as a child star, but for a more basic reason. 'We envied him his freedom,' said Eric. 'Or at least what we thought was his freedom. We all had our mothers in tow and still thought of ourselves as being tied to apron-strings.'

For his part, Ernie was quietly envying his young colleagues for the opposite reason: he envied their security. Unlike the other 'discoveries', Ernie had no chaperone, and had to make all travelling and accommodation arrangements for himself. He had to make his way between theatres under his own steam, and he had to fix himself up with digs at every venue.

For several months, Ernie coped prodigiously well. In Oxford his planning finally let him down.

By the time 'Youth' hit Oxford in 1940, the phoney war was over and the reality of hostilities had transformed the British way of life.

When Ernie arrived to look for digs during the show's run in the city, Oxford was crawling with troops and, as he soon discovered, there wasn't a room to be had anywhere. At every door he knocked on, he was told the same story – no room. By ten o'clock, he was still without anywhere to stay, and he was found by Doreen Stevens, a singer in the show who was some years older than himself. She walked with Ernie, trying some other digs he hadn't known about.

It was still the same story, and Ernie's situation was beginning to look desperate. Until, that is, he knocked on the door of the digs where Sadie and Eric were already comfortably ensconced.

By some quirk of fate – and there would be several between now and Morecambe and Wise establishing themselves – Sadie overheard the landlady apologetically dismissing Ernie. 'We can't let her turn him away,' Sadie at once told Eric, and went to intervene suggesting that Eric and Ernie shared the room's double bed, while she made do with the single.

All was agreed and, as Ernie says, 'From that moment on, the three of us were inseparable. We travelled together between engagements and Sadie took over full control of all the practical things like digs and trains. And she'd take as much control as we'd let her of our act as well.'

'Sadie adored Ernie,' says Joan Morecambe. 'When she took him under her wing, she became a second mum to him, and I think she loved Ernie just as much as she did Eric. To her, it was just like having two sons. She'd never do anything for Eric unless she could also do it for Ernie. When they were out of work for long periods of time, she went out to work herself and sent cheques to both of them.

'In his turn, Sadie told me that Ernie was always a good lad to her. He never gave her any cause for concern. She always felt in the partnership that it was Ernie who was looking after Eric: Eric was the totally unreliable one – Ernie was the pillar of strength. When they were out of work, Ernie used automatically to go to see Sadie and George rather than go home to Leeds. It was a second home to him. And that continued right up until they were mature, married men.'

Their double act evolved naturally out of their joint travelling arrangements and developed properly while they were working with 'Youth Takes a Bow' in Coventry.

The show's engagement had coincided with the week Coventry was blitzed and, since the digs they had been booked to stay in had been flattened, they had to stay in digs in Birmingham. This meant the three of them had to commute the twenty or so miles to Coventry every day by train – a journey that was painfully slow and frequently disrupted because of the appalling damage in Coventry in the wake of the blitz.

Sadie soon discovered that travelling under these conditions with two boisterous fifteen-year-old performers who were bursting with talent and adrenalin was not ideal. And she soon began to grow weary of their constant impersonations of Laurel and Hardy, Abbott and Costello and their fellow performers from 'Youth'.

Finally, driven beyond endurance by yet another impersonation, she made a suggestion. 'Look, instead of all this malarky, why don't you put your brains to better use and try and do a double act of your own? All you need are a few fresh jokes and a song.'

Eric and Ernie immediately latched on to her suggestion, thinking it a marvellous one, and began working on it there and then. Within days, their first routine materialised as a few fast gags and a soft-shoe dance to *By the Light of the Silvery Moon*.

Showing maturity and prescience beyond their years, Eric and Ernie also established the ground rules for their professional association which would last right up until Eric's death in 1984. They decided that it didn't matter who got the laughs, and everything was to be split down the middle, fifty-fifty. This was the only agreement they were ever to have between them, and it was settled on a handshake.

If they had agreed to her suggestion of forming a double act with a speed which had startled her, Sadie wasted no time in getting behind them to push it along as hard as she could.

Though Eric and Ernie still had to concentrate on the single spots they had been contracted for, as far as Sadie was concerned they were now one act: she knew that they got along well together and that they now clearly wanted the double act to work. Satisfied in her own mind that this was the way forward, she set to work.

'She was always dreaming up new ideas for us or stealing material from other comics for us,' recalls Ernie. 'Once, she even bought a tape-recorder to record our act and would offer opinions when we played it back.'

As soon as they'd put together a two-and-a-half minute act which satisfied them, Eric and Ernie took it to show Michie, hoping he'd include it in the show.

In their own minds, they were already a powerful new double act convinced they were ready to launch themselves on audiences.

3

'The great thing about a double act is you're never alone in the cold, cold world ...'

Ernie Wise

They had had to work on their double act routine in stolen moments, concentrating naturally on the solo spots for which they had been engaged.

Some of their pirated material included gags which they probably didn't even understand themselves, such as when Eric would mince on stage with his hand on his hip:

ERNIE: What're you supposed to be?
ERIC: A businessman.
ERNIE: A businessman doesn't walk like that.
ERIC: You don't know my business.

They were desperate to be allowed to perform as a double act and showed their material to Bryan Michie, who approved it in a noncommittal manner. The ultimate decision whether it could be used in the show rested with Jack Hylton, however, and they had to wait until he next came to see the show, which was in Liverpool.

When he arrived, they ran through the whole routine, ending on the soft-shoe dance. Hylton was impressed, though he had just one reservation: 'Take out that bloody awful song.'

Hylton told Michie to take one of the acts off the bill the following Friday night at the Liverpool Empire, so that Eric and Ernie could perform their double act for the first time. *By the Light of the Silvery Moon* was jettisoned in favour of *Only a Bird in a Gilded Cage* which suited their soft-shoe far better.

One Friday night in Liverpool, in 1941, the double act was born, watched proudly from the wings by Sadie, as the two teenagers grabbed the audience with what Ernie now admits was a pretty raw routine: not too raw, though, since Hylton told them they could do the act every night the following week on the next stop of the tour in Glasgow.

One aspect of the act nobody particularly liked was the name, Bartholomew and Wise. It was Bert Hicks, Adelaide Hall's husband, who came up with the solution. Discussing with Sadie the need to change Eric's name, Hicks recalled a friend of his in America, who had adopted the name of the town where he'd been born.

And without fanfare or ceremony, Morecambe and Wise was launched.

For the rest of 1941 and into 1942, Eric and Ernie still continued to do their solo spots, but did the double act whenever they were given the opportunity. Gradually they built it up into 'seven minutes of pure rubbish', as Eric would always later claim, 'or ten, if we worked slowly.' But at that time they were proud of the act, and getting enough laughs from audiences to convince them it was good.

Ernie admits Abbott and Costello were their principal role models during this progressive period. 'We did pinch some routines from their films and adapted them to our style,' he recalls, 'and we even adopted fake American accents to deliver it.' Morecambe and Wise were more slapstick in these early days; more easy to define as comic and straight man – as Abbott and Costello would successfully always be.

Laurel and Hardy, though, would prove to be their most

profound influence during the course of time, and Eric, right up to his death, would say that Morecambe and Wise aspired to their stature as comedians.

'We nearly met them in Sheffield during the fifties,' said Eric, clearly disappointed at having *not* met them. 'Missed them by ten minutes.'

'Our admiration for them,' says Ernie, 'centres on the seemingly effortless but utterly professional pace of their comedy, and the way that the extremely funny juxtaposition of the skinny fellow and the fat one is matched by the difference in their natures: the hangdog pathos of Stan Laurel neatly contrasting with the bombastic dignity of Oliver Hardy.'

Continued Eric, 'We loved Ollie's affected superiority as he lorded it over poor Stan, and his absurd pretensions to grandeur while at the same time displaying an obsequious manner to those with money or in a position of authority.'

Stan Laurel once stated: 'What we were trying to do was to make people laugh in as many ways as we could, without trying to prove a point or get into some deep meaning.'

And Oliver Hardy said in an interview, 'These two fellows we created, they are nice, very nice people. They never get anywhere because they are both so very dumb, but they don't know that they are dumb.'

This description is not dissimilar to one of Morecambe and Wise as provided by Eric Morecambe in the early 1980s. 'When we first had our own television series, Ernie was an idiot, but I was a bigger idiot. And that was the secret to our comedy.'

Stan Laurel, as Eric would do later, said ludicrous things that passed over his partner's head. A clear example of that is Laurel answering a ringing telephone. 'It sure is,' he says, as he replaces the receiver. 'Who was that?' asks a bemused Hardy. 'Just some fella saying it's a long distance from Atlanta, Georgia. I said, "It sure is." ' Instead of Hardy picking up on his partner's stupidity, he remarks that someone should put a stop to these sort of prank phone calls. Several times in their TV shows, Eric would suggest something quite ridiculous of their guest star to which Ernie would say, 'That sounds reasonable to me.'

Eric found Oliver Hardy's blank look to camera so original and enchanting that he bluntly admitted pinching and developing it himself. 'Every least thought or emotion registered in his facial expression,' said Eric, 'especially that tie-twiddling look of exasperated frustration with Laurel's ineptitude.'

In a similar use of the camera, Eric would say to Ernie, 'You have my word as a gentleman,' to which Ernie's naïve reply was, 'Well, that's good enough for me.' Eric turns to face a side-angled camera – therefore conspiring with the viewer – and says, 'This boy's a fool!' Ernie comes back with an innocent, 'Who are you talking to?' to which Eric quickly says, 'No one,' then gives the same camera – and the viewer – a fleeting, knowing little smile.

'There was a constant gibing at Ernie by Eric with the audience or camera in collusion,' says Rowan Atkinson, picking up on this point.

And Eric once said, 'Perhaps the real secret of my success is the little things I do that I don't know I'm doing.'

'You could always depend on Eric to get an audience laughing,' says Ernie, 'because it just flowed naturally from him. He had a kind of hyper-super tension inside him, and when he went on stage he was transformed and he was magic. And if, in later years, he had any doubt, he'd just fetch out the paper bag and do his trick with that, or, he'd grab me and say, "My little fat friend," and slap me on the face. And, of course, the more nerves and tension he had, the harder he used to slap me.'

Though the turning to camera idea was originally Hardy's, Eric had developed a way in which he could invite himself into viewers' homes, and, as Hardy had done with millions of cinema-goers in the 1930s and 1940s, make himself a part of those viewers' lives.

Both men were sharing a moment. In Hardy's case it was his frustration. 'Look at me,' he could have been saying, 'I'm lumbered with this incompetent fool but in truth I am unable to deal with the situation any better myself. I'm at the end of my tether, so what am I supposed to do?' In Eric's case, he could have been saying, 'Ernie thinks he's the clever one but we know different, don't we? I'll defend him to the hilt and let him think he's wonderful, so long as you and I know the truth and can keep it from him.'

Eddie Braben, who wrote most of their BBC TV shows, saw mutual affection as the secret of their relationship. 'The first time I met Eric and Ernie,' says Braben, 'I just thought they were closer than any two brothers I'd ever met. It was in Bill Cotton's office at the BBC when I'd been asked to write for them. I watched them together and could feel the affection between them. That was what came across to audiences – the affection. It was the same warmth audiences felt for Laurel and Hardy. While Eric would insult Ernie left, right and centre, he'd never let anyone else do it, and that's what the audience appreciated.'

'When we were performing shows together there was a kind of lightning thing that went between us,' says Ernie. 'You can see it in recordings of some of our TV shows where I might start to giggle or Eric might grin. That was the relationship between us: we were doing an act for ourselves within the act somehow.'

'Morecambe and Wise were the first music hall double act to talk to one another,' says Michael Grade, Head of Channel 4 and friend and fan of the double act since the early sixties. 'Previously, double acts had talked at each other or to each other through the audience. No one before had done their kind of low-level, intimate conversation which were what made them so interesting as an act.'

It's been said of Laurel and Hardy that the superiority they had over other comedy teams was that people cared about them as human beings. And how applicable that is to Morecambe and Wise. Oliver Hardy and Eric Morecambe achieved it by getting the viewers on their side – sharing their feelings – but each could only do this through his partner's skill. With Stan Laurel it was his desperate ignorance, and with Ernie Wise his being so full of mock self-importance as not to notice Eric's quiet asides. For both double acts the result was stupendous.

Perhaps the wonderful relationship both acts shared with their audiences also came from the strength of their stage and screen relationship with each other. Ernie was a dreamer full of his own importance, always certain of his superiority over Eric. Equally Eric, full of ad lib and mischief, never doubted his own superiority over Ernie. In this way each came to give the impression he was needed, if only to look after the welfare of the other.

'Eric and Ernie had pathos, real pathos,' says writer and

stand-up comic Ben Elton who, by his own admission, considers Morecambe and Wise to be his all-time favourite act. 'You really felt for those two wounded egos battling it out forever. For me, it was the intimate moments between them – Eric and Ernie in bed together, Eric and Ernie in their flat or Eric and Ernie in front of the tabs – which were the essence of the act. Although the big production numbers and the guest star routines they did were priceless moments, they weren't the whole story.

'It was Eric and Ernie together, just talking, which drew me in and, for me at least, made it such compelling television. In those scenes, they were almost surreal because they had moments of sheer madness.'

There is one very noticeable and interesting difference between the two double acts, and it had little to do with the act itself, but plenty to do with their salaries. Morecambe and Wise, from the outset to the finish would, as previously mentioned, split everything fifty-fifty, the only formal contract between them being a handshake. Not so Laurel and Hardy. Stan Laurel always insisted on being paid twice as much money as Oliver Hardy. Not because he felt he was twice as funny, but simply because he did twice the work. At the end of a day's shoot, Stan would be starting almost another full day of work, working on gags and story-lines, while Ollie would be amusing himself on the golf-course, golf being a sport he excelled at. And perhaps surprisingly, Ollie whole heartedly approved of this financial arrangement.

Funnily enough, Dean Martin and Jerry Lewis, the hugely successful American double act of the fifties, had a similar relationship to Laurel and Hardy. 'I would work on the act all day,' says Lewis, 'and Dean would play golf.'

In the early 1940s there was little true similarity between Morecambe and Wise and Laurel and Hardy. Laurel and Hardy were superstars, albeit ageing ones; Morecambe and Wise had it all still to do. At this stage, Eric and Ernie's act was merely popular enough for Bryan Michie to buy them smart outfits to perform in. They would thus appear in tailored blue blazers and straw boaters. And Ernie even managed to negotiate a pound a week rise each from Hylton. Since it was wartime, they also managed to earn some extra cash – illegally because they were still under age – firewatching all night in theatres.

In the early part of 1942, 'Youth Takes a Bow' began to suffer at the box office. Bryan Michie had been wandering around with a worried look on his face for some time, then finally a telegram came from Hylton instructing him to close, and that was seemingly that.

Eric and Ernie – all of sixteen – were convinced that Morecambe and Wise were so successfully established that they could launch themselves in professional variety with little difficulty. This was where 'Youth Takes a Bow' – which had provided them with so much good experience – revealed a weakness of cushioning. As long as they were promoted as child discoveries, they, and all other discoveries, had that aura of novelty which appealed to audiences. These same audiences were far more critical of professionals whose job was to entertain successfully. And there were no other discovery shows for the boys to cocoon themselves in.

For all her hope and ambition, Sadie saw only too clearly how potentially desperate was their plight. When Eric and Ernie began voicing their optimistic plans for their future, it was she who untypically found herself reining in their expectations.

Eric suggested they move to London. 'Agents'll snap us up.'

Ernie rapidly took up the argument, saying they'd probably make thirty or forty pounds a week between them. Not a good idea, as Sadie explained to them. 'You're only employable as child discoveries, and there's no work going. You'll have to get real jobs for a time.'

'But we haven't done an honest day's work in our life,' Eric was quick, and serious, in pointing out.

As usual Sadie had the final word, and the boys temporarily went their separate ways. Eric returned to Morecambe and employment in a razor blade factory. Ernie didn't go directly to Leeds. Despite their mutual misgivings, he decided to try his luck in London all the same. He stayed with a family of Japanese acrobats while seeking work. But variety in the capital was at a virtual standstill, and eventually he was back home in Leeds and doing the coal round.

The 'real' jobs, however, were only to last about three months. They kept in constant touch, and Ernie travelled across country to stay with the Bartholomews as often as he could.

They tried in vain to find local work, scouring the Morecambe coastline for possible venues. But no joy.

Unable to progress on Eric's patch, they tried venues around Leeds. Ernie was remembered from his days working alongside his father, and they did manage to secure a few dates in Leeds and Bradford, but it wasn't regular enough to offer something long-term.

The fact they could at least get together cheered them up. As Ernie says, 'The great thing about a double act is you're never alone in the cold, cold world. Problems are things you share.'

Around this time, Sadie, who had insisted on the attempted 'real' jobs, became more and more convinced that the boys – *her* boys – would only ever be really content if they took the full plunge into the professional world of showbusiness. And if her ambitions for them had been tempered by pragmatic reality, those ambitions still remained high. Seeing just how unhappy the boys actually were, Sadie decided that whatever the difficulties facing them – and those difficulties were multiplied by the war – Eric and Ernie deserved their chance at having a crack at success in London.

Sadie arranged a flat in Mornington Crescent, and secured them an agent almost immediately. They went to see him in Charing Cross Road, and he told them to go round to the Hippodrome where George Black was holding auditions for his new show, 'Strike a New Note'.

Ernie had met Black while staying with Jack Hylton's family. Black was, in fact, Hylton's neighbour and Ernie had often listened to them discussing their various deals and swapping stage gossip, absorbing the sheer theatricality of it all.

Ernie, of course, couldn't rely on friendship to secure him work, and Morecambe and Wise had to audition like everyone else in front of Black. But so determined were they to knock Black sideways, they gave him the full act – now nine minutes long – sparing him nothing.

At the end, they were told to change and report to Black. When they did, they found him utterly charming, but were about to learn a hard lesson in the financial jungle of professional variety.

'How much are you two boys earning?' he asked.

'Twenty pounds between the two of us,' came Ernie's honest

reply, thinking and hoping that Black would feel sorry for them.

'Right,' nodded Black, 'I'll give you that.'

In financial negotiations, the artiste must always start by asking for the impossible before scaling down to an agreed sum. It was a useful lesson, though the agent who had sent them along was furious, telling them they should have been on at least another fiver, perhaps even a tenner.

But much worse was to follow. When Black hired them, they had assumed he wanted their double act. He didn't. 'I don't want the act at all, boys,' he told them. 'I just want you in the show doing bits and pieces.'

In a move which even today makes Ernie astonished at his own impudence, he looked Black in the eye and said, 'Mr Black, if you don't want our act then I don't think we're really interested.'

Most producers would have told the two sixteen-year-olds to get lost. To his credit, perhaps because he was getting them cheap, he offered them a kind of compromise. 'Tell you what, then lads. Alex Pleon is our second comic. If he ever goes off sick you can go on and replace him.' So the boys had to resort to praying he would fall ill. But as Ernie puts it, 'In the history of stand-up comedy, Alex Pleon was its healthiest representative.' Indeed, only twice in the entire fourteen-month run did they have to go on in his place. Both times their act was received in silence by bemused audiences wondering what on earth was being inflicted on them.

Although they were little more than glorified chorus boys, their months in 'Strike a New Note' were not wasted. The show was a monster hit, and being in a highly polished successful production gave them an insight into just what showbusiness at the top could be like. There was an innovative quality about its stars and material. It made comic Sid Field, hitherto unknown outside the North of England, a huge star.

Everyone visiting London just had to see the show. Among the visitors backstage, Eric and Ernie met Clark Gable, Deborah Kerr, James Stewart and Alfred Hitchcock.

The show could hardly be described as demanding in relation to the boys, so they found themselves with abundant time to work on their act and try other things. They appeared for the first time together on BBC radio in the revue, 'Youth Must Have Its Fling'.

Originally, the producers had wanted Sid Field but, being a highly visual comic, he had said he wasn't interested. And so Eric and Ernie were delighted to step in. Some of the younger performers from 'Strike' joined the studio audience to offer support. This was noted in a review in a Morecambe newspaper.

'Morecambe and Wise told jokes in the American style. Ernie was supposed to do the feeding, but Eric complained that he took the laughs. The entire feature would have been much improved if the laughs of the young people forming the studio audience had been more spontaneous than so obviously made to order.'

'Strike' was a wonderful experience for the newcomers, but was cut short on 27 November 1943, by Ernie receiving his call-up papers to join Britain's war effort.

4

'Knowing how to react to an audience is the most important weapon a comedian has ...'

Eric Morecambe

Their call-up papers horrified Eric and Ernie. It wasn't cowardice or any perceived lack of patriotism, merely a pragmatic realisation that any time spent in the forces would inevitably interfere with their progress in showbusiness.

Ernie's papers were first to arrive. His choice had to be the army, the merchant navy or the mines. He chose the merchant navy, working for the Gas, Light and Coke Company.

Ernie acknowledges that during his time spent in His Majesty's Service, he saw little of the ocean: it was more a case of life on rivers or estuaries shipping coal from Newcastle and South Shields to Battersea Power Station. Although this work was unromantic, it was vital, and Ernie found himself with plenty of time off in between runs; he divided it between Leeds and staying with Eric's parents in Morecambe.

Eric's call-up papers were not due for several months after Ernie's, so when Ernie left 'Strike a New Note', Eric stayed on –

but not for long, the show ending soon after Ernie had departed.

While awaiting the inevitable call-up in 1944, Eric joined ENSA, and became straight man to a Blackpool comic by the name of Gus Morris.

Eric's recollections of Gus tended to display quiet respect. 'Gus had won the Military Medal in the First World War,' recalled Eric, 'and he'd been wounded by a burst of machine-gun fire. He couldn't bend his right knee. He could only bend his left knee half way. And he had only one eye. But he was a very funny man, and he was very kind to me.'

When his papers finally arrived, Eric opted to become a Bevin Boy, so going down the mines. His father, George, encouraged him to volunteer for Accrington.

George had briefly worked as a collier at Accrington after the First World War. 'You've got relatives in Accrington,' he reminded Eric. It could, maybe should, have been a sound move.

Eric lodged over a shop in Clayton-le-Moor with a couple called Mr and Mrs Birdikin. 'Mr Birdikin had been a miner himself,' explained Eric. 'His lungs wheezed when he talked and there was coal dust under the skin of his face.'

Although Eric was passed as A1 fit at his medical, he was not the strongest of young men; certainly not one at home with heavy manual work, and he was horrified by the conditions he found down the Accrington mines.

'Some of the seams were no more than two feet high, and I found myself pushing great tubs of coal along rails down the tunnels with only a Davey lamp for company.'

Eric always had enjoyed his creature comforts, and even in his youth had a dislike for physical work. Working down a mine made him yearn even more for his weekends spent at home in Morecambe, particularly when they coincided with visits from Ernie who might turn up with bacon or silverside he'd acquired from his ship's engineers.

For someone who had always had a 'poorly' look, the conditions at Accrington were going to ensure Eric lived up to it. Eleven months after going down the mines, he was classified C3 with a touch of heart trouble and duly discharged. With Sadie fussing over him – which he later confessed to absolutely loving – he slowly (though never quite fully, as the future would show) returned to health in the comfort of home.

The merchant navy had suffered horrendous casualties during the war, ferrying essential supplies to London. But Ernie admits that the worst was over when he was called up, and the only enemy action he witnessed was daylight bombing of London.

Eventually Ernie was put in the 'pool' which meant he was part of a permanent reserve of seamen available for posting anywhere at short notice. There were frequently long breaks between postings – sometimes as long as six or seven weeks on full pay. During these breaks, he was able to pick up his career as a performer, contacting agents and producers. One producer who employed him regularly during this period was his old contact Bryan Michie, who would engage him at short notice for a night or a week. Ernie would be introduced as 'A boy from the brave merchant navy', and go out in full naval uniform to do his song and dance routine. With patriotic audiences this move of course ensured huge applause wherever he appeared.

While Ernie was dividing his time between the merchant navy and snatched moments on the stage, Eric was feeling better after his ordeal down the mine. Eventually he went back to work in the razor blade factory.

But Sadie was as determined as ever that Eric shouldn't be 'tied to a whistle', as she would often say. So, while he was busy working at the factory, she was busy scanning the pages of *The Stage*, in search of any opportunities for her son. Her determination wasn't in vain. She found Eric a six-month engagement in a touring show playing straight man to a comic, Billy Revel.

All these transient showbusiness jobs must have seemed at the time as the road to nowhere-of-great-importance. But in later years, Eric would look back and realise how formative they were in honing a comic timing that would eventually lead to many accolades and stardom. Through long and varied experience, he was learning how to work to 'live' audiences, all the time developing in confidence and stature.

One of Eric's greatest concerns for comedy in general in his later years was the lack of a suitable platform for young hopefuls to learn and practise their skills. 'Knowing how to react to an audience is the most important weapon a comedian has,' said Eric. 'We really only got it from our music hall experience.'

For today's comics he saw it as being far more difficult. 'They're thrown on television within a matter of months of being "discovered", and expected to be great,' he explained. 'Some aren't bad and go on to achieve something, but for many it's the kiss of death, for what chance have these poor sods really got to polish a performance or learn to deliver lines to their best potential?'

This is an argument taken up by actress Penelope Keith who was to appear in the last BBC Morecambe and Wise show in 1977. 'One can't fail any more,' says Keith. 'Everything's got to happen immediately. When I started I started in rep, and you could be aware of what it was to fail. But it's like great bravery. Great bravery is only great bravery when you know what cowardice is.

'Performers aren't allowed time to develop. They're picked up early on, given a show or two, then tossed away. The sort of professionalism and the sort of training and hard work that went into Morecambe and Wise, seemingly doesn't exist now. It probably is out there somewhere, but nobody's looking for it because everyone's after the fast buck. No one's prepared to give any time any more.'

By the time Eric's contract was up, Ernie had been discharged without ceremony back on to civvy street. Ernie confesses now that at the time of leaving the merchant navy, he had more or less decided to opt for a career as a solo performer. 'The idea of a double act had somehow lost its appeal,' he says. 'I felt happier relying on my solo routine for my professional survival.'

But destiny was to play its hand. While in London looking for work, he bumped into Sadie and Eric walking along Regent Street. Sadie suggested, as she had done all that time back in Oxford, that Ernie joined them in their digs at 13 Clifton Gardens, Chiswick, which were owned by a Mrs Duer.

'Since resisting one of Sadie's suggestions was like fighting against fate,' says Ernie, 'I found myself once again bound up with the Bartholomew family.'

Sadie found them work in one of the more bizarre showbusiness initiatives seen in Britain: Lord John Sanger's Circus and Variety Tour.

Sanger had hit upon the unusual idea of combining two very different arms of entertainment – circus and variety. The tour was to travel the country in caravans, putting up a big top on village greens or outside large towns – anywhere where they could present their part-circus, part-variety show.

If this had looked good on paper, and it probably had in view of a war-weary nation having been starved of entertainment, in practice it was a disaster. 'It was neither one thing or the other,' explains Ernie. 'It promised audiences the best of both worlds but proved to be the lowest common denominator looked down on by circus and variety people alike.'

Not that Eric and Ernie had understood that when signing. Nor, presumably, had any of the other acts. The whole thing was put together by a Welsh concert party producer who provided the jokes and material for Eric and Ernie's act. Others on the bill included Speedy Yelding, billed as Britain's Greatest Clown, Mollie Seddon, who had appeared on the BBC, and four dancing girls: one of them, Doreen, was in the fulness of time to become Mrs Ernie Wise.

A flavour of the circus and variety mix was given in the posters which appeared ahead of the lumbering enterprise: 'For the first time on tour the best in circus, stage and radio is presented on a full size stage – Do not fail to visit the pets corner after the performance.'

Any patrons attracted to the idea of the circus by thoughts of lions and tigers were soon disappointed. 'At our height,' recalls Ernie, 'we had a donkey, a parrot, a couple of hamsters, performing dogs and a wallaby.'

The show came complete with a big top which could seat seven hundred, and all the performers soon came to realise that, as in a real circus, they were all expected to take part in the effort of erecting the top, setting out the seats and selling tickets – in Eric and Ernie's case, in full evening dress and Wellington boots! And opting out was simply not tolerated in the circus fraternity.

So, at each venue, seven hundred seats had to be arranged, and before moving on, cleared away. 'But the show was so bad that literally no one came some nights,' recalls Ernie.

Eric, particularly, hated life on the open road. Often he made himself unpopular with the others for voicing his objections rather loudly. 'I just didn't have sawdust in my blood,' he said of that time. 'Life was all right on the road for people like Lord John Sanger, with his enormous beautiful caravan. But we outsiders had to make do with converted RAF trailers which had no facilities for washing apart from a canvas bucket.'

The basic nature of their accommodation meant that even the most mundane jobs, such as laundry, became a major operation. Doreen helped out in that department, and if Ernie can be grateful to Sanger for anything, it has to be for the introduction it gave him to this dancing girl who was to become his wife.

Ernie first met Doreen at a pre-tour lunch. He claims he fell in love at first sight, but his behaviour – bravado to mask awkwardness – did little to endear him to her.

They were having soup, and Ernie was making cracks about the noise some people made when eating soup. Inevitably, Doreen made the tiniest slurping noise and Eric and Ernie fell about laughing. Doreen was highly embarrassed, and from that moment on she tried her best to ignore Ernie. Not to be discouraged, the boys set about pursuing Doreen and her friend Rose. Eventually, there was a thaw, and Doreen ended up doing Ernie's laundry, with Rose doing Eric's.

Lord John Sanger's Circus and Variety Tour ended with a not unexpected whimper, the axe falling at Nottingham's Goose Fair in October 1947; but not before Sanger tried one last desperate and exhausting (for the performers) attempt to save it.

For the three days of the fair the tent was converted into a booth without seats. The audience came in one side and moved slowly past the stage, then slowly exited the other side while the performers had to keep up a virtual non-stop performance on stage. Between them, the performers chalked up seventeen shows on the first day, twenty four on the second and a mammoth thirty two on the final day. It was a supreme effort but not enough to save the show from closure, and Eric and Ernie soon found themselves back with Mrs Duer in Chiswick, West London, with no prospect of work.

Ernie, marginally more than Eric, was feeling the frustration of seemingly getting nowhere. Eric had been getting nowhere since the beginning, so for him it wasn't a new experience. But ten years earlier, Ernie had exploded on the scene as a child prodigy. Now those heady days were no more than a fading memory as the boys found themselves just treading water. There wasn't even Sadie around to drive them on and to raise their flagging spirits. She had long since returned to Morecambe. So, now in their early twenties, no longer could they rely upon the 'child discovery' label which had served them both so well during the previous decade. Having come of age, they were trying to make it in the world of professional variety.

But would anyone in variety want them?

5

'The Americans had stand-up comics while people in England were still laughing at Dan Leno as Dame in Pantomime.'

Eric Morecambe

Variety, which literally consisted of a variety of light entertainment acts (rather cynically referred to as 'trite' entertainment acts by many of the agents) such as singers, comedians, magicians, acrobats and sheer novelty acts, really had its heyday during the early part of the twentieth century.

It had grown out of traditional tavern entertainment – like the Canterbury Hall and Wilton's Hall; halls added to the back of pubs – from where it moved into purpose-built theatres until the time when almost every English town had its own Hippodrome or Empire.

Although often looked down on by the 'legitimate' theatre, variety regarded itself as refined music hall and was hugely popular with the masses. Mass entertainment media – radio, film and, of course, television – began to eclipse variety from the 1930s onwards. But it never quite became extinct, and while the

Hippodromes and Empires may no longer be in existence, variety, itself, lives on even today in diluted form in some minor venues.

The variety world into which Eric and Ernie were attempting to get a foothold after the war was the established variety circuit which owed much to the traditions of music hall, with the order of 'billing' adhering to a set formula.

Despite a brief boom immediately after the war, which all forms of entertainment enjoyed, traditional variety resumed its slow decline in the forties. Managements then introduced nudes to make up for a lack of audience-grabbing name acts. Ironically, it was the nudes that alienated the traditional family audience, so further damaging its own future.

'Variety was still booming in 1939, when we started,' recalls Ernie. 'The old pros used to tell us that the 1920s was the heyday, and that it was already dying because of the competition from the movies. But variety was still making a lot of money in 1939.'

The real rot, both Eric and Ernie agreed, set in during and after the war. Says Ernie, 'A lot of the brilliant acts disappeared during the war. Then the [London] Palladium adopted a new policy of only using American stars as top of bill which did nothing to help British artistes. And then, of course, in the 1950s came television and the nude shows which were the death of variety.'

A typical variety show of that time would begin with a dance act. This was followed by the second spot which was where every comic served his apprenticeship. A speciality act followed – jugglers, perhaps, or a dog act – then the second top of bill, usually a comic, would close the first half. The second half of the show conformed to a similar formula. Opening with dancers, it would lead into the second spot then some kind of musical turn. Then the top of bill would appear and do half an hour or so, before the whole thing was wrapped up in a musical finale and bows from all the acts in order of merit.

Billing was crucial to performers. It determined their earnings as much as anything, and was a league table to show an individual's popularity and success. Even now, Ernie stoutly defends his place on any bill. 'I don't want to be fourth or fifth on the bill,' he says with a shudder. 'I wouldn't like the loss of face. I don't subscribe to the old showbiz adage of being nice to people on the way up because you'll see them on the way down. This business is all based on success; and if you are a failure on your way down, no one wants to know you.'

Eric and Ernie did not really begin to climb that league table of billing until the summer of 1952, and the five years after Sanger until then were perhaps the hardest of their professional lives.

The end of the farcical Sanger tour had found them back with Nell Duer, in digs in Chiswick, West London. She was a strong woman who always seemed to be smiling, and who was their salvation while they were trying to establish themselves on the variety circuit. 'She'd let us stay practically rent-free,' remembers Ernie, 'telling us we could pay her back when we were back in funds. Since we were more often out of work than in it at that time, it's only thanks to her generosity that we kept a roof over our heads.'

When Eric and Ernie were in work, it wasn't unusual for a little girl to be watching their act from the side of the stage. This little girl is now better known as the actress, Nanette Newman, who is not only the wife of film director/actor/novelist, Bryan Forbes, but was to become a star guest on one of their Christmas specials during their final years at Thames. And the reason she was standing side of stage was because her father was on some of the same bills as Eric and Ernie, in an act called 'The Courtneys'.

Like his wife-to-be, Bryan Forbes also caught Morecambe and Wise's act early on in its evolution. It was at Camberwell Palace in the early 1950s. He remembers them as being very funny, fresh-faced young boys. 'I always thought that Eric Morecambe really was in the same league as Jack Benny,' says Forbes. 'His timing always reminded me so much of Benny. Eric was a master of the slow burn, as Benny and George Burns himself were. Comedy depends on an inner ear for timing. Timing is everything. If you haven't got instinctive timing you're nothing as a comic, because you've got to know when to drop in the tag line to that pool of silence. When Ernie fed Eric a line, Eric would do those wonderful slow reactions as the penny dropped, and that was a trick of a great comedian which Eric Morecambe was.'

Having the support of Mrs Duer was certainly a plus. Sadie had some time ago returned to Morecambe and her patient husband,

George. Money was unbearably tight. Ernie was relying on his savings and Eric barely survived on the two pounds a week sent to him by Sadie.

Occasionally, when feeling very low, the boys would return to Morecambe for a week or two until they felt able to face the desperate search for work again.

To secure work in variety they needed an agent. But like all struggling performers, they soon came up against a catch: to obtain work they needed an agent; to secure an agent they needed to be seen working.

'None of them ever bothered to do anything about us until we managed to get a booking for ourselves and appeared on stage,' said Eric. 'In the winter of 1947, when we really needed an agent, not one of them wanted to know. And we tried every single agent in the book.'

Eric and Ernie were to later have very good relations with the three major agents that were to represent them, though Eric would remain very scathing about agents in general, especially many of those they had personally encountered. 'Most of them couldn't recognise talent if it slapped them in the face,' said Eric. 'And most agents at that time had started in showbusiness as bad acts and had turned to agency. They couldn't survive as pros, but they quickly realised they could survive living *off* pros, all the time despising and misusing the talent they didn't possess themselves.

'Everything seemed to revolve around keeping the agent happy whereas to my mind it should be the other way about.'

Says Ernie, 'We were very lucky with the three agents we had: Gordan Norval, Frank Pope and Billy Marsh. But agents are largely a strange fact of life in a performer's career. They're forever on the phone when you're on a good run, but hit a bad patch and they're strangely unavailable.'

The only way around their dilemma was to beg or bribe the booking manager at a theatre to get them on a bill so an agent could at least be invited along to see them perform. Eric and Ernie did try this method several times, but it was not entirely successful and their lack of progress was frustrating.

The only real variety date they got by approaching the bookers direct was a week at the Walthamstow Palace during March 1948, during which they had to call themselves Morecambe and Wisdom because there was another Wise already on the bill. (Vic Wise and Nita Lane, billed as 'The weak guy and his weakness'!) The boys flopped badly there and the booker promptly dropped them.

If the introduction of nudes was ultimately to kill variety theatre, ironically it was a booking at the notorious Windmill Theatre in Soho, home of the embryonic Soho sex industry, which was to launch Eric and Ernie's career. Not that they knew this at the time, because it appeared to be just a further set-back.

The Windmill was owned by Vivian Van Damm – affectionately known as VD by those in the world of entertainment – and he introduced to astounded audiences a non-stop show of nudity and vaudeville known as Revuedeville.

Everything that happened at the Windmill bore Van Damm's personal stamp, from opening mail to hiring and firing artistes. The audiences, especially the men, did not come to see the variety acts booked between the static nudes, so performers faced a particularly harrowing time since they came as an unwelcome interruption to the main business of the day.

Nevertheless, many of the great names in British showbusiness actually achieved their first big breaks at the Windmill including Harry Secombe, Dick Emery and Tony Hancock. Indeed, later in his career, when he came to realise just how many top stars had emerged from his tiny theatre, Van Damm decided to display on a plaque a list of the stars who had trodden his boards and owed their success to having appeared there. When he approached Morecambe and Wise to be added to his list, they refused. 'I took great pleasure in reminding the legendary VD that he'd fired us,' says Ernie.

But back in 1949, they were more than happy to trudge to the Windmill one Sunday morning and audition for VD in his tiny office with its fish tanks. Gothic lettering behind the desk read: There Are No Pockets in Shrouds. If they had any doubts about the reality of the so-called glamour of showbusiness, VD's office eradicated them. Commented Eric, 'It was the smallest room I've been in outside a loo. You could barely open a door.'

In this tiny space they ran through their act for him. He watched their ten-minute routine and agreed to book them at twenty-five pounds for one week, with a five-week option. But that was for six shows a day. And six times a day they died.

'Actually, it was a question of where you appeared on the bill,' said Eric. 'Harry Worth and Jimmy Edwards did fairly well. Our place on the bill couldn't have been worse.'

Indeed, it couldn't. Each time on their first Monday, Eric and Ernie had to follow a kind of orgy act. 'It had bare-chested men in tights cracking whips, and nudes everywhere,' recalled Eric.

To a nation just emerging from the deprivations of war, this was the ultimate in sexual wickedness. Eric and Ernie had to walk on as the curtains closed on this peep into debauched Saturnalia, and run through their routine. Unsurprisingly, they were not welcome. More than that, not one murmur came from the audience as they performed.

To make matters worse, they were immediately followed on the bill by a chorus line of naked girls who suddenly brought the audience back to life.

The same pattern was repeated on the Tuesday. Six spots delivered to six silent audiences. On the Wednesday, VD fired them.

He summoned them to his office and they walked in expecting him to tell them he was taking up the option. Eric even remarked to Ernie on their way, 'Get your pen out for that contract. Have it ready.' So getting the sack was all the more devastating as they were totally unprepared.

VD told them audiences preferred another double act on the bill, Hank and Scott, which comprised Tony Hancock and Derek Scott.

This abrupt dismissal was a double disaster for Eric and Ernie. They were banking on a six-week run to bolster up their confidence as performers. Though they might not have been getting any laughs, the Windmill was a showcase venue, allowing them to sharpen their act in front of a West End audience.

Much more importantly, they had informed several agents that they would be performing there for the next six weeks and had invited them along to watch. Now they had just four days left.

During their sacking, Ernie asked VD if they could put an ad in *The Stage* announcing that Morecambe and Wise were leaving by mutual consent. VD agreed.

As soon as they left his office, they blitzed London agents with letters enclosing a string of complimentary tickets, paid for out of their wages.

From all this effort only one agent came to see the show: his name was Gordon Norval, and it was the boys' last day there.

Norval had two minor show dates, the Grand in Clapham, and the Kilburn Empire. Eric and Ernie had hoped for far bigger dates but, under the circumstances, these were better than nothing at all.

After watching them perform, Norval agreed to take them on, and booked them into a show called *Fig Leaves and Apple Sauce*, at the Grand. More nudes, but they were accustomed to that, even though Sadie told them unequivocally she had strong objections to that type of work.

As had become their custom, Ernie dealt with the financial negotiations, something which Eric always encouraged. 'Every act has to have one bastard who can say no,' Eric later explained, 'and I thought it might just as well be him.'

Norval was offering twenty pounds a week. But for two spots, which Ernie assured him was no trouble, they would get an immediate increase to twenty-seven pounds and ten shillings.

When Norval was out of earshot the awful reality of what they had agreed to suddenly hit them. In their desperation to grab a chance at professional variety, they had agreed to do two spots of ten minutes apiece. And they knew they just didn't have the material to do a second spot.

After ten years together, Eric and Ernie's routine ran to twelve minutes maximum. Now, in less than a week, they had to devise another ten minutes out of nowhere.

6

*'Marry a girl and your fourpenny pie'll
cost you eightpence.'*

Sadie Bartholomew

In 1949, they were at the Grand, Clapham, with the two hardest
spots of any bill: second in the first half and second after the
interval. For the first spot, they had decided to go with their usual
act, the one they felt comfortable and familiar with. The second
spot was to be the new material.

Their intention was that the first spot, their real act, would give
them the springboard to launch into the new material. It didn't,
and they died, walking off again to the sound of their own
footsteps, or the 'Clapham silence', as it was known. They were
naturally dispirited as they awaited unconfidently to go out and
give the new material its first airing, wondering what chance they
had now the audience seemingly hated their 'proper' act?

But as Ernie says, 'In retrospect, having to produce ten minutes
out of nothing was the best thing that could have happened to us.
We had our backs to the wall and we just had to lock ourselves
away in Mrs Duer's and come up with the material.'

While desperately compiling the new ten minutes, they mentally

50

raided old Abbott and Costello movies, tried to recall what had worked for other double acts they had seen, plundered notebooks they had kept and then attempted to mould all this into an act they themselves could put across.

In the beginning there had been Sadie. Now they were on their own. They knew that whatever they came up with in those few frenzied days would subsequently have to be performed before a live audience at Clapham.

Moreover, this was the big chance to get on to the professional circuit. Blow this, and it was unlikely they'd get a second chance.

While working on the additional ten minutes, Eric couldn't get the tune of the 'Woody Woodpecker Song' out of his head, and they decided to incorporate it into the second spot.

The basic idea behind this routine was ridiculously simple, but like all good ideas, its simplicity was its success. Basically, Ernie would tell Eric that he was going to teach him to sing a song in which he, Eric, had the most important part. Ernie stressed that the whole secret of the success of the song was that Eric had to come in just at the right moment.

In truth, of course, Ernie had much the larger part with Eric's reduced to just a five-note pay-off at the end of each verse – a mere impression of Woody Woodpecker's chirpy cackle.

This one song was to be the turning point in the Morecambe and Wise partnership. From the grudging silence of their first spot, Eric and Ernie brought the proverbial house down.

Managements in the audience that night couldn't help but log the response, and Nat Tennens booked them straight away – 'act as seen' – for his Kilburn Empire the following week.

Wisely, they reversed the order of their acts for Kilburn. The hardest thing to get in comedy is the first laugh and Woody Woodpecker was ensuring they got theirs. So, with the audience on their side from the first spot, they found their second spot also went down very well.

After a week at Kilburn, they were then back at Clapham, and a week later back to Kilburn as top of bill. Their money had gone up to forty pounds a week, and Gordon Norval became their agent.

Since the end of the Sanger Circus fiasco, Ernie had remained in touch with Doreen Blythe. Despite their unlikely start, the two of them had been going steady for some time.

Doreen was appearing in a touring show run by Reggie Dennis, and she suggested he take a look at Eric and Ernie while they were at Clapham. Dennis saw them and immediately offered them the chance to tour in his revue, 'Front Page Personalities'. He offered them a year's continuous work.

The boys were extremely successful during this time spent touring with him. They earned good money, bought decent clothes and even began to get noticed in the local press.

The time in the tour also gave them the opportunity to really polish their act. 'We always finished the first spot with the Woody Woodpecker routine,' said Eric. 'And by now the publishers of the song had done us a special arrangement. The second spot was much the same thing, but a little more relaxed.'

They relaxed more because Woody Woodpecker was working so well and that gave them time to devote more attention to polishing the delivery of their lines since they didn't have to worry too much about their actual material. Some of the material now working well for them was, in essence, much the same as that which had not been so successful in the past. The difference lay in their delivery of it. Because they had relaxed they were able to develop and put across their personalities and relationship. 'It was all in a subtle change of emphasis or our facial expressions,' explains Ernie. 'And as we got better and better, we stopped pinching other comics' material and actually found the confidence to invent some routines for ourselves.'

As 'Front Page Personalities' came towards the end of its tour, Eric and Ernie came to the attention of an agent called Frank Pope. Pope, who booked for the two top variety circuits, Butterworth's and Moss Empires, saw them in Grimsby, and decided to take them on his books.

Pope came to an arrangement with Norval, with whom the boys had had no contract, and the first booking he secured for them was at the Empire, Swansea – where Ernie had joined 'Youth Takes a Bow' over a decade earlier.

Eric and Ernie at last had the opportunity to play the first division of professional variety, and also to enjoy the life of variety performers. Now that the hand-to-mouth insecurity of their earlier days had receded, they could appreciate the finer points of being comics who didn't need the intensive rehearsals the acrobats and dancers had to endure.

Eric, in particular, began to enjoy his work for the first time in his life. 'I never actually enjoyed performing until I became a name and it started paying,' he was to remark years later. 'Until then it was just a job.'

In later years, when they were established, both Eric and Ernie had a tendency to underplay the effort they had devoted to the act at this time. The truth was that from the time they began in the first division of variety the pressure built continuously over the next two decades and was checked only by Eric's near fatal heart attack in 1968.

But initially life *did* seem easier in variety: the fear of failure, the relentless and degrading begging for work which they'd previously endured between Lord Sanger's witless rolling farrago and dismissal from the Windmill, all that was behind them.

However, although the years of absolute failure were over, their climb to the top was to be far from rapid, and it was to be another ten years before they achieved the 'big time'. Morecambe and Wise were never destined to be overnight stars: their progress was rather a gradual development of extending their reputations and consolidating their act.

Nor were they guaranteed unlimited success at every venue in variety. The Moss circuit, consisting of some twenty well-run Empires throughout Britain, might have been in the first division of variety, but success in one Empire did not necessarily mean automatic success in another.

The Glasgow Empire especially was the most feared date on the variety circuit, with audiences notoriously hard to satisfy. Known as 'the graveyard for English comics', Eric and Ernie, like so many others, had walked off to the sound of their own footsteps when making their Glasgow debut, an experience not made any easier by a fireman in the wings assuring them, 'They're beginning to like you.'

By other English comics' standards, their Glasgow reception could have been worse and Sean Connery, who can recall being in the Glasgow Empire audience one night while serving in the Royal

Navy, remembers Eric and Ernie coping very well under the circumstances.

Certainly their exit there wasn't quite as humiliating as Des O'Connor's, who is understandably reluctant to expand on the incident. But witnessing the literal downfall of their friend became one of Eric's favourite anecdotes. Overcome by the silence which greeted his entrance, Des opened his mouth to sing and promptly keeled over, seemingly deciding a mock faint to be the quickest way to deal with the situation. His limp body was unceremoniously dragged through the curtains.

The years spent in variety were not just important for Eric and Ernie's own personal development; it would be an invaluable source of material for their later TV appearances when they would base gags on the terrible vent acts they had seen, or dance routines that had gone wrong. More than that, they also took to TV audiences a reminder of variety with their cross-talk routines done in front of the tabs. This was a feature of their work and relationship which fascinated their TV guest stars in the 1970s.

'The very first time I met them,' recalls Glenda Jackson, 'it was in one of those tiny little hospitality rooms which the BBC still had then at Shepherd's Bush. And I ached with laughter listening to their conversation – their stories and their anecdotes – about variety.

'It was a great privilege to listen to them because the whole gamut of their experience was extraordinary. The richest person in the world couldn't have recreated their careers, of starting when they did or of working in circuses and music halls. And Eric was always very honest about where they'd stolen from. He knew all the old, great double acts and said, quite openly, that they'd stolen from those acts.'

'They weren't actually plagiarists,' says Michael Grade, 'rather, they were inspired by other acts. For instance, I remember the night at the start of a summer season at Great Yarmouth, when they tried out their famous ventriloquist stage routine for the first time. Eric was terribly excited that they were going to do it for the first time, but they had no idea how it was going to go. "It's a bit of a risk," he told me, "but we've got to do some new material."

'And, believe me, they were both excited by this new bit of

material. It ran to about three or four minutes – and while they did it, Eric managed to throw in a couple of ad libs. When they came off stage, Eric was like a kid who'd discovered Christmas for the first time because it had gone so well.

'By the end of the season, that routine stretched out to about fifteen minutes. And it was fifteen minutes of pure Morecambe and Wise comic genius.

'But that sketch was also derivative, and its source was Sandy Powell who originally devised the idea of a vent act for a double act. What Eric and Ernie did was to take that idea, develop it and make it their own. In the end, it was a Morecambe and Wise routine inspired by Sandy Powell.'

'You could see a lot of variety coming through in their later work,' says Ben Elton. 'Eric's gag with the paper bag, his joke about the police siren when he said "He won't sell many ice creams at that speed," or his gibes at Ernie "Is your fan in?" They were ancient old gags which they revived so brilliantly.

'But it's wrong to suggest their success depended entirely on them having been in variety. Their success had nothing to do with variety. It was simply because they were the best comedy act in living memory and, in particular, a stunning live act.'

Of the two of them, Ernie had the more deep-rooted ambition to find huge success. Eric would always have been willing to be second on the bill with a good reputation, '... earning good money but without carrying the whole responsibility for the show,' as he once put it. And Eric went on to say, 'We met lots of old troupers; comics who'd been making about sixty to one hundred pounds a week as second tops of the bill, and who'd been doing twenty minutes a show fifty-two weeks of the year, and who hadn't changed one word of their act in three decades. Before the variety theatres began closing, a well-known comic like that could fill his date books up to five years in advance with no problem.'

The other curious aspect of variety was the speciality acts which padded out the bills but which were often of the highest quality. Trampoline acts, acrobats, knife- and axe-throwers, magicians and even acts like Wilson, Kepple and Betty, the hieroglyphic dancers brilliantly parodied by Eric and Ernie with Glenda Jackson in an early seventies Morecambe and Wise show. The parody had developed during their days in variety, often supported by comics such as Arthur Askey and Roy Castle.

During this time Eric and Ernie also forged long-lasting friendships with people who, like themselves, would reach the very top of showbusiness on either side of the footlights. One such name was Bill Cotton Junior, later Head of Light Entertainment at BBC1 during their decade-long reign as the BBC's kings of comedy.

'I first met them when they were appearing on variety bills with Alma Cogan,' says Cotton. 'I was a song-plugger at the time, working for my own company and pushing my own songs. Alma recorded a couple and I would go to see her at the theatre, and whenever they were on the same bill I used to chat to them.'

These friendships were a relief from touring in variety, which could be extremely hard work. 'Variety did have a sense of camaraderie about it which is completely missing at the moment,' says Cotton. 'Pros all used to meet up at that great railway junction at Crewe. You'd always meet another act waiting for a connection who'd been to the venue you were on your way to. So you'd ask what the boarding houses were like, what the theatre was like, and what the MD was like.'

One of Eric and Ernie's greatest friends to emerge from these variety days was Harry Secombe. A young comic himself, he had started to make a big name in 1951 as a member of the legendary 'Goons' – Milligan, Secombe, Sellers and, occasionally, Bentine. Four very funny men who after the war turned stage and radio comedy on its head for a while, just as Monty Python would do in the late 1960s for television comedy.

'After the war, all of us comics were like tadpoles in a big pond,' explains Secombe. 'Some turned into frogs, some remained as tadpoles and the rest disappeared without trace. We weren't afraid of audiences because we'd faced bullets in action. No one's going to take a shot at you from the front row of the stalls if they don't like your act. Although somebody actually once did shoot at me from the audience – but that's another story.'

Secombe first met Eric and Ernie at the Croydon Empire. Later, they did pantomime together in Coventry. 'The man who ran the theatre there had no sense of humour,' says Secombe. 'He was a businessman who sold cars some of the time. He told us he'd received a letter complaining about a comedy routine the three of us were doing together. We were quite miffed about this because it was actually going down well with the audiences. So between us we concocted a letter saying how good the show was, and we had it sent by my dresser. We used the address of a friend of the dresser's. The manager, the fool, only had one letter of complaint, so our one letter of praise negated it. He never referred to the matter again.'

Secombe remembers the variety era as an exciting one. 'It was a way of life rather than a job of work,' he says. 'Many of us had been entertaining in the services – mainly concert parties – and we had a different kind of humour to the civilian humour. And that's what we brought back after the war. The "Goon" stuff, that basically Milligan wrote, was all to lift comedy; to give it a different kind of feeling.'

Whenever Eric did seem inclined to coast along as second of the bill, Ernie was there to push him forward, just as Sadie had done before.

Sadie had for some time now taken a back seat in regard to the boys' career. She'd done all she could to nurture two young lads and put them on the road to success. The rest was up to them and fate. From now on she would keep an eye on them from a distance. But she kept in close contact, craving bulletins on how the act was progressing, and she was still quick to offer advice.

Sadie's biggest thrill, one which increased over the years, was to go to Lancaster market and natter with her cronies about what Eric and Ernie were doing. She was understandably proud of their growing reputation, and she enjoyed her new found fame, even if it stretched no further than from Lancaster market to Morecambe Bay.

The decline in variety might already have begun in the early 1950s when Morecambe and Wise joined the circuit, but the standards set in the running of theatres were still maintained by Moss Empires. There was a definite hierarchy which performers were expected to observe. The theatres were well run by managers who commanded respect from the artistes. Everything backstage was clean and well organised; the orchestras were excellent.

Every performer on the circuit had his or her own favourite

theatres, and Eric and Ernie came to enjoy playing Swansea, the Liverpool Empire and the Palace in Manchester.

They soon adapted to the internal politics of life in variety. They absorbed the protocol of band calls, made sure they kept the stage-doorman sweet, and quickly learned who were the best people to tip, or more accurately bribe, to make life just that little bit easier.

Domestically their lives at this stage were a continuous round of theatrical digs, which varied in quality enormously. They naturally had much to thank their Chiswick landlady, Nell Duer, for. Others were memorable for other reasons.

One place they stayed at in Manchester was divided down the middle: one half for entertainers, the other half for 'legitimate' stage actors. Never did the twain dare meet, although Eric and Ernie did breach the invisible barrier line to share a box of chocolates with a young actress called Flora Robson who had befriended them. Years later, Dame Flora Robson, as she became, joined up with them in two skits as their guest star in a BBC Morecambe and Wise show.

Bryan Forbes recalls one particular landlady. 'I remember her saying to me, "Have you got a good memory for faces, love?" I said, "Yes, yes; I think so." She said, "Oh that's good, 'cos there's no mirror in the bathroom." '

The established landladies were first and foremost very shrewd businesswomen, so touring pros always tried to find those just starting out who were generous in their eagerness to please. Some were also retired pros themselves and needed no excuse to suddenly launch into their own, usually long-forgotten, acts – sometimes even half-way through serving dinner.

Whatever horrors or joys awaited them at each new venue, they were faced together by Eric and Ernie. The old cliché about a double act being like a marriage is always an apt one but in Eric and Ernie's case the relationship was perhaps more like that of two very close brothers, especially since they had effectively shared one mother in Sadie during their early years together.

Even when her direct responsibility for them had waned, Sadie continued to regard Ernie as every bit as much her son as Eric. 'I've always treated them absolutely alike,' she said many years later. 'If

I knit Eric a pair of socks, I knit a pair for Ernie as well. If I ever managed to get hold of an orange during the war, I waited until I'd got two so they could have one each and eat them together. They are both my sons, and I love them both.'

Like many Northern women, both boys' mothers had warned them to keep clear of the opposite sex. Ernie recalls, 'My mother said women were either after your body or your money.'

Ever the realist, Sadie's advice to Eric was characteristically blunt: 'Marry a girl and your fourpenny pie'll cost you eightpence!'

Nonetheless, Ernie's seven year courtship of Doreen Blythe, conducted in snatched weekends when his touring commitments brought him within travelling distance of her Peterborough home, had not escaped Sadie's attention. Early in 1952, she tackled him about it.

'When are you going to marry Doreen?' she put it to him directly.

'Oh, some time, I expect,' came his noncommittal response. 'Besides, I'm not getting married until Eric gets married. I'm not going to give any woman my pay packet and have him stand there and laugh at me.'

Little did he know that within the year they would both be married men.

7

'We were powerful together.'

Ernie Wise

As they began to climb the showbusiness bill of fame at the start of the 1950s, Eric and Ernie were unaware they would be among the very last stars to emerge from traditional variety.

There had been indications in the changing tastes of audiences, of course, as the introduction of the nude shows had already proved. But it was the rise of television which was to have the most profound effect on both the entertainment industry and British society as a whole.

When John Logie Baird unveiled his new invention at London's Royal Institution on 27 January 1926, few believed that his system of transmitting moving pictures – which he demonstrated with two ventriloquist's dummies and wearing an alarming checked jacket which made him look like a cheap vent act – would usher in the age of the global village.

The crude flickering pictures he produced that day, deemed by most observers to be far inferior to anything seen even in the embryonic days of cinema, were of scientific interest but nothing more. Certainly Baird's claim that the device would one day turn every home into a theatre was regarded by most scientists as far fetched. Yet, by 1936, the BBC had begun regular TV broadcasts from Alexandra Palace.

After the interruption in television's development because of the war, TV really began to exert its dominance. Its single greatest fillip in Britain was the televised coronation of Elizabeth II in 1953 – the first coronation to be seen by millions in their own homes.

With the introduction of commercial television in 1955, TV became the single most important means of communication in Britain. As, indeed, it became throughout the world.

TV also opened up a whole new world of entertainment for many. Viewers who had never been within a hundred miles of London, had perhaps never even been inside a theatre, could now enjoy West End-style plays from their own armchairs. National celebrities were created through the medium and became a part of people's lives.

Television soon began absorbing lessons from all other media – film, theatre, radio, books – shamelessly borrowing ideas and pirating formats. But it also created its own genres such as series' featuring regular characters in self-contained half-hour or hour-long shows and, perhaps inevitably, the TV sitcom.

By 1959, twenty-four and a half million households in Britain owned a set, and the effect on other forms of entertainment was profound.

Cinema audiences were visibly hit and the movie moguls fought back with widescreen and even 3-D. Variety theatre owners, though, appeared more sanguine about the initial threat. 'Who'll bother to watch a small screen in the corner of the room when they can see acts in the flesh?' was the common theme echoed throughout the business.

This up-beat self-deception soon proved itself deeply flawed: by 1960, no less than half the British population was watching peak time programmes every night.

The impact of television was far more devastating to variety than to 'legitimate' theatre. Television plays could never truly rival 'legitimate' theatre just as Hollywood had never managed quite to eclipse the Broadway or West End musical. For devotees of 'legitimate' theatre, as for those of the musical, the real enjoyment of the product wasn't just in what was seen or heard, but in being there.

This was a hold over audiences variety couldn't boast and television could – and did – easily rival and ultimately outstrip anything variety could provide. Indeed, it is no coincidence that the first night of regular BBC transmissions in 1936, and the first night of ITV in 1955, both featured a programme called *Variety*: two early warnings that TV could do variety as well as any theatre.

This changing climate was as obvious to the artistes themselves as it was to the producers. 'By the mid 1950s, more and more people were looking at television,' Eric remarked. 'People were making their names on panel games, and it soon became obvious that no one could ever ignore television again.'

Nevertheless, although both Eric and Ernie were keenly aware of the rising popularity of television in the early 1950s, they were content to consolidate their hard-won inroads on the variety circuit.

Since the war, their lives had, for the most part, been a shared round of digs and variety dates, but with the passing of time, their thoughts were distantly pondering domestic security.

It was a question of which of them would tread the path to the altar first. Since Ernie was romantically entangled, the odds favoured him.

For variety acts, constantly on the road, marriage was not something to be undertaken lightly. By nature a cautious man, Ernie had nearly lost Doreen during their long courtship when she had briefly contemplated following another boyfriend to South Africa. She had also complained he never sent her love letters. Instead, he sent her his tour list so they could arrange meetings when their trains crossed.

Ernie now claims he was 'inexplicably slow' at proposing. 'When we first met, Doreen thought I was pushy and obnoxious, dedicated only to performing and making money. And I suppose I was. But Doreen has been the only one for me.'

Ernie proposed on Valentine's Day, 1952. They were married the following January. But not before Eric had found the altar first.

'Minutes after we were introduced,' says Eric's widow, Joan, 'Eric told a mutual friend of ours that I was the girl he was going to marry.' Quite definitely like mother, like son.

It was June 1952, and the venue was the Edinburgh Empire. Joan Bartlett was a dancer, a former model who had turned to showbusiness. After her debut in a musical, she began touring in variety, and in 1952 joined the show at Edinburgh as last minute replacement for a girl who'd gone down with appendicitis. Also on the bill were two comedians – Morecambe and Wise – whom Joan had heard of but never seen.

Eric's first sight of Joan was at band call on the Monday morning. 'I saw this tall girl who was very beautiful with wonderful eyes, and who had a wonderful kind of sweetness which made your knees buckle,' he recalled. 'I knew at once that she was the one for me for life. It was as sudden as that.'

'At times in his life, Eric took the big decisions very quickly,' says Joan. 'He went off instinct and had the happy knack of getting it right.

'Eric was impatient, impractical and didn't like the everyday problems of life. He later told me that he knew he needed to marry someone who would give him confidence and would be a calm influence. He was convinced that if he'd married someone like himself it would have been a disaster. Now how anyone can determine all that in one single glance is beyond me. But Eric did, and the pursuit was on.'

Like most only children, Eric was accustomed to getting his own way, and even an existing boyfriend in Joan's life did not deter him. By the end of the week, Eric had proposed to Joan. And he continued asking her at the rate of about once a fortnight – until she finally said yes.

On the surface, Eric's pursuit of Joan might appear selfish, but it was driven as ever by pragmatism. 'From the very beginning,' recalls Joan, 'Eric told me he had to have a woman in his life. And by 1952 he had reached a stage where he was very restless.'

There had, of course, been one woman in his life already – Sadie. The bond between Sadie and Eric was particularly strong, though never smothering.

Says Joan, 'Sadie realised that when Eric was no longer a child, her role as mother, minder and manager was coming to an end.'

Like that of Ernie and Doreen, Eric and Joan's courtship was one of snatched Sundays between venues. One week, while Eric and Ernie were performing at Margate, they stayed at a hotel owned by Joan's mother and father. That same week, Joan was appearing at Morecambe, and she stayed with Sadie and George. 'And they told me all of Eric's secrets,' she smiles.

Eric and Joan became engaged towards the end of 1952. Unlike Joan, who had always believed in saving a little of whatever money she made, Eric had never bothered too much about savings. He did, however, believe in buying nothing but the best. This was reflected in his purchase of a beautiful solitaire diamond engagement ring – to purchase which he'd had to borrow from Sadie. Sadie, who would have willingly sold up everything and gone to live in a tent to assist her adored son, was more than willing to lend him the money. But she did wonder aloud, 'What does Joan see in our Eric? It can't be money, he hasn't got any!' And although delighted he had found himself a beautiful and sophisticated 'southern girl', she was for many months bemused that Eric's feelings for Joan could seriously have been reciprocated.

Sadie was disappointed at what she saw as the unnecessary haste of arranging the wedding. Eric and Ernie were booked into the Theatre Royal, Sheffield, for pantomime at the end of 1952. Just before they had to travel up to Sheffield, Eric and Ernie, who had otherwise been booked for work solidly for every week of the year, had the unusual luxury of a couple of days off because they were due to make a broadcast with Tessie O'Shea for Radio Luxembourg from the London Palladium on 12 December. Eric called Joan and suggested they got married on the Sunday before. Then they could travel to London together to combine the honeymoon and his broadcast before catching the train to Sheffield.

'Not very sensibly, we decided to make the most of the opportunity,' says Joan.

There was a week to make the arrangements. With the help of Joan's mother, the whole operation was put into gear. Fortunately, because her family was in the hotel trade, catering was not a problem, but any idea of a beautiful white wedding dress was abandoned due to lack of time. Even the vicar of St John's Church, Margate, had to be persuaded to marry them on a Sunday.

Both mothers were less than pleased at the impromptu marriage, especially Sadie who had always wanted her son to marry in a grand ceremony in Morecambe. Worse, Sadie had just put an ad in the *Morecambe Visitor* announcing the engagement; now suddenly she was confronted with news of the imminent wedding. Never one to hide her feelings, she tackled Eric about it. 'Why are you rushing things? How disappointing that you can't wait and have a proper big white wedding.'

Eric had to use all his persuasive charm to ensure Sadie and George even came down to Margate for the wedding. But typically, as soon as they were there, Sadie made friends with everyone she encountered, having a wonderful time in the process. And she never stopped talking about it for months.

Joan and Sadie were to develop a very close life-long friendship, one which went beyond that expected of mother-in-law and daughter-in-law. To Joan she became another mother, indeed Joan would always call her mum, and to this very day says that she misses her terribly at times, especially in the absence of Eric.

John Eric Bartholomew and Joan Bartlett were married at three p.m., 11 December 1952. Ernie was best man, and Joan recalls he looked somewhat shattered at the sheer speed of events.

Almost in shock response, just over a month later, Ernie and Doreen were married in Peterborough. Because of their ten-week run in pantomime – *Dick Whittington* at Sheffield – they too needed to be married on a Sunday. Unlike Joan, Doreen was unable to persuade her vicar to marry them on the Sabbath, and so the ceremony ended up being conducted in a Baptist chapel on 18 January, 1953. And Eric was best man.

By this time, Doreen had given up performing and was running a dancing school. One of the reasons she cites for their decision not to have children was that the children she encountered there put her off for life.

Once married, Eric and Ernie's lives were to take very different paths. For over a decade their time had been spent mostly together. From now on, outside of rehearsals and performances, they would spend little social time together. Marriage also heightened huge differences in their personalities. Eric and Joan soon started a family; Ernie and Doreen, having made the conscious decision not to, enjoyed their time as a couple.

The sharp distinction between their professional and private lives, apparent from 1953 onwards, also explains why Morecambe and Wise stayed together so successfully for so long.

Many double acts have been notorious for their public rows between partners – Laurel and Hardy, Abbott and Costello, Martin and Lewis, Cannon and Ball – the ferocity of the violent arguments sometimes achieving legendary status. Money, billing, even who got most laughs have all been the basis of much antagonism. In extreme cases, it has led to the act breaking up.

It was not like that with Eric and Ernie. There was never jealousy between them, just a determination to perform to the best of their ability. All that mattered was the final product: making an audience laugh. Their pairing worked because they were so at ease with each other.

'We were powerful together,' explains Ernie. 'And we had a great camaraderie. That's where a lot of other double acts fail: they don't talk to each other.'

Michael Grade, who got to know both Eric and Ernie well after he began working for their agent, Billy Marsh, in 1966, also highlights the business approach to the partnership, evident almost from its conception, as the real reason for their professional longevity.

'When it came to their basic relationship,' says Grade, 'they were very sensible. You see, they had a central fear which always kept that relationship businesslike: they didn't want to end up like all the other double acts they'd seen over the years who'd ended up loathing and screaming at each other. Whatever differences they might have had, they both maintained this very mature and sophisticated view that theirs was primarily a business enterprise. The key to that was that they simply just had to keep on doing it and to come to terms with each other, however different they might be. They knew that the whole thing would collapse if they fell out.

'Now, in all the years I knew them, I was never aware that they fell out. But I can't believe that they never did. I expect there were strains. The thing was, though, if they did have any differences between them, they kept them private, very much to themselves. Those differences never spilled out publicly.

'The other reason for their success was that they always worked on the basis that they both had to say yes to something, even if one of them thought it was wrong. And Eric was particularly good at deferring the business to Ernie. You see, he was acutely aware that, as the comic, he was the one the public identified with more. Therefore, he was very happy to create a large role for Ernie on the business side of the partnership. He would always leave it to Ernie to discuss the contracts. And, believe me, Ernie did that very well: he was a very tough negotiator and a difficult man to do business with. That, I feel, was a particular clue to the way they felt about each other.'

Shortly after Eric's death, the actor Robert Morley said in a radio interview that during rehearsals they would, '... very occasionally break off and try a sketch. Ernie never remembered it, so Eric used to whisper to me, "He never remembers the gag lines, but he's very good with the money." I always rather liked that.'

Theirs was a pragmatic approach to the business of being a double act which, Grade noticed, was born both of their mutual common sense, and of the struggle of their first decade together. But more important than even their business sense was the fact that they had spent the most formative years of their lives together.

This fusing of minds was the bedrock of their act. And it was such an intrinsic part of each man that the greatly reduced time now available to be spent in each other's company affected their professional relationship not a jot. As soon as they came together in a theatre or rehearsal room, they were at once as one.

This ease with each other also put them at ease with fellow performers, and Eric and Ernie were soon among the most popular entertainers on the variety scene.

They were witty, quick and, according to Joan, able to radiate a youthful exuberance which gained them friends wherever they appeared. Their dressing-room was always full of other artistes or visitors who'd come along just to enjoy their company and share a laugh.

From their earliest days, other comics had taken to the young double act, offering nuggets of advice, some of which they followed, some they ignored. One of the most memorable stars to take an interest was Max Miller, who once told Ernie, 'Remember, lad, in this business when one door shuts they all bloody shut!'

For Joan Morecambe, their time spent touring in variety was

possibly the single most important part of their career, the training ground and the foundation upon which everything which was to follow could rest.

'The first time I saw them was in variety and from that moment on I knew they'd become big stars. I can quite honestly say I never ever saw them not do well or not be funny with a variety audience. Even as second spot comics, which is a very tough spot to fill when you have to get the audience warmed up for the people who follow on.

'And they really did benefit from those variety dates. All that experience. When they were touring in variety, Eric and Ernie used to be on the road all the time. They never had a week off – not even when we were married.

'The death of variety took that away, and I know Eric was sad about that. He used to say that modern comics had no audiences to practise on. "They've nowhere to go to be bad," he told me. When the variety theatres closed, all that was left were the clubs.'

That change in culture – from variety theatres (which, though they had blue comics like Max Miller, were predominantly for family entertainment) to clubland (which was essentially an adult domain) – explains, according to Bryan Forbes, the noticeable decline in stand-up comedic standards in the latter half of this century.

'What often happens to a comedian who works clubs is that he plays down to that audience,' says Forbes. 'He starts to give them what they want, whether it's his style or not. Inevitably, it becomes scatological and dirty. It becomes, in effect, a stag night. Now, okay, some comedians are very good at stag nights: but it's not exactly comedy at its highest form, is it?'

One other consequence of the decline in variety was the eventual eroding of the tradition of camaraderie between acts which was created by the endless touring, of digs and the seemingly endless travelling between venues.

Sometimes, friendships forged between performers on the circuit were to last a lifetime. One such friendship occurred between Eric and Ernie and another young hopeful comic whom they came across at the Regal, Hull, in 1953. It was just before his 'Glasgow fall', and his name was Des O'Connor.

'The first time I came to see them was when I heard a lot of laughter coming from the audience, so I went to see what their act was all about,' recalls O'Connor. 'They were very good even then. Eric was a good faller. He did a fast and funny dance routine kicking his legs to one side while just keeping on going. He'd fall to the floor as if he'd been poleaxed.'

Morecambe and Wise, and particularly Eric, had a profound effect on Des O'Connor. 'There are only a few genuine wits around, and Eric Morecambe was one. All good comics have a stock of gags and lines in their head applicable to whatever situation. But added to that, Eric also had the ability to genuinely ad lib witty repartee or responses. I don't think I've ever met that many who have this ability, and in my career I've met all the big names: Jack Benny, Phil Silvers, Groucho Marx. I think there were strong similarities in style between Groucho and Eric.'

Bryan Forbes sees greater similarities between Jack Benny and Eric and, interestingly enough, Ernest Maxin (who choreographed all Morecambe and Wise shows for the BBC, and in the mid-1970s also became their producer in place of Johnny Ammonds) also likens Eric to Jack Benny rather than to Groucho Marx.

As a young man, Maxin had the opportunity to produce a Jack Benny show made in England. 'Benny was a master of comedy, and working with him I saw that quality of the untouchable celluloid star which Hollywood used to make. Those stars were almost unreal, slightly larger than life and yet, at the same time, everyone feels they know them which means you love *them* before you love what they do. And yet, you know, at the end of the show we did together, Benny confessed he, too, was star-struck and loved rubbing shoulders with the likes of Clark Gable.

'The moment I met Eric in the early 1960s in Torquay, I felt he had that same aura as Benny. I remember saying to him, "You know what you've got? You've got that celluloid look. People can draw cartoons of you like they can of the big stars." It was that world of make-believe – which in a sense they both had all the way through – which made them different from anyone else I've worked with or seen, and explained why everyone, be it a big star or a shop assistant down the road, rose to them the moment they walked on.

'Their other secret was that everything they did came from the heart. You know, those dance routines we did in the 1970s – the spoofs on *Singin' in the Rain* and *South Pacific* – showed Eric and Ernie doing things that nobody else was doing at that time. And although they weren't great dancers, they actually did those routines far better than a lot of professional dancers I've worked with. And they could only do that because it was all coming from the heart.'

'It was also honest,' says Ben Elton. 'And the only rule of comedy is honesty. Some say it's timing but it isn't. Timing's obviously important but it has more to do with understanding the right moment. Honesty is belief in what you're doing.

'Whether you're doing something which is based on a fairly complex idea, like I do, or if you're doing a piece of work based solely on your own exuberance, such as Eric shouting "Arsenal!", you've really got to believe in it, really got to know it's funny. You can't just believe they, the audience, will think it's funny.

'It's honesty which counts and you just knew that Eric and Ernie believed in that act. They believed in it so much that it ceased to become an act as such at all. Sometimes the bickering of a double act is so wooden – but the one thing Morecambe and Wise never were was wooden. You know, if their talent had been play-writing or classical acting, they'd've been knighted: in a different discipline they would have been studied at universities. That was the level of their achievement and it came from their honesty.'

For his part, Des O'Connor, by working closely with Eric and Ernie and becoming close friends with them, was able to observe the working relationship of the team. 'Eric Morecambe was always there, solid as a rock. Ernie Wise, too; always there and just as solid. They were undoubtedly the Laurel and Hardy of television. And Ernie didn't seem to mind – though privately perhaps he did – that Eric was getting seventy-five per cent of the limelight and ninety per cent of the laughs. You've got to give Ernie great credit for that. He would set Eric's lines up like a golf ball on a tee.'

The friendship, which was to last a lifetime and give forth a wealth of anti-Des O'Connor jokes that would turn into a national pastime, developed from taking tea together at cafes while touring. 'Later, they gave me lifts from theatres back to the digs I was staying at in North London,' remembers O'Connor. 'Eric would make gentle gibes at my expense, but purely between the two of us in private.'

It was while he was topping the bill in 1967 at the Bournemouth Pavilion that all that was to change and the private joking was to go public.

'I met up with Eric in a café; Morecambe and Wise were working Bournemouth as well that season. I told him, "I want to become an international star." He nearly choked on his tea. "International star?" he gasped. "I'd like to have an affair with Brigitte Bardot, Des, but all things are not possible." But after a few minutes he asked me how I was going to go about it. "I'm going to be a singer," I told him. Eric just stared blankly at me a moment then said, "And I shall join the Royal Ballet." I told him I was serious. "I know you are," he said, "that's why I'm going to join the Royal Ballet." '

That Des O'Connor went on to sell over twenty-four million records worldwide in the years that followed, only fuelled what had become one of the longest running gags in television – Morecambe and Wise jokes about Des O'Connor's singing.

The first televised anti-Des joke went out in 1972. It was a Royal Flying Corps sketch involving DJ Pete Murray. A phone rings, Ernie answers it then turns and says, 'I've got some great news.' To which Eric replies, 'What? Has Des O'Connor got a sore throat?'

'What had started out in 1953 as a private joke between two mates had suddenly become a national campaign,' O'Connor explains, 'and it remains so to this very day. I can't get in a taxi without the driver saying, "Where do want to go to, Mr O'Connor? Now you're not going to start singing, are you?" And Eric would ring me in the middle of breakfast to say they were playing one of my records on the radio. "Do I have to go upstairs and get the bucket?" he'd joke, and all that sort of nonsense.'

O'Connor remained impervious to the jokes and insults which he acknowledges in the long term seriously helped rather than hindered his own career and public standing. And although at first he wasn't so keen on being the brunt of their gags, by the late 1970s and at the height of it all, he would either contact or spend time with the boys devising anti-Des jokes, many of which they used. 'I'd say something like, "I've become a limited company," and tell

Eric to reply, "That's good, because you have limited talent." Eric would quickly scribble it down saying, "That's a good 'un, Des." '

Des O'Connor never wholly approved of the way other comics took up the joke. 'It was something solely relevant to Eric and, much later, to Morecambe and Wise. I didn't mind Russ Abbot taking it on, because I don't think Eric would have minded.' Russ Abbot, who once, when in the duo's company, described himself as 'the new boy', was quietly admired by both Eric and Ernie.

Even to this day, if there's a national or international crisis, the press fall back on a Des O'Connor joke. An example of it backfiring was the cartoon a national paper used at the time of the Tiananmen Square uprising in China. It depicted a Chinese general standing over a record player with one of his records in his hands. He is saying: 'If you do not disperse immediately, we will take serious action.' As O'Connor says, 'It *was* funny. But not so funny the next day with thousands of students lying dead.'

It wasn't until Des O'Connor himself appeared on the Morecambe and Wise show that the public appeared to understand for the first time that really they were friends, and the whole thing was just a bit of fun and nonsense. And after a while O'Connor found himself anticipating the gibes. 'One year I was watching their Christmas show waiting for the inevitable insult. Well, there wasn't a single one. Straight after I rang Eric and complained.'

Royalty joined in the Des-baiting. Introduced to O'Connor some years ago, the Duke of Edinburgh said: 'Ah yes. You're the chap always on the Morecambe and Wise show.'

'I naturally replied, "Well, no, I'm not always on it, sir, but I'm always mentioned on it",' says O'Connor. ' "Ah yes, I see," he nodded and then asked: "And are you really that bad?" '

Back in the 1950s, when Morecambe and Wise and Des O'Connor first met, Eric and Ernie began thriving. In addition to variety commitments, there was panto, summer season and before long they managed to secure regular radio work.

Their first broadcast together had been back in 1942, when still in 'Strike a New Note', and they had graduated to *Workers' Playtime*, which brought them to a much greater audience.

On the strength of this, they were auditioned by a radio producer from London for the programme *Variety Bandbox*. This was the southern equivalent of *Variety Fanfare*, which was broadcast from Manchester. The result of that audition was a slightly dismissive, 'You sound too much like Jewel and Warriss. Come back in five years.'

Undaunted, Eric and Ernie persuaded a friend to leak the news that they were about to be signed up as resident comics on *Variety Bandbox*, hoping it would reach the ears of Ronnie Taylor, the producer of *Variety Fanfare*.

'It did,' said Eric, 'and the ruse worked. He signed us up for a succession of *Variety Fanfares* which eventually ran into forty-five.'

They followed this with a series of their own, also broadcast from Manchester, called *You're Only Young Once* – or *YOYO*, as it became affectionately known. It was to prove to be one of the busiest periods of their lives as they had to combine broadcasting the shows live from Manchester each Sunday while touring the country in variety the rest of the week. And for the first time they had the services of a writer called Frank Roscoe, whom they had to share with fellow comedians Ken Platt and Al Read.

Their producer on *YOYO* was Johnny Ammonds, Ronnie Taylor having been promoted to Head of Light Entertainment, BBC North. It was Ammonds who was later to produce many of the Morecambe and Wise shows in the 1970s, before handing over to Ernest Maxin.

'In many ways, as a team, we were pioneering in creating Morecambe and Wise on the radio,' recalls Ammonds. 'Eric and Ernie would bring their gag books with them, and each show was virtually put together on the Sunday. Speed was essential.'

Several recordings of both *Variety Fanfare* and *YOYO* survive and it's interesting to compare these earlier broadcasts with their later TV appearances. Despite many of the sketches being on the thin side, it is astonishing how polished Morecambe and Wise were even in their mid-twenties. Eric, in particular, could always perform miracles with the most mundane material, and from both performers comes a feeling of relaxed confidence.

Recalling those shows Eric said, 'Ernie and I were Abbott and Costello without the American accent. He would call me Morecambe, and I would all but call him "Chuck" and say, "Him a bad boy!" We thought we were being original. Even then we thought we did high-class rubbish.'

The tendency for British acts in the 1950s to adopt an American accent was almost impossible to resist. 'All that generation of entertainers did it,' says Ben Elton, 'because it was considered glamorous after the war. It was a result of the Yanks coming over. They were the most exciting thing the British had ever seen. They had money, they were sexy and they got the girls. No wonder kids in showbusiness thought America was everything and started adopting this semi-transatlantic slang.'

Even in the 1950s, though, Eric and Ernie had started to shift away from the traditional American model of funny man and feed into something much more subtle; an evolution was in progress which would continue until they became the act most recognisable to their television audiences.

Their success in radio should not be underestimated. Radio, which had really grown into its potential during the war, had the power to make stars almost overnight. And despite their steady career progression in variety from 1951 onwards, it was through their radio appearances that most people, including producers, really came to take notice of Eric and Ernie.

'By 1954, we were a success in variety and radio,' said Eric. 'We were beginning to make an impact. The only accurate barometer of success in showbusiness is the money you make, and we were making it.'

'Sometimes we'd appear with top-of-the-bill acts who weren't as big as we were,' Ernie says. 'If it was a singer, we didn't mind. But if it was a comic, there'd be just a little bit of edge which would concentrate our minds.'

It was inevitable they would at some time come to the attention of television producers and, after a brief appearance they made for BBC TV which was broadcast from the Tower Ballroom Blackpool, they were approached by a producer called Ronnie Waldman. Waldman was the then Head of BBC TV Light Entertainment, and he offered them their own series assuring them they were natural television material.

The series was to be called *Running Wild* – the biggest professional opportunity they had had in their careers up until that point. They were convinced it would propel them into the big time; that it would make them into huge stars.

Running Wild, however, was not only a disaster, it provided Eric and Ernie with the worst reviews they had ever gathered. Indeed, it came perilously close to ending the careers of Morecambe and Wise once and for all.

8

*'... Contrary to how the public saw him,
he (Eric) was a very insecure person at
heart.'*

Ernie Wise

As late as the 1950s there was still a North-South divide in comedy,
and the perceived wisdom in the business was that a comic from,
and successful in, the North, would not work well with a southern
audience.

Ronnie Waldman did not subscribe to this outdated paro-
chialism and, largely on the strength of that brief routine they'd
done for the BBC in Blackpool, resolved to devise a networked
television series around Morecambe and Wise.

Eric and Ernie were signed to a series of six half-hour shows with
the first one scheduled to be broadcast at 9.40 pm on a Wednesday
in April 1954.

As soon as they had signed the contract, they were
understandably convinced it was the launch-pad to superstardom.
With a television series under their belts, they would be able to
expect top billing on the variety circuit and to demand five hundred
pounds a week from managements.

Their radio work for the BBC had demonstrated they were more than able to broadcast to a wide and appreciative audience, and television was the next logical step forward. Their career, which had sometimes progressed at a rather more sedate pace than they would have liked, had now ignited.

Alarm bells, which later in their careers would have started sounding from the outset, stayed silent at this heady time, and Eric and Ernie didn't see the warning signs until it was far too late.

Bryan Sears was signed as their producer for the new series, and he travelled up to meet them in Sheffield, where they were appearing in variety. Eric and Ernie had some ideas of their own for the series and related them to Sears. Politely, but systematically, each idea was rejected in turn.

It was subtly suggested to Eric and Ernie that their hiring was something of a problem for the BBC, and that Ronnie Waldman was surely a little off his head in taking them on. The difficulty, they were told, was that they were Northern, and as such were unlikely to appeal to a national audience. Still, the problem might not be insurmountable if they could get the right writers for the series.

In itself the perception of Morecambe and Wise as a Northern act was not unreasonable. They were, of course, both born in the North, and most of their work on the variety circuit had been in the North. And they preferred to work in Northern theatres, which they felt suited their temperaments. But they had also worked successfully enough in other places, and the response they'd received from audiences at theatres like the Brixton Empire proved they could score south of the imaginary dividing line just as well.

Ronnie Waldman clearly appreciated this though many of his colleagues were nervous of launching a Northern double act on a national television audience, and remained unconvinced throughout preparations for *Running Wild*.

It was eventually deemed necessary to hire no fewer than six writers for the first half-hour show in order to breach the supposed North-South comedy divide. Alma Cogan, who had been a good friend to the boys and a hit on the radio show *Take it From Here*, and was on the verge of stardom herself, was hired as resident singer for additional insurance.

'When Eric and Ernie did what they believed to be right for them, they seldom put a foot wrong,' says Joan Morecambe. 'The only times they went astray were when they did what other people told them to do.'

But on *Running Wild*, everyone was telling them what to do. In 1954, Morecambe and Wise were not a major act with plenty of clout and so lacked the confidence to argue with the producers of the show when pushed in a direction they didn't feel comfortable with. TV was a new medium for them. Everyone on the production team was far more experienced in TV comedy than they were. Eric and Ernie therefore concluded that they must listen to the experts and that if they did as they were told, the series would be a success.

On the morning of Thursday 22 April, 1954, the day following the first edition of *Running Wild*, they learned in the hardest way possible that they'd misplaced their naïve trust as they waded through the most vitriolic set of reviews they were ever to receive in their careers.

It was to have been so different, of course. The previous evening everyone who knew Eric and Ernie had taken their phones off the hook and settled down with keen anticipation to watch their first step on a short road to national television stardom. Ernie had even bought Doreen their first TV set so she could watch the show uninterrupted.

At the end of the show, Eric and Ernie's family and friends – like the boys themselves – knew there had been shortcomings. No one, however, was prepared for the storm that was to strike during the following twenty-four hours.

The basic problem with *Running Wild* was the script. By 1954, Eric and Ernie had a couple of twelve minute spots which served them perfectly well in theatres, but which couldn't be used without a great deal of alteration on television. These alterations were done with the help of the scriptwriters for the first show. These scriptwriters, though, were unfamiliar with the boys' style of comedy and, as a result, imposed an alien format on the routines with which they were not comfortable.

Running Wild was certainly no classic. The first show lacked originality and was decidedly thin. But Eric and Ernie were working to a TV script for the first time and acquitted themselves well enough. They had rehearsed tirelessly until the spots were timed down to the split second; and despite the unfamiliarity of the medium, they had delivered everything that had been asked of them, as it had been asked of them. That was not to save them when the reviews came in.

Limitations in the script were pounced on by the critics as evidence of severe limitations in the performers themselves, and these same critics mutely agreed to indulge in a feeding frenzy of unprecedented ferocity:

'How do two commonplace performers such as these get elevated to the position of having a series built round them?'

'This was one of the most embarrassingly unfunny evenings I have spent in front of the home screen for some time.'

One critic wondered in affronted prose: 'How dare they put such mediocre talent on television?' Another believed that, 'Alma Cogan stood out like a sunflower on a rubbish heap.'

The most cutting notice of all came from a reviewer who devised his own definition of the week: 'TV set – the box they buried Morecambe and Wise in.'

While still stunned from this succession of verbal lefts and rights, Sadie phoned them from Morecambe. Having had so much pride in her boys, when she learned of the dismal response to the TV series she was hit particularly hard. In fact, the critics might just as well have attacked her personally, because if you pricked the boys, Sadie bled as well. The only way she could deal with her disappointment was by letting Eric and Ernie know exactly how she felt about *Running Wild*, dressing nothing up. So, never one to tone down her criticism, she bluntly asked them, 'What the devil are you two playing at? Everyone's talking about it round here. I daren't show my face outside the house, and I can't go shopping in Morecambe for fear of who I might see. We'll have to move. We'll have to change our name.'

'The trouble was, Sadie and George lived in a small confined community,' explains Joan. 'People could therefore be very cruel to them without realising it. If someone came up to them in the street or market and said, "I didn't think much of Eric and Ernie's show last night," that was like a stab in the heart to them because, basically, their lives revolved around Morecambe and Wise.'

Quite why the critics expressed such hatred for *Running Wild* has never been satisfactorily explained, but there was more than a lingering suspicion at the time that the abuse was orchestrated for no reason other than that the BBC was trying to promote Northern comics across the country. Certainly, in retrospect, *Running Wild* seems a rather inconsequential little programme to have engaged the massed guns of the critical establishment.

For Joan Morecambe, the mystery remains to this day. 'The funny thing is,' she says, 'I watched *Running Wild*, and I didn't think it was that bad. And, usually, I was a very good judge of their comedy. I never understood the reaction. It really was as if the press had banded together and decided they were going to shoot this young couple down in flames.

'What made it worse for Eric and Ernie was that they had accepted that they were new comics on the scene and so had done exactly as they had been told. They had had no say in *Running Wild*.

'Looking back, I suppose it was a bit dated and a bit hammy, but you could still get a laugh from it and, to me, the criticism *Running Wild* received was totally unjustified. Part of the problem was that they were ahead of their time: even when they first went on radio their material was advanced.

'Eric never forgot the mauling they got for *Running Wild*, and at the time he told me he would never do another TV series.'

'We're Northern,' Ernie said at the time as he tried to come to terms with the volley of attacks, 'and you can't win if you're Northern.'

Eric and Ernie were devastated by the initial abuse. But it was Eric who was hardest hit by the failure, admitting years later to having been 'utterly appalled' by the show's reception. At times of crisis the fundamental difference between the characters of Eric and Ernie was apt to become more obvious.

Eric was a perfectionist and a worrier. Both comics put a hundred per cent effort into every performance but each appearance drained Eric emotionally far more than Ernie who was much better equipped to go home and relax after work than his partner.

In the days following their critical drubbing, Ernie found

himself having to bolster up Eric. He had taken the abuse personally and fallen into a state of temporary depression as a result.

'He became terribly morose and lost his sparkle,' Ernie can recall. 'Eric did have a tendency to take things far more personally than I did. And it caused him a great deal of stress. Contrary to how the public saw him, he was a very insecure person at heart.'

At the start of his career, Eric had had Sadie to push him along and give him confidence when the going got tough. Then Ernie had gradually assumed Sadie's role, but the *Running Wild* debacle came hard on the heels of Eric's marriage to Joan and subsequent birth of their first child, Gail. Eric was a married man with a family to support. He had responsibilites to others and the failure of *Running Wild* suddenly brought these responsibilities into sharp focus.

Ernie, by his own admission the one with the harder shell, privately acknowledged that *Running Wild* had done them a great deal of harm, but resolved to remain outwardly sunny and optimistic in Eric's presence. He was also able to take a much more detached view of the disaster and believed they should just carry on with their careers and resolve not to let *Running Wild* drag them into negative recriminatory introspection, which might destroy their act.

Deciding positive action was needed, Ernie told Eric that their top priority should be to get the remaining five shows cancelled. Perhaps if they could stop the series they wouldn't lose too much ground with variety managements and audiences.

Eric agreed and they went to see Ronnie Waldman at the Shepherds Bush studios. Waldman refused to take the show off the air. He claimed he had quite liked it, and any problems were easy to iron out. They persisted, revealing to him they were terrified of doing any more of the series. But again Waldman refused. He insisted they fulfilled their contractual agreement.

'I'm not doing this because I'm bloody-minded,' he assured them. 'Or because I can't find anyone else. I'm doing it because I believe you two are first-rate TV comedy material. Stick it out. I have faith in you.' His faith, though not misplaced, was some years premature, and if the scripts had remained the same, then there would never have been Morecambe and Wise as we remember them today.

Eric and Ernie found it very hard to 'stick it out', but being contractually obliged, and with Waldman seemingly unmoved by their pleas, they had little option.

At the end of *Running Wild*'s run their morale was the lowest it had been for a long time, and as they prepared to return to the familiar sights and sounds of variety, they were convinced the series had set them back many years.

As though to confirm their worst suspicions, their first job after *Running Wild* was a booking at the Ardwick Hippodrome in Manchester. They were placed fourth on the bill – even though they were the only act on the bill to have appeared on television. After all the high expectations of TV stardom this final humiliation left them feeling they had a fight on their hands merely to survive as an act.

Harry Secombe remembers feeling very sorry for them at this time. 'A lot of people who knew them well understood what a setback it was,' he says. 'But every comic needs a disaster. It makes you more street-wise – more able to handle audiences. Through the great chemistry of their relationship, and the innate pathos in Eric that made you want to reach out and hug him, they were able to worm their way into the heart of the public, and they stayed there. This meant that when they came back from the *Running Wild* disaster, they were virtually unstoppable.'

There were important lessons to be learned from the experience. What *Running Wild* had exposed, more than anything else, was their need for well-written scripts. Material that worked well in variety did not necessarily transfer successfully to television, and even scripts written specially for television had to be strong to register. Furthermore, if they were ever to make their mark on television, Eric and Ernie had to have material tailored for them, and to develop their own style. In essence, they had to be themselves.

The other great worry was that television had a voracious appetite for material. In variety, it was relatively easy to have a couple of twelve minute routines which remained more or less constant from venue to venue. And it was accepted that material was sometimes pirated by one comic from another. On television, once a gag had been used it couldn't be repeated or, if it was, it had to be considerably reworked.

They had already learned lessons about material the hard way when developing a second ten minutes to meet the terms of their contract for *Fig Leaves and Apple Sauce*. And there had been a regretable incident at Blackpool a couple of years before *Running Wild*, an incident which had left Eric and Ernie both highly embarrassed and acutely aware of the lack of comedy material they held in reserve.

They were appearing at the Winter Garden Theatre with Alan Jones – father of singer Jack Jones – who was topping the bill. The air at Blackpool has always caused throat problems for singers appearing there, and from time to time, Jones would lose his voice and have to be replaced at short notice by Eve Boswell from the Opera House.

The producers of the show, George and Alfred Black, had told Eric and Ernie that if Jones had to cry off a performance, they wanted them to fill in at short notice until Eve Boswell arrived to take over. Eric and Ernie said nothing, but privately knew that it was impossible for them to do so. Their two routines would be used up in their normal spots. They had nothing in reserve.

One day the inevitable happened. They were in their dressing-room and heard Alan Jones break off mid-song and apologise to the audience that he couldn't carry on. Panic-stricken, Eric and Ernie stripped off all their clothes so that when Alfred Black dashed in and ordered them on stage, they couldn't go.

The ruse gave Eric and Ernie no pleasure. They knew they'd let their producers down. Not only was it a paucity of material, but an inability to just go out in front of an audience and chat. They learned their lesson then and there and, in the aftermath of *Running Wild*, knew that to maintain any chance of developing as comics beyond the TV fiasco, they would have to continue developing their material.

As Eric pointed out, '*Running Wild* taught us that we needed a new act with new material. We'd been too static up to that point. More than that, we also decided to put our own personalities across more. We decided to try and be more like ourselves rather than just two comics telling jokes.'

Their first test following the television series, the date at the Ardwick Hippodrome, Manchester, showed their reconstituted act. Their reception proved that, contrary to all expectations,

Running Wild had done them very little damage with audiences. They received a standing ovation that night and it did a great deal to restore their confidence. Eric trundled home in a fixed daze after the show: the spectre of their television disaster had finally lifted.

'That did wonders for their confidence,' says Joan. 'And I always remember a write-up they got for that show which said: "These can't be the same two I saw on television the other night because these guys are brilliant and are going places." '

In truth, only agents and managements had really been aware of the critics' onslaught. Variety audiences either didn't know or didn't care about *Running Wild*. Audiences – the 'bums on seats' of theatre-world, as Arthur Askey always referred to them – were on their side, and evidently loved their style of comedy. And when the public is on its feet and cheering you, what do the acrimonious remarks of the press matter? In later years, Eric would often say, 'The hardest thing to find is yesterday's newspaper!' Most of the papers bearing reference to *Running Wild* were consigned to the dustbin or fish and chip shops.

Pausing just long enough to ensure that the series hadn't damaged their standing with audiences, managements were not then slow to promote Eric and Ernie as television comics. So, despite all the criticisms levelled against *Running Wild*, and the disappointment it had engendered, they found themselves billed as 'those inimitable TV comedians Morecambe and Wise', or even 'Morecambe and Wise of that brilliant TV series, *Running Wild*'.

The wounds inflicted on Eric through this brief flirtation with television, though, still ran deep and it would be seven years before there would be another Morecambe and Wise television series.

The transformation in their style of performing after *Running Wild* was profound. The more they put themselves across to audiences, the more audiences loved it: and the more audiences showed their appreciation, the more confident and relaxed Eric and Ernie became.

The disaster they had once believed had come close to finishing them off for good had, ultimately, revitalised them. *Running Wild* had breached a barrier. Not the artificial North-South comedy divide which existed mostly in the minds of producers and would be blown away by television anyway within a decade, but the final barrier between Eric and Ernie and their audience. Clawing themselves back from the precipice seemed to encourage the love of their audiences all the more. They came out of what appeared a nightmare situation with greater credibility and greater stature.

Nevertheless, as they picked up the pieces and expertly reassembled them into a superior act, in the months immediately following on from *Running Wild*, they were acutely aware that they had been lucky to escape professionally unscathed.

Eric and Ernie clearly understood that another flop like *Running Wild* would really finish them off.

9

'There's never been any tension between us ...'

Eric Morecambe

The two most important dates in any variety performer's diary in the 1950s were summer season and pantomime. Both involved approximately twelve weeks' work and, therefore, twelve weeks' regular income. With those bookings confirmed, performers knew they were unlikely to starve for the rest of the year.

Morecambe and Wise were no exception, and both before and after their *Running Wild* debacle, considered summer season and panto essential elements in their performing year. And when it came to summer season there was really only one place any performer wanted to play: Blackpool.

'If you got summer season in Blackpool you'd reached the Mecca in showbusiness,' emphasises Ernie. 'It dispelled all the memories of cramped railway compartments, unreliable motorcars and grim digs at a stroke. It was a twelve- or fourteen-week season of sheer joy and not a little glamour.'

As Eric once noted, there simply was no other place in the world quite like Blackpool in the 1950s, when it was still on the crest of its own extraordinary wave of success.

When Queen Victoria came to the throne, Blackpool was a small town with few more than seven hundred inhabitants; by the time she died it was firmly established as the major seaside resort in Britain. As the railways brought travel within the reach of everyone, so resorts such as Blackpool began to benefit from visitors from the industrial cities.

The resort really began to develop with the establishment of the Winter Garden Company in 1875 and then, eighteen years later in 1893, the supreme confidence of the town was confirmed for all to see with the building of Blackpool's famous tower, constructed just a couple of years after Paris' own Eiffel Tower.

Soon the Golden Mile, Blackpool's promenade comprising fortune tellers, fairground attractions and Punch and Judy shows, was stretching south from the tower in a mile or so of cheerful, honest vulgarity.

Always eager to outdo rival resorts, Blackpool was soon able to boast not one but three piers all with their own theatres and amusement arcades.

Blackpool existed to entertain its visitors and by the 1950s, when private motoring became an option for the majority and thereby supplemented the holidaymakers travelling by rail, the town's population would be swollen by over a million people during the height of the summer season. And those people had but one thing in mind: having fun.

As a result, Blackpool at that time was able to support more live shows than any other resort in Britain, and its theatres became some of the most sought after venues for performers. There was the Opera House and the Winter Garden, the Hippodrome, the Tower and the Palace and, of course, the Central, North and South Piers. These were in addition to the countless cinemas and nightclubs and fairgrounds for visitors to escape to for their annual fortnight away from the drudgery of industry.

'You could see our audiences all at once on a fine day,' Eric once said. 'All you had to do was to stand on a pier and look down on the sands in either direction. And a pro couldn't fail at Blackpool in those days. There was regular employment, good money and the whelk-and-belch audiences would applaud anything that moved.'

If the air at Blackpool was notorious for interfering with singers' voices, it also seems to have had the ability to blunt audiences' critical faculties, and after a strenuous day along the Golden Mile, or an arduous day constructing sandcastles on three square feet of claimed beach, punters were eager to be entertained by anyone or anything.

Conditions of employment for performers were not so universally sunny in Blackpool. The North Pier, for instance, always seemed to bear the brunt of the crueller elements which frequently assailed Blackpool, and performers, like audiences, had to walk the length of the pier to get to the theatre. 'On a clear day you could see the ocean,' says Ernie. 'On a windy one, you were in it. And if it was raining you'd arrive at the theatre soaking wet. So would the audience. In those days, though, we'd do anything for the money.'

Nevertheless, Ernie, like Eric, always loved playing at Blackpool because there was always something happening, always something going on to make life interesting. There was also a great camaraderie between the pros playing the various theatres in town and most would regularly meet up each morning for coffee and, more vitally, gossip at the Savoy or Winter Garden restaurant. That sense of extended family was always important for performers of all kinds, but was perhaps even more acutely cherished by travelling variety artistes.

If, as Eric believed, there was nowhere quite like Blackpool, there was also nothing like success at Blackpool to boost a performer's confidence. Long runs in front of capacity audiences gave acts like Morecambe and Wise not only financial security but also the chance to really work on their material.

Eric and Ernie, particularly after *Running Wild*, always took opportunities to develop as they moved increasingly from the early years of largely pirated material to something far more sophisticated and original. And the more they developed, the more their individual strengths came together to make their act unique.

There was a danger in these long runs however. Without the usual distractions of travelling or finding digs, the more insecure double acts had time to brood over real or imagined tensions within their partnership.

It's in the nature of every performer to strive to be number one and that can be where tension often germinates in a double act. During an extended period of success, such as summer season, external tensions can be added when audiences or critics go beyond appreciation and begin analysing the act or start making comparisons.

'They'll look at a double act and say: "Well, he's better than him",' explains Ernie. 'And they would say about Morecambe and Wise that one of us was funny and the other one wasn't.'

Ernie admits he grew tired of people remarking that Eric was the funny one. 'It could be hurtful to hear them add, "He's so funny he doesn't need the other one",' he says. 'Such a remark shows a basic failure to understand how a good double act works. Each partner was more than half the sum of the two. People who wondered what Wise would have been without Morecambe, were asking themselves the wrong question, because there was truly no answer to that. What the act would have been without one of us – whichever one – is simple: not half so good.'

Ben Elton says anyone who does not recognise Ernie's importance to the act basically knows nothing about showbusiness: 'Because of Eric's job in the act, his talents were by far the most comedically exuberant and this means that a lot of people have, quite absurdly, said that they were a one-man show. It tended not to be said at the time so much because it was so obviously not the case. But ignorance has grown over the years, especially from people who don't know the act.

'So you hear stupid comments from people who say Reeves and Mortimer are like Morecambe and Morecambe because they're both funny. The truth is that Ernie's role when Eddie Braben was writing their scripts was a very complicated one. That character of the vain playwright was quite brilliant – and Ernie played it quite brilliantly.

'I'm not saying that Ernie was my favourite because, if truth be known, Eric will always be everyone's favourite in that act. The point is, though, Eric could never have been your favourite without Ernie. The act was the act and Eric needed Ernie just as much as Ernie needed Eric.

'Personally, I find Ernie's comic character of the frustrated playwright who has no conception of his own limitations endlessly fascinating and I think it was one of the great comedy creations. It was just magical and, because of that, you can't just think of Ernie as Eric's foil.'

While comments about who was best could be hurtful, they never affected the fundamental relationship between Eric and Ernie. The conflict outsiders saw between the roles of funny man and feed simply didn't occur to Eric and Ernie because, like Ben Elton, they didn't regard their individual roles in the act as being so clear-cut. Rather, they considered the act to be two different sets of humour and skills which simply came together and gelled. An example of this was the dance routines which would develop into a major facet of their TV shows and for which many viewers still remember them most fondly.

Ernie freely admits that though Eric's biggest worry was getting the laughs – which was their end product – he himself was always happiest when they were singing and dancing because that was his background. 'I was a better dancer than Eric,' he says, 'and Eric always used to say I was a lovely little mover. But when we sang and danced together we made it look so professional, and we got away with it somehow.'

That was the true essence of it. They were not perfect dancers or singers, but far better than anyone would have expected from a comedy double act.

In an interview during the 1950s, Eric stated, 'There's never any tension between us ... That's the secret. Ernie makes me laugh and I know precisely what he's thinking. That's important.'

Their scriptwriter, Eddie Braben, believes their almost telepathic reading of each other's mind meant that the 'and' of Morecambe and Wise could have been dropped altogether. 'It should have been MorecambeWise,' he says. 'Because that's just how they were.'

Bill Cotton, Head of Light Entertainment during Morecambe and Wise's BBC decade, agrees. 'Ernie was one half of Morecambe and Wise. No more, no less. He was as vital to Eric as Eric was to him. Don't forget that Ernie is one of the best straight men ever to tread the boards.'

It could be added that had Eric felt Ernie was not equal to

himself, he had in total forty-three years in which to have done something about it. Naturally he didn't, because the longer they remained together the less obvious were the signs of funny man and feed. In the public's eye, Eric was certainly the most loved comic, but that doesn't make Ernie any less of a comic himself. One has to realise that Eric was more loved and admired than probably any comic this country has ever seen. Several times he has been described as the funniest thing ever to have stood on two legs. Ernie had a hard time therefore to get the acclaim he justly deserved. Ernie also had an immense talent for making his partner look even better than he already was, which is an additional reason for the raw deal he got from public opinion.

Interestingly, to the true Morecambe and Wise connoisseur, it is Ernie who inspires the most curiosity. Eric was obviously a very remarkable funny man. As Jimmy Tarbuck once said, 'Eric was a giant of comedy who had the rare gift of not only being able to look funny, but of saying funny things.' Ernie, however, especially through Eddie Braben (as Ben Elton has pointed out) developed the more fascinating characteristics. The best of these, apart from his play-writing, was his willingness to interrupt the patter of their shows to sing or do an impression of John Wayne or Jimmy Cagney. He was not just convinced he was good enough to inflict his impressions on the viewing public, but assumed with total presumption he was the best and that it was just what the audience wanted. And always he carried the air that he was a true artiste who had to put up with a meddling partner whom, strictly speaking, he would have been better off without.

This aspect of their relationship was, in fact, developed into a TV routine. Ernie tells Eric he's getting rid of him. Eric glumly says, 'Well, I'm off now – I'll be going then.' Ernie offers the briefest of acknowledgments – amusing in itself after forty years together – saying, 'Okay, goodbye then,' and at once readdresses the audience.

Ernie's role in the Braben scripts is to show a man who is total self-confidence; a man who believes that as playwright, comedian and actor, he's one of the most talented ever to have lived. Dame Flora Robson asks, 'How long have you lived in this house, Mr Wise?' Ernie replies, 'Ever since I became a highly successful writer. All my life.' In another routine Ernie says of guest star Cliff Richard, 'Cliff surprised me in that play.' Retorts Eric, 'I told him to be careful with that umbrella.' Explains Ernie, 'I meant he can really act. Just a little more style, a little more sophistication and he could well be another me.' A shocked Eric says, 'Never.' Ernie with a patronising shake of the head says, 'No, I suppose you're right.'

At other times they would be seen discussing past and prospective guest stars. Ernie says how lucky they were to have had Dame Flora on the show and that he wouldn't be surprised if they made Glenda Jackson a Dame. 'No, she won't do pantomime now,' jokes Eric. 'She's internationally famous now, she's got half as many awards as you.' Reflects a serious Ernie, 'I didn't know she was *that* good.'

Most of the humour is derived from Ernie being unaware of the shortcomings that both the audience and Eric can only too plainly see in him – yet Eric is there to defend him.

Equally interesting is Ernie's fickleness to Eric. Supportive of each other much of the time, Ernie often changes when in the company of a star guest he wishes to impress – not unlike Oliver Hardy's pretensions to grandeur while at the same time being obsequious. He goes into grovelling mode which perfectly deflates and discards Eric. With Sir John Mills on stage staring blankly at Eric, Ernie hisses gleefully, 'He doesn't know you, go and get ready.'

And Ernie is equally capable of getting the better of Eric, emphasising that he was always more than just a straight man, and that Eric wasn't there purely to spout funny lines and get all the laughs. An example of this is when Eric comes on as an old man. Ernie tells Eric he really didn't notice the difference. A hurt Eric says, 'But they've been very nearly four hours making me look like this.' To which Ernie retorts with a laugh, 'If they'd waited another month or so they wouldn't have had to bother.'

Conversely, Eric could make Ernie look silly, while Ernie reveals his 'Oliver Hardy' style stupidity at the same time. Says Ernie, 'But what about my audience?' Eric answers, 'He rang earlier – he's gone to bingo.' Ernie shrugs, 'Oh, all right.'

'Every comic would like to have had a "feed" like Ernie, and

Abbott and Costello meet Mr Morecambe and Mr Wise.
(*Thames Television*)

Youth taking a bow: the very beginning of the double act, 1941.

An early variety routine, Finsbury Park Empire, 1951.

Eric goes for the high note in 'The Woody Woodpecker Song'.

Summer season, Blackpool, 1957. A traditional publicity pose.

Supporting Stan Stennett at the
Hippodrome in Derby.

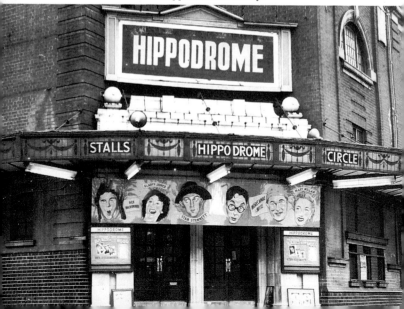

every "feed" would like to have had a comic like Eric,' comments Harry Secombe. 'Eric had a quick-silver brain that not every comic has. He was a multi-faceted man; a great comforter and listener, which many aren't. And he had a natural aptitude for all sorts of things. Ernie, in a way, was taken for granted. And he shouldn't have been, because the quality of the "feeder" reflects the quality of the comic. But for Eric and Ernie it was the perfect chemistry; a little like the "Goons" coming together.'

Though there was little or no tension between Morecambe and Wise, Ernie himself does recognise that the public, even back in the 1950s, had the order of billing firmly fixed in their own minds. 'I was always, "and Wise". Of course, that might just be in my imagination, but I think that's the pecking order people put us in.'

In many ways the greatest test of their ability to remain almost telepathically linked arose from their marriages. The old cliché about a double act being like a marriage is, like many clichés, true. And how can a marriage survive when other partners come on the scene?

In the beginning, Eric and Ernie had faced the world together, after marriage they faced only audiences together. Their relationship with each other – their daily shared routine – had significantly changed; and so the differences between them were more sharply accentuated.

'We went everywhere together and shared everything when we were first in showbusiness,' says Ernie. 'After we were both married there was a new situation and we were apart much more. Early on we messed together. But later we got separate rooms and we ate separately. This was far more sensible, really, when we both had different sets of friends and relatives visiting.'

This fragmentation of their domestic lives did not affect their working relationship however, mainly because the important years, the formative years, had been spent together. After they had found success in variety and honed their craft in front of demanding, sometimes downright hostile, variety audiences, it was no longer neccessary to spend their off-stage hours in each other's company.

The years of shared digs, of trudging from one agent's office to another in a desperate search for representation, of enduring the privations of the Sanger fiasco or the humiliation of being sacked from the Windmill, had ensured the foundations of their partnership were impregnable. If the worst was to happen, that they would go separate ways, then it would have happened then, not now as they began an exciting if not hurried rise to the top.

While Eric and Ernie had grown up sharing a remarkable bond of trust, friendship and understanding, it is curious to note it had not been the same for Laurel and Hardy.

Stan Laurel wrote of his partner soon after Hardy's death, 'Funny, we never really got to know each other personally until we took the theatre tours together. When we made pictures, it was all business even though it was fun. Between pictures we hardly saw each other. His life outside the studio was sports – and my life was practically all work, even after work was over.'

In later years, when Eric would sit down to watch their own shows, he would savour the whole feel of them, taking everything in. When Stan sat and watched old Laurel and Hardy movies, he would see only Oliver Hardy, never focusing on himself. Watching Hardy would make him laugh and laugh.

One rather unexpected development soon after Eric and Joan's marriage was that Joan became pregnant. Eric and Ernie were still travelling round the country to various venues but now they were travelling independently with their respective spouses.

After a spell living in Doreen's parents' spare room in Peterborough, Ernie and Doreen bought a small house there which gave them not only a base, but also a sense of some kind of financial security. They were hardly ever there though, and their conscious decision not to have any children clearly fitted in with their appreciation of a touring life.

Unlike Ernie and Doreen, Eric and Joan quickly decided there was no point in them setting up a home anywhere at that time. They couldn't afford to buy a house and thought it pointless renting anywhere when they would hardly have time to live there. So they remained on the road.

There was another complication. Eric couldn't drive. While Ernie and Doreen travelled around by car, Eric and Joan still had to rely on British Railways with frequent changes of trains and long bouts of waiting in stations for connections. This did little to ease the trials of Joan's pregnancy. Eric was soon forced to take driving lessons and save madly for a car.

The summer season booking at Blackpool in 1953 did ease things for Joan. The baby was due in September, so they were able to rent a small house in the town and at least the later stages of Joan's pregnancy did not involve the frequent travelling that had characterised her first few months.

In Blackpool that summer, Eric duly learned to drive and passed his test at his first attempt. Eric and Joan's first car was an Austin Hereford, and would take them to Sadie and George virtually every Sunday where Sadie would serve up a traditional and enormous Sunday lunch.

Joan had decided she wanted to have the baby at her in-law's house and during labour the midwife was convinced Eric and Joan would have a boy. This promised boy did not arrive at the expected hour of twelve noon, and the hours began to drag on. That evening Eric and Ernie had a show to do at the Winter Gardens theatre, where they were appearing with Alan Jones, but Eric was loath to leave Joan until the baby was born.

As the afternoon wore on, it appeared he had no choice. Somehow he would have to find the inspiration to run through the act that night.

The baby finally arrived at seven that evening and Sadie immediately telephoned the theatre. The news was given to Eric the moment he stepped off stage and he was given permission to leave the theatre before the finale. It was left to the star, Alan Jones, to explain away Eric's absence: 'Ladies and gentlemen,' he beamed, 'I'm thrilled to be able to tell you that Eric Morecambe's wife, Joan, has just given birth to a six-month-old baby girl!'

On arriving home, Eric had his first glimpse of his new daughter, christened Gail. 'And as I looked at her,' he recalled, 'I came face to face with a major reality in life. I knew our lives had changed.'

If domestic life could be hell for partners of touring variety stars, the addition of children only added to the complications. Frequent changes of home with a baby and its full complement of requirements, plus Eric's renowned lack of all-round tolerance, meant life in the Morecambe household was that much more testing.

Gail's first Christmas found Eric and Ernie back in pantomime at

Sheffield with Stan Stennett top of the bill. Eric and Joan struck up a long friendship with Stennett and his wife; rather poignant, for though they did not see much of each other in the intervening years, it was to be while making a solo guest appearance on Stennett's stage show that Eric would collapse and die in 1984.

Camaraderie in panto was as great as in summer season. And panto represented twelve weeks' employment during the expensive winter months. It wasn't always comfortable, however. As variety began to decline, so some of the theatres began to decay, and Eric and Ernie, like many other artistes, endured some pretty bleak dressing-rooms. The alleged glamour of showbusiness that variety desperately continued to peddle to the punters was as ephemeral as a desert mirage. Backstage, pros were only too well acquainted with the squalor of showbusiness.

The greatest disadvantage of pantomime was that it happened in winter, so the deprivations of backstage life, tolerable in the balmier, longer days of summer, appeared all the more harsh. And the winter weather did nothing to calm Eric, who had visions of being so snowed in he wouldn't be able to reach the theatre and perform.

Pantomime was, and remains, an essential part of the theatrical Christmas, but Christmas itself could be a tough time for pros in the 1950s. Traditionally, business was always slack in the run-up to Christmas, and pros who hadn't worked were broke before starting pantomime. But since panto usually started on Christmas Eve or Boxing Day, and pros needed to have worked a full week before being paid, they were usually broke over the holidays as well. So, even if they were inclined to return home, wherever home was, they often couldn't afford to.

Added to that was the reluctance of theatre managements to allow their performers to travel too far from the theatres in case a sudden worsening of the weather prevented their getting back. It was hardly surprising, therefore, that a great camaraderie grew between pros thrown together, and to facilitate this, Ernie and Doreen would often throw a Christmas party for fellow cast members who couldn't get home to their families for the festivities.

For Ernie and Doreen, these gatherings became something of an extended, substitute family. Naturally, Eric and Joan's home life, geared around a baby, was somewhat less gregarious.

Joan, unable to join Eric at the theatre in the evenings, became lonely, though far from bored, in a succession of rented houses. Inevitably, any novelty found in touring with a baby soon began to pall, and Eric hit upon what he thought was a brilliant idea to solve their problems: a caravan.

It was Stan Stennett's own success with caravanning that had inspired this idea, but as Joan, who readily went along with it, points out, they forgot one thing: Stan knew what he was doing. 'Stan had once driven lorries,' explains Joan, 'and was a very useful mechanic. He could even fly a plane, whereas Eric could just about manage to drive a car.'

Nevertheless, not letting themselves be dissuaded, and fired up by the thought of having a home they could tow behind them, they ignored any nagging doubts regarding lack of caravanning experience and took the plunge.

When the sun shone endlessly (and it seemed to in a long summer season in Blackpool) with the caravan parked in the grounds of a holiday camp, the whole family thought it fun. But confined to the limited space of a caravan in one of Manchester's characteristic weeks of torrential downpour with drying nappies, it was more like living in a mobile laundry and the joys of caravanning soon began to pall.

Not long after Gail was born, Eric and Joan decided to have another child and some serious decisions had to be faced about their future home life: not only where they were to live, but what sort of environment their children were to be brought up in. Both Eric and Joan had a horror of their children growing up under the influence of showbusiness. They wanted to establish some kind of family life away from the instability of touring life.

Two and half years after Gail was born, Joan gave birth to Gary. Joan's family had by now left Margate to run a pub in North Finchley, so to be near them, the growing Morecambe family bought a Victorian house there; a useful solution to the long weeks when Eric and Ernie disappeared to tour.

The very first piece of furniture to be delivered the day they moved in was a large television set. Joan still recalls Eric walking into the empty flat, pulling up the one and only chair, switching the set on and himself off from everything else going on around him.

Suddenly, the television set had become the most important item in the house. For Eric knew, as Ernie knew, that he was looking at the future of entertainment in Britain.

Together they had now hacked their way through pantomime, summer season, radio and, above all else, touring variety. They were now an established act with a growing reputation. But like the band playing on as the *Titanic* went down, there would be little future if they didn't escape their dying medium. Basically, they had to jump ship and they could only do that by putting all the horrific memories of *Running Wild* behind them and trusting their own instincts.

The contrast between Eric and Ernie's domestic arrangements during the mid-1950s couldn't have been greater, but together on stage they remained as seamless as ever. When Eric remarked, 'You can't see the join!' in reference to Ernie's 'wig', he could have been referring to the act itself.

In a dressing-room at that time, Eric confessed to a journalist that, though their act had been very successful for a number of years, 'if we don't make it really big soon, then the real success will never happen. We will forever coast along being very comfortable without becoming big stars.'

Together, now highly confident of what they could seriously achieve as a well-known double act, they made their most important decision to date.

It was time to return to television.

10

*'Morecambe and Wise were remarkable in
the way they bridged the gap between
variety and television.'*

Rowan Atkinson

Although it is their ten year association with the BBC between 1968
and 1978 which is regarded as the pinnacle of Morecambe and
Wise's achievements on television, it was at Lew Grade's ATV with
Two of a Kind that they finally established themselves as major
players in British comedy.

The years between the failure of *Running Wild* and the start of
Two of a Kind in 1961 had seen a sea-change in British
entertainment attitudes.

The 'Northern comics' label which had previously been so
limiting and, ultimately, damaging in regard to *Running Wild*, was
now a positive advantage in a culture which had suddenly
embraced the North of England.

In the cinema, Laurence Harvey had already reached for the
Room at the Top against the bleak industrial landscape of
Yorkshire, while Rita Tushingham was enjoying a brief *Taste of
Honey* in an equally grim Salford: in the theatre and on television

so-called working-class kitchen-sink drama was steadily replacing, or living alongside, middle-class drawing-room plays. And *Coronation Street*, 'doomed from the outset', according to a *Daily Mirror* critic, because of its 'grim scene of a row of terraced houses and smoking chimneys', would soon prove unmissable for audiences the length of the country. Northern voices and working-class situations were suddenly in vogue, and this permeated through to humour as to every other facet of the media.

Changes of this nature in cultural fashion allow many performers to suddenly appear and burst out on to the national scene, as Rowan Atkinson explains:

'Fashion and fad are just as great a part of comedy as they are in clothes. That's why comics like Benny Hill and Frankie Howerd – people who were a different confection altogether from Morecambe and Wise – went through such cycles in their appeal. Performers who have one basic comic act can't, without incredible ingenuity on their part and subtle marketing on that of others', avoid that.'

There is no doubt that Morecambe and Wise fitted the early 1960s penchant for Northern and/or working-class humour. But because they did not perform one basic comic act, as Atkinson highlights, once Eric and Ernie were established with television audiences, they were able to ride across the numerous and sudden changes of fashion for more than twenty years. Having been able to seize their opportunity when it presented itself, they now had the talent and the opportunity both to hold on to it and to develop it.

This was largely due to the fact that their act had been continually evolving to concentrate on the relationship between the two men: by 1961 that is precisely what they were about.

The start of *Two of a Kind* coincided almost exactly with the twentieth anniversary of Eric and Ernie's first appearance together as a double act. When the series started in 1961, they were well known to radio and variety audiences, but *Two of a Kind* saw them reborn into the widest possible fame. And because of the essential relationship they had established, audiences were quickly able to identify with them. This audience-performer rapport was arguably the single most important part of their act, and it gave them an edge over other entertainers.

'There have always been soft, middle-of-the-road entertainers on television who, in theory, have a broad appeal,' says Rowan Atkinson. 'But because there's no edge to what they do and what they do isn't genuinely funny, except to a relative minority of middle-aged viewers, no one really cares much about them. They're inoffensive and viewers just accept them for what they are: there just isn't enthusiasm for them, and they're there like wallpaper.

'Morecambe and Wise were never offensive and yet they had an edge to them which was sharp enough to get teenagers involved just as much as older viewers. Adolescents enjoy rudeness and Eric and Ernie were rude enough to each other or to their guests to interest young people. It was that kind of relationship we tried to achieve in the *Blackadder* series – particularly the second one.'

It was in *Two of a Kind* that this essential part of their appeal was first unleashed on television audiences, and Philip Jones, then a producer and director with ATV and later Head of Light Entertainment at Thames, cites the show as possibly the single most important step in Eric and Ernie's careers.

'Everyone now associates Morecambe and Wise with Eddie Braben and the BBC,' says Jones. 'But those *Two of a Kind* shows, written by Sid Hills and Dick Green, and produced by Colin Clews, were terribly important in establishing Morecambe and Wise on television.

'It's easy to forget now that they were done on minimum budgets. All black and white, of course, and although not performed live as such, they were taped as live in the days when you didn't do much editing anyway.

'And yet they produced really memorable routines which was the reason why the BBC bought them in 1968. So I think in fairness to Sid and Dick and Colin Clewes, we should remember the great job they did in the founding of Morecambe and Wise on television.'

Two of a Kind was the culmination of the decision Eric and Ernie had made to return to television, recognising that they needed to crack the new medium if they were to have any future security in comedy.

But two things had directly led to this superior era for the double act – Winifred Atwell and Australia.

Their first TV work after *Running Wild* came in 1956 with guest spots in Winifred Atwell's series for ITV. The writer on the series was Johnny Speight – who believes Morecambe and Wise were ahead of their time when they emerged in the mid-1950s – who was later to create TV's favourite bigot, Alf Garnett. The scripts were good, as was the money, but Eric, haunted as ever by the failure of *Runnng Wild*, was extremely nervous. So jumpy was he that Dickie Leeman, the producer for the show, was forced to take Eric to one side.

'He told me to relax,' said Eric. 'That it was only a TV comedy show. And he asked me what I'd be like if I was on Death Row and due to be executed the next day. I told him that if I was going to "die" I wanted it to be on stage. "That's what I like to hear," he told me. "As long as it gets a laugh on my show." '

Their appearances on *The Winifred Atwell Show* had proved popular, and the good notices received went a long way to eradicating the memories of the critical lashing of their first major TV outing. Their success led to an invitation to join Atwell on a six-month tour of Australia.

Eric and Ernie had now been together as a working double act for seventeen years. They were tired. The treadmill had certainly produced its livelier moments, but they were growing disgruntled with the business – and, occasionally, even with each other.

The prospect of working in a whole new continent was exceptionally tantalising and couldn't have come at a better moment. They could refresh the act and themselves from a completely removed situation, and for the first time in their working lives, consider what they really were and where they really wanted to go.

But there were problems. Eric and Joan had two children, their second no older than two years. Taking them on such a trip was not realistically conceivable in those days of archaic air travel. The idea, therefore, was that Joan should stay at home for the duration. Sadie, characteristically blunt, would have none of it. 'What about your marriage?' she demanded of Joan. 'You're just asking for trouble. Your husband should come first.'

It was agreed that the children should stay back with Sadie and George for the six-month tour which meant that Sadie, whose role in the Morecambe and Wise partnership had taken a back seat since Eric and Ernie had acquired wives, was now, once again, able to contribute positive practical help.

Their six-month tour of Australia, though a personal success and hugely enjoyed, merely pointed up the changes rapidly occurring in the British entertainment industry. And the most obvious change of all was that the decline of variety had suddenly accelerated.

For Eric and Ernie, the Winifred Atwell tour had by chance come at the worst possible time. Six months was a long time to be out of the public eye at that time, and they returned in 1959 to a summer season at Blackpool but an otherwise empty date book.

'Variety theatres everywhere had begun shutting their doors,' says Ernie. 'But it was worse for us because the Butterworth circuit of theatres – for which our agent Frank Pope had the sole booking – had closed down. This left him with virtually nothing to offer us.'

The rapidly dwindling number of variety dates available meant that the competition from other acts was becoming increasingly fierce and, like other first grade variety acts, Morecambe and Wise found themselves offered second and even third grade dates to which they were now unaccustomed.

A crisis of sorts had developed. They knew there was no doubting they were a good solid act. But they were a good solid act that was now not getting the best work. It was clearer than ever that television was the only way to stardom, and so they saw no option but to concentrate their efforts on conquering it.

Once that decision had been made – and it was a simple one to make because their incentive to crack that medium had resurfaced in recent months – another, altogether more painful decision, had to be faced.

To conquer television they required an agent with excellent contacts in that genre. And that agent wasn't Frank Pope. Reluctantly, for they had become good friends with him, Eric and Ernie saw the only way forward was to leave Pope and seek other representation. It was not a decision either of them relished.

'They were both upset at having to end their association with Frank,' says Joan. 'So was I, because we'd all become personal friends. But this was make-or-break time in their careers and there could be no room for sentiment.'

Eric and Ernie put an advert in *The Stage* saying, in effect, that Morecambe and Wise had terminated their association with Frank Pope by mutual agreement, and were looking for representation. Within days they'd been contacted by virtually every major agent in the business – and joined the biggest one: Billy Marsh.

Within the showbusiness fraternity, the name Billy Marsh was already fast on its way to becoming legendary. Marsh began his own personal success story in 1942 when he joined Bernard Delfont's agency. Marsh's skills were so acute that Delfont let him run, carte blanche, the Delfont agency, while he himself concentrated on being an impresario. Marsh proved a genius in the light entertainment field, booking artistes and knowing just how to massage their often sensitive egos. In 1969, he would move to the West End of London, to Regent Street, and buy out London Management – one of three agencies within the Grade Organisation – with Dennis Van Thal and Leslie Grade. And there would begin what were to be his halcyon days in the entertainment industry, seeing him stage summer seasons, pantos, tours and, what he enjoyed the most, the Royal shows. On top of this he would have a stunning list of big star names from light entertainment for whom he would have sole representation.

Marsh was never a glory-seeker and, unlike the Grades and Delfonts (except for Leslie Grade, who also preferred to keep a low profile) he would remain virtually unknown beyond the invisible wall separating showbusiness from the real world.

When Morecambe and Wise strode into his office one day, Marsh gave them a warm welcome – by now Eric and Ernie's act was gaining respect in the business – said he would represent them, picked up his phone and rang ATV. Immediately, he got them a spot on the ATV show *Sunday Night at the Prince of Wales*.

Morecambe and Wise stayed with Marsh from then on, and from the very first day there was no contract between them. As with Eric and Ernie themselves, just a handshake settled it.

Almost at once, Marsh's impeccable television contacts brought in an enormous amount of small screen work for Eric and Ernie. Three more spots on *Sunday Night at the Prince of Wales* followed before their next summer season and, by the end of 1960, they had chalked up over twenty more guest spots in other TV variety shows. Not for nothing did *TV Times* comment that Morecambe and Wise, without actually having a series of their own, were two of the most televised comedians.

But numerous appearances on television created an unexpected problem. In variety, performers, even top of the bill stars, could get away with doing the same basic act for years. Stars like GH Elliot and Jimmy James hadn't changed their essential routines for several decades. But comics simply couldn't get away with that on television.

'Remember, television's not like variety,' Marsh pointed out during their first meeting. 'Television gobbles up material and once you've used it you can't use it again. Your stage experience won't help you much except perhaps with your timing. Television's a totally different medium, something very few stage people appreciate. But as long as you can keep coming up with good fresh stuff, I can get you all the television work you want.'

Marsh's advice, though sound, was marginally erroneous in the case of Morecambe and Wise. Because of their long stage experience, rather than in spite of it, for their television appearances they were able to draw from the well of previous routines which they adroitly blended with new material. And, in a sense, their experience of variety was carried forward to television, particularly in their BBC years when traditional curtains – tabs – gave the impression that the shows were coming from a proscenium arch stage rather than a TV studio. It not only became their trademark, but an indication of the tradition from whence they came.

Even a classic routine like the famous kitchen dance Eric and Ernie performed to *The Stripper* in a BBC show had its origins many years earlier, as Ernie explains: 'We always had a notebook for ideas when we were working variety, and when we moved into television we continued using one to jot down ideas for sketches and routines.

'One day, I suggested we make breakfast in a flat to the sound of *The Stripper*. Eric thought it was a great idea and it went into the notebook. But it was twelve years before we used it, and then it became one of our most successful and popular routines.'

'Morecambe and Wise were remarkable in the way they bridged the gap between variety and television,' says Rowan Atkinson.

'They came out of variety and took it on to television. They went on for such a long time with that variety tradition in their shows and there was nothing about that tradition which people felt was out of date.'

'Morecambe and Wise were the first of the vaudeville double acts who really honed their act on the stage and brought it to television,' Bill Cotton adds. 'They were of their time, working with the tabs and the black ties. Right back to the days of Ted Ray and the *Billy Cotton Band Show*, TV producers had worked with the proscenium arch and the tabs. Morecambe and Wise came right at the end of that tradition but were still very much part of it. In fact it's probably because they perfected it to such a successful level that they finished it off. It's significant that the Two Ronnies – who came just after them – were much more TV studio oriented.'

Perhaps Eric and Ernie perfected the double act because they became virtually one performer comprising two contrasting personalities. As presenter and writer Paul Gambaccini once observed, it was as though Morecambe and Wise were joined at the hip.

Adapting their act for television was not easy since, as Ernie points out, their stage act was something which they had been doing for twenty years and had by then perfected. 'But when it came to television,' says Ernie, 'we had neither the experience nor the writers.' In effect, once they had decided to take on television, the exacting disciplines of the small screen had to be learned.

'And they did learn them,' says Glenda Jackson. 'There's such a difference between working an audience in the theatre and working for television. You can't just do a stage show for television. They learned that and were able to adapt to it.'

With growing experience and confidence, it wouldn't be long, as *TV Times* had more or less indicated, before Morecambe and Wise were contracted to their own series.

The call came during summer season at Torquay. And it came from Lew Grade. Marsh had approached Grade suggesting it was high time Morecambe and Wise had their own series. Lew Grade disagreed. 'Maybe they are good,' he told Marsh, 'but they don't warrant a series of their own.'

Marsh never fully knew what made him change his mind, but

Grade rang back a few days later. He told him he wanted to sign Eric and Ernie for a series of thirteen half-hour shows which would be transmitted live.

Eric and Ernie were both excited and horrified. This was an unexpected second chance in view of the *Running Wild* debacle, and with that spectre still lurking, they knew that another attempt to succeed on the small screen would require the best script-writers.

One of the main failings of *Running Wild* had been the paucity of good material. They were no longer inexperienced, which had also been a problem, but assurance would mean nothing without decent scripts. Thirteen half-hour shows meant six and a half hours of material was needed. No amount of raiding past variety routines would fill such a vacuum.

Eric and Ernie both admired the work of Sid Green and Dick Hills, who had written successfully for Jewel and Warriss, Harry Secombe, Roy Castle and Bruce Forsyth. Via Marsh, Eric and Ernie made it plain they would do the series if they could have Hills and Green – and to produce, Colin Clews, someone else whose work they greatly admired.

'Money doesn't come into it,' Eric told Marsh. 'We've simply got to have the right people this time round.'

Grade and ATV wouldn't agree to these terms. They could have anyone they wanted – apart from the people they'd named. Eric and Ernie took the risk and dug their heels in. For a while it looked as though the whole deal might be off. But ATV relented and Hills and Green were assigned the role of writers, with Clews producing.

The title of the series – *Two of a Kind* – came from a record by Johnny Mercer, which also became the theme song for the series.

The relationship between Morecambe and Wise and Hills and Green, was to last for seven years and would include not just the *Two of a Kind* ATV series, but also the three feature films they made for the Rank Organisation in the mid-1960s, and the first series they would do after their move to the BBC in 1968.

Although an extremely successful and fruitful pairing of two double acts, the relationship was not always harmonious. The creative process has long been littered with bruised egos, imagined slights and hurt pride – and *Two of a Kind* would prove no exception. Eric and Sid Green, in particular, found it relatively easy to bristle on occasion, and Ernie often found himself in the position of peacemaker between comic and gag-writer.

Nevertheless, each partnership appreciated the professional excellence of the other, and Dick Hills recalls the joy he and Sid Green felt writing for Eric in particular:

'His brilliance was his infinite capacity to see himself in a funny role in any situation. This was such a challenge to us; one which opened us up into giving him every situation we could possibly do. One minute he'd come on as a magician, pretending he was good at it and conning everyone he was good at it and ending up with dove feathers flying all over his suit: the next minute he was conducting the whole orchestra in *Peter and the Wolf*, and when Ernie came on to do the recitation, he thought he was just trying to tell a joke and tried to stop him.

'He could play all these nuances of character – anger, frustration, madness, cunning. He was a great comedy performer.'

Hills' comments echo Kenneth Tynan's observation of the sheer range of Eric's comedy moods which were given full rein in *Two of a Kind*. Watching Eric and Ernie perform live, Tynan noted that Eric could shift through a series like alarm, aggression, collapse, recovery, snide insinuation, all in about four seconds. 'Morecambe's reflexes,' he wrote in the *Observer* in 1973, 'the effortless speed and timing with which he changes expressions and tones of voice ... are among the wonders of the profession.'

Despite their initial enthusiasm for their script-writers, Eric and Ernie were disappointed with the very first script Hills and Green wrote for them, which went out in October 1961. Their disappointment was most keenly felt in one sketch – a spy spoof – which Eric and Ernie felt didn't suit their style at all.

'There were so many people in that sketch that I couldn't even find Ernie,' grumbled Eric at a post mortem on the show. Morecambe and Wise always believed that they were seen at their best when it was just the two of them together on stage. It was their relationship that mattered. As soon as they were part of a crowd scene, they felt their natural talent was stifled. Obviously, they knew they couldn't expect every TV sketch to feature just the pair of them, but overall, as far as Eric and Ernie were concerned, less meant more.

Their instincts about this proved infallible for, as Rowan Atkinson explains, 'Morecambe and Wise weren't really sketch actors at all. They tended to look at the audience as much as they did at each other which is a true indicator of the theatrical tradition. This is in contrast to, say, the Two Ronnies – and Ronnie Barker in particular – who were real actors and very much sketch-oriented. That's why in *The Two Ronnies* shows there was only room at the beginning and at the end for them to address the audience directly.'

Hills and Green thought differently. Clearly believing themselves to be more experienced than the stars of the show in television comedy – and at that time they were – they disregarded Eric and Ernie's concerns over the number of actors clogging up the sketches. So, despite the fact that Morecambe and Wise had barely registered with the viewing public in the first *Two of a Kind* show – something which Eric and Ernie blamed solely on being virtually invisible in the over-populated spy sketch – they went ahead and wrote a sketch for the second show which featured even more actors.

The problem wasn't that the script was unfunny – there were some good lines for both Eric and Ernie – but they instinctively felt that, again, the script wasn't right for them.

The solution to this basic disagreement came rather unexpectedly. The actors' union, Equity, chose this moment to go on strike; a strike that was to last twelve weeks – exactly the running-time scheduled for the rest of the *Two of a Kind* series.

As members of a secondary union – The Variety Artistes Federation – Eric and Ernie were unaffected and could continue to appear in the show without any problems. But no other actors who belonged to Equity could appear with them.

The result was that the Hills and Green sketches which, to Eric and Ernie, seemed to have scarcely fewer cast members than *Gone With The Wind*, were out – for the duration of the strike.

It was the big break they wanted – an act of God – for by the time the Equity strike came to its end, Morecambe and Wise were stars.

To have abandoned the series at such a critical time would have been disastrous for everyone concerned, not least ATV who were contracted to provide ITV with a full series. So it was decided to continue the shows by writing sketches with a much reduced cast; usually Eric and Ernie with Sid and Dick themselves playing other parts. This was perfect because it meant that the scripts were then tailored individually for Eric and Ernie. There was much tighter economy in the comedy and audiences were able to focus firmly on Eric and Ernie.

The result was a show which suddenly clicked with its audience and Hills and Green were forced to confess that this enforced working pattern had, however inadvertently, led them to a winning formula.

And as the show became more popular, so Hills and Green were inspired to write better and better scripts. As the scripts got better, so Eric and Ernie's confidence grew which led, in turn, to them coming up with ever more inspired ideas for routines and gags. It became a fertile creative environment.

'I'm not saying we didn't have arguments,' Eric said. 'There were plenty of them. But, funnily enough, ideas came from differences of opinion.'

Two of a Kind became increasingly successful and began to attract high ratings and big name guest stars including, on one famous occasion, the Beatles.

By 1963, the series was second only to *Coronation Street* in the top twenty TV ratings; Morecambe and Wise were voted TV Light Entertainment Personalities of the Year; their summer season at Blackpool was one of the most successful in history; and the newspapers began reporting that the two men were now the most highly paid double act in the country.

Two of a Kind ensured that Morecambe and Wise could do no wrong. In this new phase of their careers, their slow, steady progress suddenly accelerated as never before.

'In the end, it was the intelligence of Eric and Ernie, the understanding of their craft, which enabled them to make the transition to television,' says Michael Grade. 'That was a result of them coming up through the hardest school of all – music hall. They were personalities of their own background.

'If I had to single out one reason why they were so successful, it would be that they were great judges of their own material. They knew what was funny and what would work. A prime example of that was a Hills and Green sketch they did at ATV, involving Spanish dancing, in which Eric was the dancer and Ernie the guitarist. When it was written, it was intended that each should play the other part: Eric doing the guitar and Ernie doing the dancing. But in rehearsal they decided to switch roles. That was their genius, because anyone writing that sketch for them today would do it exactly as Hills and Green did it. But if you watch that sketch, you can see it works so much better the way Eric and Ernie decided to play it.

'It's just like Arthur Lowe and John Le Mesurier being originally cast in each other's roles in *Dad's Army*. Today it looks obvious that Arthur Lowe should be Captain Mainwaring and Le Mesurier Sergeant Wilson, but at the time it wasn't.'

The TV shows were churned out at thirteen a year and getting better all the time. With this, they combined summer season, pantomime and countless other appearances on shows like *Sunday Night at the London Palladium*.

'We were very hungry in those days,' Ernie admits. 'We did everything that was offered us and turned nothing down.'

Constant demands were made of them. When they weren't performing, they were opening fêtes or judging competitions or making after-dinner speeches. Added to these pressures, they were now aware of being a public property and felt a compulsion to 'be' Morecambe and Wise. This is something their friend, Penelope Keith, explains:

'I first met Eric and Ernie at ATV in the 1960s when I was working there for a time. And I found it extraordinary the way how, when Eric in particular walked into a room, everyone looked round and smiled. Now we weren't demanding that he be funny, but because we all smiled, he obviously felt the need to respond through this amazing comic gift he had. And it must have been awful for him, because he must have been thinking, "Oh hell, they want me to be funny."

'But he did it. And both of them were always kind and courteous to all the people they encountered on their shows. Having led a company on a sit-com, I know just how tiring that can be because you have to make sure that anyone who comes into the room is made to feel at ease.

'I remember on the Morecambe and Wise show in which I appeared, a group of army gymnasts arrived to rehearse some falls for a routine. Eric made a point of going over to them to say hello and have a joke.'

While at ATV, Keith saw how Lew Grade's company nurtured Morecambe and Wise, allowing *Two of a Kind* to grow steadily in popularity. And she contrasts this professional nurturing with 1990s practices.

'It was just like the BBC allowed us to do with *The Good Life*,' says Keith. 'When we made the first series, no one talked about viewing figures. We did a series, then another, then another, and by the fourth series we were established and doing very well. We were allowed to grow.

'That doesn't happen today which is why I don't think you'll see the like of Morecambe and Wise again. No one invests in talent any more; all they're interested in is the instant returns, and entertainers aren't allowed to grow.

'Morecambe and Wise couldn't have been picked up by *New Faces*, say, and instantly given a successful show. They needed all those years of training – and sometimes failing – to create the final product.'

Bryan Forbes agrees with Keith's feelings on this matter. 'There's no real training ground anymore,' he says. 'My generation was lucky; there were two thousand repertory theatres in this country, whereas it's hard to find twenty now. And drama schools aren't the answer because we're a practical medium, not a theoretical one. You can't teach people to act and you certainly can't teach people comedy. You're born with an instinct. And today where do they get their training? Television is instant and has a voracious appetite.'

There's no doubt that *Two of a Kind* facilitated the evolution of Eric and Ernie into the most powerful double act on British television and that the prevailing producing culture at the time allowed that evolution. Had the 1990s ratings obsession dominated producers' thinking in 1961, it's possible the pressure on *Two of a Kind* to provide instant success would have adversely affected the quality of the shows. Instead, supported all the way, the shows continued to improve.

But it wasn't easy. However important Hills and Green, Colin Clews and, indeed, Lew Grade were in ensuring the highest quality, it remained, essentially, Eric and Ernie's personal success. And since both men were almost pathologically determined to ensure that each series, each show in fact, topped the last, they worked incredibly hard perfecting each gag and each routine.

'Eric always seemed to be the driving force,' remarks Penelope Keith. 'He was the one who was always working, working, working. I'm not suggesting Ernie wasn't working hard as well. Of course he worked at the shows. But it always seemed to be Eric who was controlling it, especially on the creative side.'

Eric and Ernie's working relationship was highly different from Laurel and Hardy's. Laurel crafted their films with the writers, while Hardy preferred to be out on the golf course. And since the contribution of all the best straight men is largely invisible, Ernie's share in ensuring the success of their shows was easy for most observers to overlook.

Nevertheless, there is little doubt that the shows, like the rest of their subsequent television work, drained more energy from Eric than from Ernie.

'In his work, Eric was a perfectionist,' says Joan. 'And once he and television had found each other, he was hooked. It set him new challenges and he loved it. He enjoyed the positive side, too – the popularity and the rewards.'

And so did Ernie. After all, it was what they had been working towards for over twenty years. But while Ernie could leave all thoughts of work behind at the studio, Eric found it increasingly difficult to do so. And the amount of work which both he and Ernie felt necessary to put into each *Two of a Kind* show meant that Eric often couldn't relax.

'Sometimes,' Joan says, 'he could be so unrelaxed that you couldn't get him to sit still long enough to have a meal.'

The tension caused by their television work was to stay with Eric for the rest of his life. And the effort they put into their shows was never to diminish – only increase.

Their producer at the BBC from 1975, Ernest Maxin, recalls just how tense Eric could be for much of the time.

' "Nothing Like A Dame", from *South Pacific*, with the

newscasters, is a good example,' says Maxin. 'Eric was loving it, then about two days before we were due in the studios, he said, "It won't work, because we've never had all the people rehearsing together." That was true: they had other commitments and we could only rehearse them in twos. The only one who turned up day in, day out was dear old Peter Woods, who just wanted to be where Eric and Ernie were.

'Eric seemed a bit down about the whole routine. I promised him the routine would work, and that if it didn't, we would take it out. But he still didn't want to do it. Then Ernie said, "Look, give it a go, Eric. It might work out fine."

'This wasn't like the Eric of old, but he was getting very apprehensive, and a touch concerned, about his health at this time. And there were overtures from Thames, and all those sort of things building up on him.

'The night before the show, when I was still editing, Eric was so worried about this *South Pacific* routine that he came down at about midnight to get a sneak preview. I sat him down and he was a bundle of nerves, tapping away at the arms of the chair with his fingers, and very pale-looking. He watched it and said, "Bloody hell fire, it works." He put his arms around me, and all the pink colour returned to his face, and that brought a tear to my eye, I can tell you. But he was such a perfectionist, and he knew that if it didn't work the whole show could be pulled down because of it.'

'I've heard rumours that Eric was a bit of a depressive,' says Ben Elton, who never had the opportunity of meeting him. 'Manic, unable to turn off and having certain Hancockian tendencies. That would back up a theory I've always had, which is that comic geniuses who don't write their own material have a difficult path to tread because if you're truly brilliant but not entirely in control of the medium of your own brilliance, then that's a very tense life to live.'

Happily the rumours Elton has heard are, largely, gross distortions of the truth since those who knew both Eric Morecambe and Tony Hancock could not conceive of two comic giants who were so unlike. Indeed, Kenneth Tynan, (interviewing Eric for the famous *Observer* profile in 1973) specifically looked for signs of melancholy and said he could discern none.

Certainly, though, Eric was a perfectionist in his work, something which became increasingly reflected in the extensive rehearsals he preferred in all the TV work he did with Ernie.

'Never were sketch-based programmes more rehearsed,' says Philip Jones, talking of Morecambe and Wise shows ranging from the *Two of a Kind* era, to their final series for Thames. 'I was a producer and director at ATV in the 1960s, working with Mike and Bernie Winters, who were lovely guys, but not on a level with Morecambe and Wise. So I saw them working on *Two of a Kind*. And then, later, in the 1980s, as Head of Light Entertainment at Thames, I obviously kept a close eye on everything. So I saw them at work in the studio pretty often over the years and, believe me, they knew what they were doing. Especially Eric. He knew precisely how a joke was going to work; whether it was too long or not.

'They made it all look as though there had been no rehearsal, which was so deceptive. Dialogue which sounded as though it was a bantering tennis match between them was finely honed in rehearsal and Eric, with that lightning mind of his, would pick up on any deviation from the script which Ernie might inadvertently make and, boy, he'd capitalise on it. The speed of Eric's comedy reactions was sensational on television. He didn't miss a trick and it was fascinating to watch him do it without putting Ernie down in any sense.'

'At rehearsals, if Ernie had trouble with his lines,' says Penelope Keith, 'Eric would always finish them. And that always made me laugh because it looked as though it was part of the act when, in fact, it was for real.'

Though totally as one in their work, they appeared, to outsiders, to have little else in common. And yet the telepathic gelling of minds and performance not only remained but grew ever more telling over the years. It was a contradiction which would perplex producers and guest stars alike from their ATV days, through the BBC and finally to Thames.

'Their remarkable relationship was all the more remarkable when one learned that they didn't socialise together,' says Bill Cotton. 'I mean, it was obvious they liked each other a lot. And in many ways I think there was a form of love between them. But they didn't see much of each other when they weren't working together. And yet when they were working together, Ernie knew precisely what Eric was going to do next and vice versa.'

'Eric and Ernie were amazing because they never *seemed* to talk to each other,' says Penelope Keith. 'They'd arrive at different times and there was none of this "Hello, how are you? What did you do last night?" which you're always doing as an actor. They never seemed to have any communication and their outside life just didn't seem to exist when they were together.'

In the 1960s, it was virtually impossible for their outside lives to penetrate the lucrative but draining cycle of success they had entered, which they both described as a treadmill.

Still, neither of them could complain at the time, and having conquered the domestic entertainment scene, their ambitions naturally took them to consider finding fame beyond Britannia's realm. In the movies, perhaps? Or the USA?

By the end of 1964, they would have entered both those arenas.

11

'If you've always worked in front of live audiences, the sudden shock of doing comedy on a silent stage, where all you can rely on is your director, is a major leap.'

Bryan Forbes

Eric and Ernie had wanted to make it in the movies for about as long as they could remember. They'd been brought up on the movies and their lives and careers had been inspired by movie stars – not just other double acts, but the likes of Buster Keaton, Harold Lloyd, Cary Grant and Fred Astaire and Ginger Rogers.

So, when the Rank Organisation approached them in 1964 with a contract to make three feature films, it was an offer they naturally couldn't refuse, despite the treadmill of work they were already on. The three films were *The Intelligence Men* (1965), *That Riviera Touch* (1966) and *The Magnificent Two* (1968). They were not good films, and only served to interrupt their otherwise soaring careers.

It was an experiment in a genre they were never destined to conquer. While they were thankful to have had the opportunity, they were even more thankful that they'd emerged virtually unscathed as far as their TV image went.

Their biggest problem was having no audience feedback. The double act had always soared and dipped according to audience reaction. Over many years they had honed their act on live variety audiences. This cinematic departure from what they did best appeared to trivialise their talent. Someone must have remarked that Morecambe and Wise were very funny, and what a good idea it would be to make a film with them starring in it. The thought process hadn't been followed through to its inevitable conclusion before someone powerful at Rank had signed them up.

'If you've always worked in front of live audiences, the sudden shock of doing comedy on a silent stage, where all you can rely on is your director, is a major leap,' remarks Bryan Forbes. 'Sid Field and Tony Hancock could be bracketed with Morecambe and Wise. When they were on their individual roll, they had moments of genius, as indeed did Peter Sellers. But Peter, you see, had done bits of variety, but he wasn't really a stage performer. He didn't really have the discipline for it. He worked primarily on big screen. He didn't really do any television apart from interviews and a few bits of "Goon" stuff, which was self-congratulatory.

'But for most comedians, without the physical reaction of an audience, it's very difficult to time comedy. The comedian has got to trust the director's taste. That's the only thing he can go by. There is no other audience. If the comedian doesn't make you laugh on the floor then he's not going to make you laugh when it's trapped on the celluloid. On the other hand, you can't have an in joke where everyone laughs at the rushes. Usually that ends up as a puerile film. You've got to stand away from it and say, this will be funny when we put it all together; it's not necessarily as funny now because we haven't dealt with it.'

Forbes recalls working with Sellers in *The Wrong Box*. Sellers played a character called Dr Pratt. 'After the first day when he saw the rushes he wanted to re-shoot it all. I said, no. It's marvellous. I had to talk him back into it and convince him that it was good. He did the same on a film I produced, not directed, *Hoffmann*. When he'd finished it he rang me and said, "I want to buy back the negative and remake it." I said, "Peter, you know it's just not possible." He then gave an interview to the press saying how bad the film was so killing the film stone dead. This didn't do me or anyone involved any great service.

'But Peter was a very split personality. He wasn't a simple character by any means. When you met Eric Morecambe socially, he could not only make you laugh but you liked the man. That again is a great test of a comedian. If you don't like them then it's an uphill struggle to make the audiences laugh.'

Fortunately the slickness of the double act remains intact on film; though the retakes for close-ups often meant a little look here or there which Eric was renowned for would either be lost or exaggerated when edited in later.

The British film industry boom, which had actually begun at the end of the 1950s and would eventually peter out at the end of the following decade, was in full swing by 1964. So when they reported to Pinewood Studios in the autumn of that year for the first day's shooting of *The Intelligence Men*, it was to a studio riding on the crest of its own confidence and success.

Seventeen miles to the north-west of London, Pinewood was built in 1935 by an entrepreneur, Charles Boot, and eventually sold to the Rank Organisation. By 1964, Pinewood was known domestically as the base for the Carry On series and, internationally, as the home of the James Bond films. And arguably the two best examples of both series – *Carry On Cleo* and *Goldfinger*, respectively – had been in production at the studios the same year that Morecambe and Wise were making their film debut.

Eric and Ernie knew they were major players in the game now. Within just three years of becoming regular TV stars, the movies had come knocking at their door. Making movies was an ambition they'd both shared and they really had high hopes of changing the style of British film comedy.

Eric commented at the time, 'We want to bring to the films the same originality we've brought to television. We don't want them to be just typical British comedies with all the usual ingredients.' Alas, someone with clout didn't share Eric's sentiment.

To facilitate as successful a transfer as possible from small to large screen, Rank also signed Dick Hills and Sid Green to write the screenplay, thus ensuring that the entire team which had made

Two of a Kind so successful on television would be available to duplicate that success on celluloid. Harry Secombe sees this as a big mistake.

'They were hyped, just as I've been hyped in films before now,' says Secombe. 'But most importantly, the writers should have been screen writers. Sid and Dick were television writers. That was the area they worked in.

'But back then there was no one to advise us. It was the blind leading the blind. Now we know that less is more. It's what Michael Caine has always told us. He does as little as possible – doesn't even blink.'

As added insurance, it was further decided that the film should capitalise on the spy boom that had exploded with the release of the first James Bond movie, *Dr No*, in 1962, and which was then approaching its zenith.

Influenced by this, Hills and Green created a scenario in which Eric and Ernie would play two incompetent spies who blunder their way through a series of increasingly mindless adventures. It was a weak spy-spoof with Eric and Ernie finding themselves recruited by MI5.

Though spy stories were very much in vogue in the 1960s, pastiches in general had not been up to much. Spy-spoofing was, and is, a dangerous occupation in film-making terms, for unless executed with the all-round brilliance of a Blake Edwards Pink Panther film – a series that starred the incomparable Peter Sellers and so stands up as strongly on its own today as it did back in the 1960s – you end up with an inferior and mildly embarrassing impersonation.

Robert Asher, who had earlier helmed mild British comedies like the Norman Wisdom vehicles, *Follow A Star* and *On The Beat*, was signed as director; and a strong supporting cast, which included Warren Mitchell, Francis Matthews and William Franklyn, came along for the ride.

On paper, *The Intelligence Men* looked fairly promising. The script, written to order, was professionally crafted and certainly a notch or two above most of those written for the Carry Ons.

It was unfortunate that the theme of Eric and Ernie's first film outing was spying for this had been the theme of Hills and Green's very first sketch for *Two of a Kind* which had so disappointed Eric and Ernie at the time.

But by 1964 Hills and Green were intimately familiar with Morecambe and Wise's style and there was no reason to suspect that Eric and Ernie would be any less effective in an extended narrative – in effect, a 104-minute sketch – than they had previously been in the endless stream of short sketches Hills and Green had come up with for *Two of a Kind* since 1961. Besides, the spying theme had been decided upon by everyone – producers, writers and Eric and Ernie themselves – before one word of the script for *The Intelligence Men* had been committed to paper.

One obvious new factor was that Eric and Ernie would be called upon to act characters. They had, of course, performed in pantomime over the years, but subtlety is hardly the hallmark of pantomime, and caricature is the most that is required for this seasonal attraction used by producers to fill their theatres in what would otherwise be the thinnest time of the year.

In their TV sketches, Eric and Ernie were, essentially, themselves and were not actors in the accepted sense. They were, instead, performers. For pantomime or a sketch-based TV show, this was fine. But they would have to be directed properly to achieve success in a full-length film – a totally different discipline. Harry Secombe believes they were ill served in all three of their film outings.

'I don't think people knew how to handle them in this medium,' he says. 'Theirs was a raw talent in some respects and sometimes that's too big for the screen. But Eric was capable of underplaying if directed properly and though these three films weren't great, they weren't bad, either.'

Despite the unfamiliarity of the territory, they quickly managed to adapt to it. Penelope Keith, who first met them around the time they made *The Intelligence Men*, says no one should be surprised at just how quickly they did adapt.

'Any clown can play Hamlet – but not every Hamlet can play a clown,' says Keith. 'You see, actors have support which stand-up comics just don't have. An actor has the script, the director and fellow actors. But the stand-up comic has no one to fall back on if something fails; no one else to blame. The stand-up is up there totally naked. That's why you'll find actors have the most enormous respect for stand-up comedians and why comics have this ability to adapt to serious acting.' Norman Wisdom, Dawn French, Griff Rhys-Jones, Russ Abbot, Rik Mayall and Robbie Coltrane are all recent confirmation of her belief.

'In fact,' says Keith, 'there's nothing worse than seeing straight actors trying to be funny, and I'm convinced that Shakespeare wrote his clowns intending them to be played by clowns like Eric Morecambe, like Frankie Howerd, like Bill Maynard.

'Frankie Howerd was the funniest Shakespeare clown I have ever seen when he played Bottom at the Old Vic. Sadly, it seems to me that actors are held in higher esteem than they deserve and it's really only recently that great actors have acknowledged what great actors comedians actually are.'

Keith demonstrates her point with John Osborne's *The Entertainer*. 'I've seen Olivier do the play and I've seen Peter Bowles do it,' she says. 'But the kind of person who should have played Archie Rice was someone like Eric Morecambe. When I saw Olivier doing it, I remember thinking, "How wonderful, he can sing and dance, and isn't he daring to tell these awful jokes." But I shouldn't have been thinking that. That's not what the play is about – it has to be worth more than that. In the end, of course, it just comes down to the play surviving and John Osborne having the great coup of securing Olivier.'

John Thaw agrees with Keith. 'I think Eric would have been marvellous in *The Entertainer*,' he says, 'because he had, in repose, a sadness about him. I don't know what it was, or why it was, but you could certainly see it.'

Bryan Forbes is marginally more wary of comics performing outside their own specific genre. 'Audiences can be mean,' he says. 'If you don't give them what they expect they can turn on you. With Eric and Ernie, Morecambe and Wise was the act.

'They all wanted to play Hamlet. Peter Sellers wanted to be Mastroianni, a romantic lover, and really he was a fat Jewish boy and brilliant. And the moment he slimmed down and had his teeth fixed his persona altered.

'Tony Hancock was similar. He fired his writers, Galton and Simpson, got another writer and wanted to do serious things.

Basically, he wanted to play Hamlet. And the public didn't want him to play Hamlet. They wanted him to be with Sid James and be that brilliant character in East Cheam that he had honed over the years.'

Harry Secombe, who has personal experience of straight as well as comic acting, echoes Penelope Keith's thoughts on why straight actors tend to think so much of good comics. 'It's because they're not so good at doing comedy themselves,' he says. 'Ask actors to do a comic role and they usually panic. An actor comes on and his entrance is built up before he even starts. Comics go out there and look directly at the audience and try to win them over, with no guarantee. But also a comic has to be an actor. You've got to pretend to be funny and happy whatever happens.'

And of Eric Morecambe he goes on to remark, 'He was unfulfilled. He could have done other things – the Shakespearean fool he would have been brilliant at. Let's face it, it's far easier to play Lear than to play Eric Morecambe. Basically, he died too young, just like Sellers.'

'Eric had a unique talent,' says Forbes, 'and I could see as a director how skilfully he worked. With some comedians you can see the wheels going round but Eric always had the knack of surprising you, even though you were familiar with the material. You waited for those more familiar things, and there was an added pleasure when they did come.'

Of course, a largely-forgettable bit of cinematic tomfoolery like *The Intelligence Men* did not require intense performances from Eric and Ernie and, sadly, none of their other films would do so either. But Keith is right in pointing out that the ease with which they adapted to the regime of a film studio – something unknown to them before that time – reveals that had they ever been given the opportunity to do some real acting, in the right production with the right script and the right director, talent was something which wouldn't have been lacking. In the 1980s, after Eric died, Ernie did appear in a straight role in the West End musical, *The Mystery of Edwin Drood*. It is perhaps a pity that the pair were given few opportunities other than the Rank films to act in character.

It's entirely possible, however, that the Rank films were the very reason that few other offers came their way in this field: put simply, the three films did Eric and Ernie no favours at all in the genre, particularly with the critics who mauled each one.

There were many reasons given for the failures, not least the meagre budgets allotted to the films. Despite the apparent buoyancy of the British film industry, appearances were deceptive. The superbly crafted, big-budgeted Bonds, and Oscar-winning films like *A Man For All Seasons* and *The Lion In Winter*, might have been made in Britain, but they were financed by American money and distributed by American studios.

There was no American money for the small, indigenous film aimed squarely at the domestic market. These films – and it is a category into which Morecambe and Wise's Rank films indubitably fell – found themselves suffocating beneath their own mediocrity and limitations. Like the Carry Ons and the relentless Norman Wisdom efforts, the films Eric and Ernie made for Rank in the 1960s were notable chiefly for their cheapness of budget and production. Alas, unlike Norman Wisdom – who was a genius of pathos and slapstick – Eric and Ernie were not suited for this market. Even worse, for a double act who had always chosen a mildly sophisticated approach to comedy in preference to slapstick, they found themselves being used as Wisdom's chosen successors to perpetuate the British comedy farce on the big screen.

The cheapness of their own productions became blatantly clear to Eric and Ernie while they were at Pinewood in 1967. While shooting *The Magnificent Two*, they were horrified to learn that just one set built on an adjoining lot for the Bond movie, *You Only Live Twice*, cost more than their entire picture.

Disillusionment turned gradually into embarrassment, and in later years Eric and Ernie found it difficult even to watch their Rank efforts if they were screened on TV on the occasional Sunday afternoon. But the desire to try again would never leave them and would, in 1978, be their motivation in switching channels from the BBC to Thames, through whom they would take a retrograde step in regard to their film efforts by starring in *Night Train to Murder*.

Despite all the negative aspects of their three Rank films, they all seem rather more impressive thirty years on than they did at the time of their initial release. Partly this is because, since they were made, Morecambe and Wise have become much more familiar to

Two legendary acts which started in Liverpool.

The Ed Sullivan Show, 1964. Morecambe and Wise battle to win over
American audiences.

Typical poses from Morecambe and Wise at the BBC in the 1970s. *(BBC)*

Robert Morley preferred to bring his own lunch. *(BBC)*

Eric had impeccable manners . . . he always apologised to André Previn before slapping him. (*BBC*)

Christmas 1976. A mix-up in wardrobe? (*BBC*)

Two Freds and a Ginger: with Glenda Jackson. *(BBC)*

us; partly it's because there is a certain 1960s naïvety about them which is much in vogue in the 1990s. Certainly, the second of the three productions, *That Riviera Touch* (1966), has become something of a minor cult.

Again produced by Hugh Stewart but this time directed by Cliff Owen, it became their most fondly remembered film and in later years when people remembered Morecambe and Wise it would be for their Christmas specials and *That Riviera Touch*.

It begins with a woefully contrived situation that finds Eric and Ernie as errant traffic wardens apparently feeling forced into taking a vacation in the South of France, where they become hapless holiday-makers in ludicrous situations. Expecting sun-soaked beaches and beautiful girls, which they do manage to find later, they arrive at an eerie mansion in the pouring rain to encounter dead bodies that appear and disappear in the style of traditional British farce. Later on, Eric is misunderstood by the croupier at a casino, and in consequence wins a fortune. He keeps this in a money belt which the villains of the piece continually attempt to relieve him of. Too much back-projection in an otherwise enjoyable water-skiing finale does little to enhance the film. But its strengths lie in its locations and, as with all three films, the quality of the supporting cast.

The film was generally better received than *The Intelligence Men*, and even those people who didn't much care for Morecambe and Wise on television seemed to enjoy this one. An entry in Kenneth Williams' diaries published by HarperCollins in 1993, describes Morecambe and Wise as his least favourite comics – though that was an opinion he amended in later years – but then makes encouraging sounds about *That Riviera Touch*.

'There were some very funny original things in this film, which was very well done,' he writes. 'These two came out of it very well indeed – very much "innocents abroad" and at times a real note of pathos established.'

Rowan Atkinson echoes Williams' comments when he says he recalls 'enjoying it hugely and finding it very funny.'

One of the more interesting features of *That Riviera Touch* was that the title song was sung by Morecambe and Wise: echoing *Two of a Kind*, and foreshadowing the yet to come, and most famous of all their eventual repertoire, *Bring Me Sunshine*.

Had Rank built on the slightly more solid foundations of *That Riviera Touch*, their film career might have developed beyond their final outing for that company. But the last film – *The Magnificent Two* – emerged as a very odd mix of styles which ultimately never gelled when released on an indifferent audience in 1968.

It was produced by Hugh Stewart with Cliff Owen directing again. It also starred Cecil Parker, Margit Saad and Virgilic Texera. Again written by Hills and Green – with Peter Blackmore and Michael Pertwee also contributing – we see goodies and baddies, men and women, shoot each other dead and get blown up at regular intervals: violence beyond one's expectation in what was supposed to be a lightweight comedy. As one critic observed when the film was screened on British television twenty-five years later, (13 June 1993) '… There are vague and unsettling undercurrents of nastiness running through the story.' Certainly not the type of thing found in any Laurel and Hardy film, true, but in fairness to this Morecambe and Wise effort, it is one of its saving graces. For although Eric and Ernie remain improbable bunglers, all around them is realistic mayhem.

The background action is further authenticised by good, straight acting from the supporting cast. No one else around them is out to get a laugh: the comedy is Eric and Ernie, but the situation deadpan and not altogether unbelievable.

The basic story line has Eric mistaken for Torres, the leader of a resistance party planning a banana republic overthrow in South America. The real Torres, who bears a passing resemblance to Eric, is murdered on the same train Eric and Ernie are travelling on. When Eric and Ernie, travelling salesmen, arrive at their destination, Eric is coerced into taking on the deceased's mantle in Parazueilla – a rather too obvious Pinewood backlot.

Again, despite severe limitations in the script, there is some good comedy in *The Magnificent Two*. For instance, Eric in conversation with the beautiful Major Carla: 'I will always be the woman behind you,' she tells him, and Eric enquires, 'You'll come round the front now and again, won't you?'

Ultimately, though, *The Magnificent Two* was just another mediocre Morecambe and Wise film to put with the previous two and in a sense Eric and Ernie should have been prepared for the disappointing results of these big-screen outings.

When they finally took off as television stars, it was after they had proved they worked best alone, not cluttered up with cast and sets. Despite the small budgets of the films, they were definitely swamped with cast, sets and a lot of nonsense that might have worked better for a Carry On production. The story-lines, as is often the case when comedians are put on big screen, are very weak.

For Eric and Ernie and wives, the plus side of filming *That Riviera Touch* was location work, and locations don't come much better than the South of France. There was a carnival atmosphere which lasted the several weeks necessary to get the French scenes in the can.

Joan Morecambe describes this time as probably the happiest memory of her life with Eric. They met scores of people, including film stars Tony Curtis and Omar Sharif, and became good friends with Warren Mitchell.

Film star Eli Wallach was staying at the same hotel. He was a big star with whom Mitchell had briefly worked a short while back. 'Get me to meet him; that would be great,' said Eric. 'Sure, okay,' shrugged Mitchell. One morning, Eric and Warren Mitchell were sitting in the lobby when Wallach came striding through. The opportunity had nicely presented itself. Mitchell stood up all smiles and extended a hand. 'Hiya, Eli,' he beamed, in an 'old chums' sort of way. Wallach gave him a cursory glance without faltering in his step, said a curt 'Good morning,' and strode on and out of the hotel. Eric fell about laughing, and after that moment, whenever he saw Warren Mitchell, he opened their conversations with, 'Hiya Eli!'

Though *That Riviera Touch*, is the one most remembered, it is *The Magnificent Two* that comes closest to being a reasonably good film.

That Morecambe and Wise could act, given the right ingredients, was made clear in their most successful foray into drama when they appeared as guest stars in the very last episode of TV's *The Sweeney*.

Starring John Thaw and Dennis Waterman, *The Sweeney*, which lasted from 1974 to 1978, and spawned two feature-film spin-offs, was one of the most successful British police series of the 1970s. Blasting away the gentle legacy of Jack Warner's *Dixon of Dock Green*, *The Sweeney* focused on the tough cases tackled by Scotland Yard's Flying Squad, and was routinely accused by TV watchdogs of wallowing in bad language, violence and corruption. Viewers appeared to disagree and John Thaw's leading character, Jack Regan, became a TV icon of the cynical 1970s, while the series itself clocked up huge ratings week after week.

The Sweeney was, on the face of it, an unlikely place to find Morecambe and Wise; but such was the popularity of Thaw and Waterman, whose off-screen friendship allowed them to create an on-screen chemistry which, in its own way, almost matched Eric and Ernie's, that they were invited on to the Morecambe and Wise Christmas Show in 1976.

The return match – Eric and Ernie on *The Sweeney* – came as a direct result of that Christmas Show, and was the personal suggestion of John Thaw.

'I remember it clearly,' says Thaw. 'After we'd done the recording of the Christmas show, we all went up to the bar. I half-jokingly said to them that in their side of the business performers regularly appeared on each other's shows. In that case, I told them, now that Den and I had been on their show, they should come on ours.

'It was Ernie who picked it up immediately. "What?" he said. "You mean come on *The Sweeney*?" I said, "Why not?" "God, I'd love that," said Ernie. And it was the same with Eric: they were both fired up with this idea.'

Thaw admits that at first he wasn't quite sure what he'd done. 'I had only said it half-jokingly, and here they were virtually asking when they had to start filming.'

A week later, Thaw and Waterman returned to work on what was to be the last series of *The Sweeney*. Thaw mentioned his conversation to the series producer, Ted Childs, wondering what Childs' reaction would be.

Says Thaw, 'He said, "What a great idea. But do you think they'll do it?" I told him that they'd said they would, but that was, of course, in the bar after a show.'

John Thaw left the idea with Childs who came back some time later with the news that Eric and Ernie were indeed serious and would do an episode, subject to script. Childs immediately set about commissioning a script which, in the event, was an add-on to the last series: usually *The Sweeney* team made thirteen episodes a year, but Eric and Ernie's adventure came in at number fourteen, and was the last episode ever made.

To accommodate the inclusion of Morecambe and Wise in the story-line, the script for this final episode was uncharacteristically farcical, revolving round a professor with a bad heart, Arab princes, showgirls and a chase scene which had Eric and Ernie hurling boxes of kippers from a van into the path of pursuing Arab baddies, reminiscent of scores of Keystone Kops' movies from the 1920s and 1930s.

'It was a more light-hearted episode, to be sure,' says Thaw. 'A kind of end-of-sentence gift to Den and me from Thames.'

Nevertheless, their performances in that episode render meaningless any claims that Eric and Ernie couldn't act in character – even if they were basically playing themselves – and that their failure with Rank was solely their responsibility.

John Thaw, for one, believes *The Sweeney* episode provides clear evidence that Eric and Ernie could have developed into more dramatic roles had the right scripts come along.

'If you look at that episode now,' he says, 'it proves that Eric, in particular, could deliver a line straight. He didn't have to be funny all the time, and he didn't have to try to be funny all the time. He was perfectly capable of standing on a set and delivering a line.

'I'm of the belief that if you're an actor – be it a comic or a straight actor – you can, to a large extent, perform anything if you've got that inherent timing. Now there's no question that they both had that timing, so there was no reason for them not to have done more acting – providing it had been tailored to them.'

The Rank films, alas, were not tailored to Eric and Ernie and, in retrospect, seem curiously ill suited to their style, despite the input of Hills and Green. As a result, they appear ill at ease, and this is undeniably conveyed to the audience.

This is not the case in the episode of *The Sweeney* they made. Why was that hour of TV drama the most successful departure they were to make from their usual work? John Thaw believes it's because of the way *The Sweeney* was produced.

'I'll be honest, on the first day of shooting they were initially nervous,' explains Thaw. 'Just as Dennis Waterman and I had been on the first day on their show. But the big difference between their show and *The Sweeney* was in rehearsal. On the Morecambe and Wise Show, they insisted on rigorous rehearsals. On *The Sweeney*, there was no rehearsal. You just arrived in the morning and read through the scene a couple of times. Then it was a case of "you stand here and you stand there", a run-through and then a take. And I could see that this made them nervous.

'So all Den and I could do – and what we did do – was to try to relax them by mucking about. We tried to get across to them that it wasn't overly serious and we weren't out to win any prizes: the secret was to be relaxed and natural. We told them that it didn't matter if a take went wrong. We could do it again, and keep on doing it until we were happy with it.'

This campaign launched by Thaw and Waterman certainly worked, for as the first day of shooting went on, and Eric and Ernie got to know the crew and the director, they visibly relaxed, and as the stress evaporated, so their performances improved.

'What you've also got to remember,' adds Thaw, 'is that on *The Sweeney* we had a team, a crew, that had been together on the programme for four years. It was like a family. Most of the scripts were good, but when they weren't so good, this crew could all pull together to make it look better than it was.

'So there was a strong family feeling to the whole unit and Eric and Ernie were made to feel part of that family: everyone surrounded them and said, "Hey, this is going to be good. This is a successful programme, we're proud to have you on it and it'll be as good as, if not better than, anything else we've done in the series." And I just think that helped to bring out what they had to offer which was, for God's sake, a great deal.'

Though Eric and Ernie scored well in that jokey finale to *The Sweeney*, they were never again invited to make similar appearances on other series. Neither were they offered a drama or sit-com series; a challenge, notably in Eric's latter years, they would have dearly liked.

Glenda Jackson, one of their most famous and certainly most regular guest stars, believes this to have been the one great disappointment of their careers.

'It really is a shame that no one ever came up with a script for them,' says Jackson. 'If you look at their BBC shows, it seems to me that at the centre of their appeal were the Eric and Ernie characters you saw in the flat. Not just the jokes. They could have done it but they never did find the sit-com they had always wanted.'

For Eric and Ernie, though, their less than auspicious film career, which would remain logged as no more than a flirtation with that particular medium, would inevitably be a personal regret.

Not long after *The Magnificent Two*, however, Eric was to be struck down by a storm which had, unbeknown to them, been gathering for a while and which would finally put success and failure and the relentless treadmill on to which they had willingly stepped, into perspective once and for all.

12

'Comics don't live as long as straight men.'

Ernie Wise

In addition to talent, good fortune and the ability to take opportunities when they present themselves, what every performer needs to ensure a long and successful career is good health.

The physical demands made on performers can be extraordinarily harsh, particularly in the early years when he or she may be travelling long distances between venues, accepting everything going in what is often a vain hope of becoming established.

The unhealthy life-style adopted to accompany those long, unsociable hours has often returned to plague many a successful performer in later life. The unremitting loneliness and boredom of living in digs far away from home has led more than a handful of entertainers to frequent some local hostelry before, after and, in some cases, during a show. There the inevitable alcohol and nicotine intake, so necessary in the manufacture of the enforced camaraderie required by pros, has been far in excess of what any doctor would recommend. It's perhaps no coincidence that the plastic red nose of the clown has long been a superfluous prop!

Even for those like Eric and Ernie, whose family commitments did not lead them to the nearest boozer, the pace of the work, the travel, the tension could still prove detrimental to health. Of warm, invigorating summer seasons spent at Yarmouth, Bournemouth and Blackpool, Eric used to say he felt more like a vampire, always in the dark, and when he faced daylight it took half an hour for his eyes to adjust. With showbusiness, perhaps uniquely, pressures mount rather than diminish with increasing success, so, short of turning down work, which at this time both Eric and Ernie were incapable of doing, the pressures on them were going to be constant.

With double acts, the need to remain healthy is doubly important, since one member of the act succumbing to illness interrupts the career of both partners.

Bobby Ball, of Cannon and Ball, probably Britain's most successful double act to follow Morecambe and Wise, puts it well. 'If Tommy Cannon died tomorrow, my life would be finished. And it would be the same for him if I died tomorrow. That's the underlying reality of a double act.'

The tension involved in appearing in front of live audiences is really understood only by those who do it, but it is perhaps felt most keenly by comedians, many of whom, like Eric Morecambe, die from stress-related illness before reaching the accepted three score years and ten. Others, Tony Hancock being a notable example, have taken their own lives during stress-induced depressions. As Les Dawson said in an interview in 1973, 'Being a comedian is no joke.'

'What is that pressure on comics which makes them die so young?' Philip Jones wonders. 'You think of Eric, Frankie Howerd, Tommy Cooper, Dick Emery, Les Dawson – the list is endless. But why Eric and not Ernie? It can't only be that Ernie had the ability to switch off more than Eric.

'I think part of the answer lies somewhere in the motivation of being a comic. That's the biggest mystery of all with funny men. What motivates, what triggers, what frightens them? I mean, Eric used to tell me that going out to perform on that stage or in that TV studio was all down to fear. His constant worry was a tap on the shoulder and a voice saying to him: "Well, come on; you've had a good run, but you've got to give it all back now." '

The fact was that throughout the 1960s inner fear drove Eric to work too much, smoke too much, but not relax enough.

'I don't know any comics in our business not driven by fear who are any good,' says Bill Cotton. 'It shows itself in all sorts of ways. Some are arrogant, some are mean and some are over-generous.

'One of the reasons I think I had success in television as a producer and then as an executive was because I once took my father's band on a sixteen-week tour of Moss Empires theatres when he was ill. So I got to know exactly how you feel just before the curtain goes up and you're not sure whether this audience is going to stand up and applaud or throw things at you. And you never get over the possibility that they might just be the audience which gives you the bird.

'Now that's bad enough as a band leader – although my father's act did have a degree of comedy in it. But the real recipients of that are the people who set themselves up to make audiences laugh, because if audiences don't laugh, then the comic's just talking gibberish. There's no doubting the sheer pressure and hard work involved in being a comic. It's the nature of comedy. There's no doubt in my mind that the bravest men in the world are comedians.'

Although the 1970s is the decade most people associate with Morecambe and Wise, it was the 1960s which first established them nationally with television audiences. But, they could not yet concentrate solely on television work. Instead, Eric and Ernie worked solidly in TV, summer season, pantomime and in what was left of variety. They turned nothing down as they established and then consolidated themselves as one of the country's leading comedy acts. They didn't dare turn anything down, both convinced that they'd have a couple of good years at the top, but then it would be back down to reality. And for Ernie, as much as Eric, that thought was horrific. 'I would honestly hate to start on the slow spiral downwards,' he said in the mid-1970s. 'It's not so bad being second or third on the bill if you're on the way up, but it must be soul-destroying the other way.'

For Eric, there was a severe price to be paid for taking on such a gruelling workload. The day of reckoning came in November 1968 when, at the young age of forty-two, he suffered a massive heart attack that all but left him dead.

He was lucky. He was given a second chance, and he went on to make a slow, but full, recovery. Their most successful decade then followed, but the damage done to his heart led to a further attack in 1979, a by-pass operation and, ultimately, his premature death in 1984.

'He wore himself out,' says Ernie. 'Simple as that. When he was on stage he was very dedicated. I don't have the same temperament as his, and I've always held something back. I don't go flat out when I'm performing, but Eric did. When he came on stage, he gave the audience everything he had. And he didn't relax or hold back enough and that's what killed him. It was stress. Of course, the fact is that as the straight man you're not the end product. You are helping to push that end product but it's the comedian who has most responsibility to get those big laughs.

'As a straight man I worked to get laughs wherever I could, but the onus is always on the comic. And I think that's why comics don't live as long as the straight men.'

Though, in retrospect, Eric's coronary seems an inevitability biding its time – particularly since he already had a recorded minor heart problem from his time as a Bevin Boy during the war – when it happened in 1968, the attack came as a bolt out the blue or, in Ernie's own words, 'a hurricane'.

Says Joan Morecambe, 'In 1968 they were in demand from every quarter. They'd broken records with a summer season in Great Yarmouth, made an LP and left ATV to sign up with BBC2. By October, they were scheduled to do a TV appearance in New York and then an eight-week theatre season in Glasgow. They even had to turn down a request from Bernard Delfont to do four spots in a Royal Command Performance show because they just didn't think it was humanly possible.'

Delfont, however, persisted and the boys did finally relent but, for the first time, Joan began to notice the strain on Eric as he confessed that he didn't think he'd be able to cope.

Reflects Joan, 'Perhaps it was then that he concluded that all comedy is based on fear. You see, Eric lived on his nerves and was always concerned that he must live up to people's expectations, never to disappoint and never do an off show. And then there was always that nagging thought at the back of his mind that it could all end tomorrow.

'As for his smoking, I never really thought much about it. His parents smoked and Eric had been a smoker all the time I'd known him. Being the kind of man he was, though, Eric took to smoking heavily. It was quite normal to see him with a cigarette in his hand and in the studio he was rarely without one.'

Indeed, being the kind of man he was meant that he had great difficulty in coming to terms with any moderation. It was always either to excess or not at all.

'Certainly he was smoking between sixty and a hundred cigarettes a day and living on his nerves,' says Ernie. 'But I don't think anyone who worked with him – and I include myself – quite appreciated the pressures he was under. You see, on the surface Eric had a very bland manner and, at the same time, he was a hypochondriac who never had any qualms about letting you know of every twinge he suffered.

'Looking back, it's quite obvious we were crazy to accept the volume of work at that time. We were swamped. But we had everything. From those very humble beginnings we'd achieved financial and material success, popular and critical acclaim, and even respect from the business itself. And when BBC2 started in August 1968, the bookings really started to pour in.'

Forced to make the choice between starring in a West End show or doing a tour of Northern clubs, they opted for the club circuit. 'There's more money to be made in the Northern clubs,' as Prince Philip had once jokingly told them.

Club work was not something that greatly appealed to them as no one could guarantee they'd have the full attention of the punters. For every person watching the act, there would be another at the bar chatting to a mate or ordering drinks. Some patrons would be drunk, and the smoky atmosphere of clubs – many years later thought to be the cause of Roy Castle's lung cancer – did little to alleviate the discomfort.

Worst of all were the hours which usually meant an act did not start to perform before eleven pm. Small wonder Ernie says, 'We always preferred working in theatres to clubs.'

Jimmy Corrigan's club in Batley, West Yorkshire, was a date they couldn't resist, however, for several reasons. It was probably *the* major, prestigious venue of its type and it attracted the biggest names in the business. They had known Corrigan, who came from a fairground family in Leeds, for many years, and finally, they had been offered the sum of four thousand pounds for one week's work.

They opened the week on 3 November 1968, doing an act of an hour and a quarter which didn't start until midnight. On the Thursday of their week-long engagement, Eric felt unwell during their performance.

'I'd had a twinge all week,' he said much later. 'It was in the right arm and felt a bit like tennis elbow or rheumatism. Whenever I pressed that arm in the area of the funny-bone I got a shooting pain.'

The pain continued throughout the week and, in truth, he didn't feel well for the whole week. But the pain was much worse when he woke up on the Thursday morning and persisted during that day into the evening and right through their act, which he somehow managed to stagger through.

'I could see from the look on his face that something was wrong,' remembers Ernie. 'But I had no idea, and nor did he, that he was actually having a heart attack there on stage in front of a packed audience.'

At the end of their show, Eric asked Ernie to deal with the autographs and set out for his hotel in his car, a Jensen Interceptor, which fortunately came with power steering and automatic gears.

Even so, Eric soon found it increasingly difficult to drive since the pains in his chest and back suddenly became acute, and he decided that he really ought to try and find a hospital. From that moment on, the whole saga of Eric's well-documented heart attack took on farcical qualities which could not have been bettered by the most inventive comedy scriptwriter.

Pulling into Leeds at quarter to two in the morning, Eric saw a young man, Walter Butterworth, walking home. He stopped the car and asked:

ERIC: Could you direct me to the nearest hospital?
WALTER: Ah, let me see ... Oh yes, go up this street here – it's all one way which makes it a bit awkward. Then take the third right – no, take the second right. Then carry on and take your

third, no, your fourth left … Then you'd better ask again because it becomes complicated.
ERIC: Look, I don't feel very well. Could you drive me there?
WALTER: Well, I'm in the Territorials. I've only ever driven a tank!

Walter, nevertheless, climbed into the driving seat and somehow drove Eric to the nearest hospital. It turned out not to accept emergencies. At Leeds Infirmary, Walter left Eric in the car at the bottom of a hill and went to find help. At the hospital, he found the wrong entrance and was re-directed to Casualty.

Eric, meanwhile, was feeling much worse and so got out of the car and struggled up the hill to Casualty. There, he had to endure a seemingly endless questionnaire, again of farcical proportions, before he was finally admitted.

Then at last, injected to dull the pain and slipping gently into sleep, Eric felt a tug at his arm. It was Walter.

WALTER: 'Look, my mates'll never believe me. Do me a favour, could you sign this for me before you go?'

Succumbing to unconsciousness, Eric's last memory was of scrawling 'Eric Morecambe' on the piece of paper Walter had laid on his chest, convinced he was signing his last autograph.

The first Joan knew about the drama was a telephone call in the early hours of Friday morning from Leeds Infirmary. At first she thought it was a cruel practical joke. But when she checked with the hospital, she learned that Eric had indeed been admitted with a suspected heart attack, and that she should be ready to travel up to Leeds immediately. A later call emphasised the urgency: 'You'd better hurry, Mrs Morecambe, or you may be too late.'

Indeed, the doctor who had said that to Joan was convinced that Eric was about to die. Although the news was put out that Eric had suffered a slight coronary thrombosis – and that was what he himself was told – he had, in fact, suffered a major one from which it was initially thought he might not recover. The first forty-eight hours were crucial.

'The doctor told me that if he lived through that period, he'd probably recover,' says Joan. 'But it was touch and go.'

When he first came round, Eric found himself in a plastic oxygen tent. 'For a moment it crossed my mind that I'd died, and was passing out of this world into the after-life,' he said. Later, when he had recovered consciousness fully, he saw Joan through the plastic and reassured her. 'I'm going to be all right, love. I'm not going to die.'

Ernie was staying with Doreen at another hotel when the news reached him. By the time he reached the hospital, Eric was sitting up in bed not looking too gravely ill. Appearances, though, were deceptive, and Eric eventually needed six months' recuperation before returning to work. For a time he even seriously considered retiring altogether.

Everyone thought it necessary to keep Eric's spirits up, and the severity of his illness was kept from him for a long time.

So, when Ernie stepped into see Eric for the first time, his opening comment was, 'You'll do anything for a laugh.' They continued the light banter for a few minutes with Eric saying that the flowers Ernie had brought would do for the wreath. Ernie did a sterling job in hiding his despair at seeing his partner so fragile and incapacitated. Only later did Joan tell Eric that Ernie had left the room in tears.

If Eric and Ernie had needed any further proof of just how popular they were with the British public, Eric's illness gave it to them. Interest in his condition was enormous, and journalists camped outside the hospital awaiting news, though one managed to disguise himself as a member of the medical staff to take a sneak picture.

'The hospital was deluged with telegrams, letters, flowers and all kinds of presents,' says Joan.

One well-wisher even sent a Lourdes medal, which Eric wore on his watch-strap after his return to work.

During the two weeks following his heart attack when, though still understandably very weak, Eric had been getting stronger, he couldn't wait to get back home to Harpenden. In fact, the doctor treating Eric had long been of the opinion that the best way to deal with patients who had suffered coronaries was to get them out of bed and walking about as soon as possible. So he had not been confined to bed during that two-week period.

But when the moment finally arrived to leave hospital for home, Eric panicked. Always the archetypal hypochondriac even when in the best of health, he now set his mind to worrying about what would happen if he had another attack. At the hospital, he was just seconds away from specialists and intensive care: but at home, he reasoned, he would be too far away to be helped.

'Doreen and I saw him not long after he got home,' says Ernie. 'He looked just as he'd felt on the day he left hospital – old and sick. But he soon began to enjoy all the fuss: breakfast in bed, taking things easy and just pottering about.'

'He gradually began to recover his strength,' says Joan, 'but he continued to feel vulnerable for a long time. After any exercise, he thought he was going to have another attack. He started going for short walks and began to take an interest in bird-watching to make the walks more interesting. But his inclination was to hang about the house where he felt safe.

'One day our GP, Dr Price, appeared on the doorstep and threw his car keys to Eric. "Here," he said. "You need some exercise. So we're going to the golf driving range at Watford and you can take me in my car." "But I'm not ready for that." "Yes, you are. It's just what you need."

'Eric returned from that trip a changed man. He was no longer thinking like an invalid, and by the time he reached home was even contemplating a return to showbusiness.'

Recalls Ernie, 'He rang me up bubbling with enthusiasm. It was wonderful to hear the old Eric again.'

'They'd had a pretty good career up until Eric's first attack,' says Joan, 'and I think everyone at the time thought that was the end of it. That's what so amazed the profession: they didn't just bounce back, they bounced back bigger and better than ever. What Eric had done, you see, was to use the enforced break to make himself really well so that when they returned to TV their shows were not just as good, but further improved.

'Many people thought Eric was finished in 1968, but I believe Eric, himself, never doubted that he would go back and do some work. But to go back and score so well? To be such a huge success and to keep it going from series to series? I don't know if anyone really thought that was possible.

'Mind you, even without the heart attack and his recurring health problems, that's something he could never have known himself. Comics just never know what the future holds, which is why most of them are such pessimists about the future. There's always this nagging worry that if the public don't like the next performance it could be downhill from then on. That never happened to Eric and Ernie, but there was a strain in having reached such a high peak and staying there. And that strain never really left them. It's one thing going up: it's quite another avoiding coming down.'

Eric was not hasty in deciding upon a full return to the treadmill of work. Pondering on the stress, the fear involved in performing comedy, he let the doctor make the decision on how long he should remain away from the spotlight. When told that the average case involved being off work three months, Eric said, 'In my line of business it's impossible to work without tension. You need it to make a show come alive. So I'll stay off work for six months.'

Naturally enough this proved to be a very difficult six months for Ernie who, although in the best of health, found himself forced not to work through his partner's ill health. Indeed, for the first few days following Eric's coronary, it wasn't clear whether he would be able to return to work at all, putting Ernie in a very difficult position.

'If the doctor had said there was no chance of him ever working again, that would have put a completely different complexion on to things,' says Ernie. 'But as it was I had to stand by him, just as he would have done for me. I couldn't very well go out and start doing things on my own until something definite was settled about Eric's future.'

Plagued all the time by the question, 'How's Eric?' from well-meaning well-wishers as well as journalists, Ernie took to wearing a badge at functions which read, 'Eric's getting better. PS: I don't feel so good, though.'

Through the enforced sabbatical, Ernie kept the Morecambe and Wise partnership alive wherever he could. Just prior to Eric's illness, they had recorded both their own show for BBC2, broadcast on Boxing Day 1968 and a guest appearance on *Night With the Stars*, broadcast on Christmas Day itself. These went some way towards keeping the act very prominent in the public eye during those early weeks of recovery.

But in the late 1960s, Morecambe and Wise were still in the ascendancy, and it was important to keep their image in the nation's consciousness. No matter how much colleagues wished Eric a speedy recovery, competition is cut-throat at the best of times. Other acts, sensing a gap in the market, would hardly need encouragment to muscle in on the opportunity. The last thing Morecambe and Wise wanted was a serious break in their momentum and a one-day comeback that would find them labelled 'old hat'. So Ernie embarked on a nationwide PR job for the act while Eric recuperated at home.

'I talked about Eric at ladies' luncheon clubs, guested at schools and Girl Guide concerts, did a few radio programmes and went on the Eamonn Andrews show. And at every event I made a point of talking about Eric.'

During this period they were greatly encouraged by the support of Bill Cotton at the BBC. He promised not only to honour their contract until Eric was fully fit but also, in a unique demonstration of faith in them, offered another contract for July 1969.

Cotton had been delighted with their first series for the Corporation – and particularly by the audience reaction to it – and he was determined to wait until Eric had recovered to continue their series.

Morecambe and Wise finally returned to performing in August 1969 at a Sunday concert at the Winter Garden Theatre in Bournemouth. Their return was welcomed with a five-minute standing ovation, further proof of the affection now felt for them by British audiences.

Eric had been given the severest warning possible, and he and Ernie were forced to reconsider their entire working pattern.

From now on television would dominate their time, with theatre bookings taking a back seat and summer seasons and pantomimes dropped completely. Eager to keep their stage relationship with audiences alive, they would do the occasional tour of one-nighters – 'bank raids', as they liked to refer to them.

Eric also adapted his life-style. Cigarettes were jettisoned in favour of a pipe – he was named pipe-smoker of the year in 1970, an award he shared with Manny Shinwell – and he allowed himself more time to indulge in hobbies. Bird-watching was the newly found pleasure, but fishing, his life-long love, he now pursued as often as he could.

'The thing about Eric was that he was so relaxed when casting a fly,' recalls Philip Jones, who often went fishing with him. 'And he was very good at it. I was fishing with him on the River Test on the Thursday before he died, and it was a really good day. He was totally relaxed.

'I don't think I caught anything that day, but he did. And in a fishing book on that stretch of the Test is his entry for that day. I wrote it in the book and I remember putting his name down as Bartholomew rather than Morecambe in case someone tore it out. I hope it's still there.'

'My one escape in life is fishing,' Eric once wrote. 'It gives me a total serenity I can't get anywhere else – so long as I'm left alone. If people recognise me or want to make a fuss then it defeats the object of the whole thing as far as I'm concerned.'

Says Joan, 'From that first attack onwards, we were very sensible about Eric's condition. And he adapted very well to all the new disciplines, never questioning that he had to give up cigarettes or take pills for the rest of his life.

'Of course there was the constant fear at the back of his mind, and mine, that he might have another heart attack if he carried on working. And that was an extra stress. But as the years went by, it did seem as though he'd made a complete recovery. It was a naïve assumption.'

The first indication that Eric's health was not all as it should have been came in September 1975, the day before his daughter, Gail, was married. Eric woke up that morning feeling totally numb down his left side and unable to control his arm or leg. The paralysis led him to believe that he must have suffered a stroke. Following an examination, medical opinion was that he'd suffered a spasm of a blood vessel.

Advised to cancel all immediate work, Eric went through his daughter's wedding supported by a walking-stick. To the inevitable questions about it from the press, he blithely claimed to have had a minor fall.

Eric recovered very quickly from this temporary seizure, and remained in good health until March 1979 when, eleven years after his first heart attack, he suffered his second. Though again it was touch and go as to whether he would survive, Eric seemed mentally better equipped to weather this latest setback than in 1968.

He underwent detailed checks both in London and at Harefield Hospital. Magdi Yacoub, arguably the finest heart specialist in the world, gave Eric the verdict in May 1979 at Harefield. 'We've looked at all the evidence and seen the results of the tests. And our recommendation is that you should have a by-pass operation.'

Eric naturally inquired what would happen if he didn't have the operation. 'Then I wouldn't expect you to live more than a few months,' came Yacoub's reply.

'What're you doing this afternoon?' said Eric.

Although apprehensive about the operation, Eric calmly accepted the possibility that he might die and was more worried about the effect it would have on his family – and Ernie. 'If I die, I shan't know anything about it,' he told Joan just before going into hospital. 'I'll have the injection and the happy pills and that will be that. It's you and the family who'll suffer. I know you'll grieve for me and I want to be missed and remembered. But I don't want there to be any long faces.'

The operation – then in its infancy – went well for Eric Morecambe (alias hospital patient, George Wilson). Before the operation his life expectancy had been measured in months: now he would go on to live a further five years during which time he would lead a normal and active life.

Yet again, and it was something Eric was beginning to dislike as it clashed with his comic persona, his ill-health was national news. The cards, the letters, the flowers flowed in. When he left Harefield, sporting an uncharacteristic moustache, he felt compelled to put on a sparkling show for the gathered newsmen.

'No one could have ever known just how much he would have loved to slip away quietly from the hospital without any fuss,' says Joan. 'But Eric always managed to conceal his deeper emotions and on the spur of the moment found something witty and original to say to the journalists.'

But, the fatal addiction to comedy which had gripped him all his life and which he knew had brought him to the brink of death twice had still got hold of him. The fear of not performing comedy outstripped the fear of performing it.

Ironically, it was only towards the end of his life that Eric was finally to shake off the obsessive need to perform when he became convinced that to continue would probably kill him. But making the decision to stop would prove impossible for him and, besides, it was too late anyhow.

For the beginning of the end had occured in Batley back in 1968, when comedy began stalking one of its most celebrated victims.

13

*'Sometimes you get a person in the front
who is so bored by your show it isn't true.
As he looks at you you can feel the
hate ...'*

Ernie Wise

The Rank films were not the only diversion from the relentless pressure of *Two of a Kind* throughout the 1960s. Between 1961 and 1968, Eric and Ernie also made several visits to the USA to appear on the Ed Sullivan show. These American appearances are generally remembered as having been largely unsuccessful, the prevailing wisdom being that Morecambe and Wise somehow failed there. This is not strictly accurate, and any failure was largely self-inflicted, and inflicted by Eric's perfectionism.

Sullivan, a former newspaper columnist turned TV linkman, had been on American television from 1948, and his show for CBS was the foremost showcase for vaudeville acts in the States, with an estimated audience at that time of well over fifty million. Despite a rather bumbling on-screen manner, Sullivan was one of the most powerful and influential figures in the American TV industry. He could book the biggest names to appear on the show – Frank

Sinatra, Elvis Presley, Bing Crosby – but if they didn't satisfy him, he'd fire them without compunction.

Sullivan first saw Morecambe and Wise while they were appearing with Bruce Forsyth at the London Palladium in 1961. He liked them and immediately made an offer of five thousand dollars a show to make three appearances for him.

Eric and Ernie, with their wives, were flown over to New York and feted as major celebrities: a status which, by the very fact they had been invited on to the show, they were entitled to in America. And despite some quibbles over their material which was felt to be too blue for the Midwest (there was very little that wasn't too blue for the Midwest), Eric and Ernie enjoyed a warm relationship with Sullivan himself.

Introduced by Sullivan initially as 'Morrey, Camby and Wise' – later they would be 'Bartholomew and Wise' – Eric and Ernie were launched on to the American public who responded with respectable, if less than overwhelming, applause.

For Ernie, it was a good start. Despite being influenced by US-grown acts, such as Laurel and Hardy and Abbott and Costello, Morecambe and Wise would remain forever identified as a British double act to perennially parochial American audiences, and therefore had to work that much harder to register.

That, coupled with the tampering with their material, necessitated both by the change of locale and the nervous whims of Sullivan's production staff, meant that they had done as well as could possibly have been expected of them. But for Eric, that simply wasn't enough.

'Eric hated not getting the laughs,' says Ernie. 'And he didn't like walking the streets of New York, and not being recognised. He needed the recognition, and needed to be told he was funny.'

'I remember seeing Eric and Ernie do a sketch in their BBC series where they did nothing but sit on a bench,' says Glenda Jackson, 'and I was literally rolling about on the floor with laughter.

'When I met them later, I told them how much I'd enjoyed that sketch, and Eric turned to me and said, "But it was awful. The studio audience didn't laugh once." I found that extraordinary because I thought it had been a brilliant piece of TV humour. But then, Eric did have this attitude which many comedians have: you only know if you've got it right if the audience laugh. If the audience doesn't laugh, it's failed.'

The problem certainly wasn't that the American audiences weren't laughing but, for Eric, they weren't laughing enough, and at the end of each Sullivan show, the thought of returning to England grew in appeal.

For a while the shows were a source of disagreement between Eric and Ernie. Ernie remains convinced to this day that they could have built on their admittedly moderate success with American audiences to crack that country eventually. Once Eric had had his heart attack, any attraction left in making it in America evaporated.

Ernie admits that he became impatient with Eric's lack of on-stage assurance, which they both knew was communicating itself subtly to the American audiences. Nevertheless, Sullivan was sufficiently satisfied to issue repeated invitations to appear on his show, and they made several visits between 1964 and 1968. Their very last appearance for him was in a ninety-minute gala produced by Sullivan to mark the eightieth birthday of Irving Berlin. It was a singular honour to be invited on to such an American-centred show: it was introduced by the then US President, Lyndon B Johnson, and also included Bob Hope and Bing Crosby in the line-up.

'Had they settled in America, I've no doubt that Eric and Ernie would have become enormously successful eventually,' says Joan Morecambe. 'But Eric simply would not change and become Americanised. He didn't like using words like elevator instead of lift, and he felt that it was this country which had made them stars. He knew they had worked so hard for so many years to become stars in Britain, that if they concentrated on America, they'd be throwing away all they'd struggled for at home.

'All right, so they might have made a lot of money in America, if they'd become international stars, but Eric could never have settled out there. And it would have been an uphill struggle for both of them because audiences would have had to get to know them all over again – and it took the British a long time to get used to Morecambe and Wise.

'Eric certainly wasn't comfortable working in New York, and

they weren't always allowed to perform what they would have liked. On the other hand, they were both aware that it was a great accolade for Ed Sullivan to keep inviting them back, because he could be ruthless with acts.'

Ben Elton believes Eric's disenchantment with performing in the States sprang from an inner conviction that Morecambe and Wise could never have made it there:

'I suppose it's possible, but I have to say that I think it's very unlikely. And I'm sure Eric must've known that. Let's face it, it must be difficult for any performer who knows he can pull in over half the population in Britain – which has never been done before or since except perhaps by the Queen – to go over to the States as a five-minute act trying to prove its worth.

'To make it in the States as a live act you've got to keep working there for years. Perhaps if they'd spent twenty years there they could've made it, but what would have been the point? I'm a great Ernie-defender against those people who can't – or won't – acknowledge his contribution to the Morecambe and Wise act. But I do know he has this obsession with making it in America. Why can't he be satisfied with being the greatest post-war entertainer in Britain? When you've got twenty-eight million viewers watching your Christmas show, surely even America becomes just another audience to play to.

'Far too many British entertainers break their hearts worrying about success in America. Look where it got Hancock. I think that Morecambe and Wise in the States would have become worse and worse and ended up as an impression of an American act which would have been ludicrous. As it is, Ernie has a tendency – charming in England – to slip into that awful 1950s mid-Atlantic hoofer accent which pretends it's in some kind of Frank 'n Dino situation.

'Of course, he's not the only one to do it because it came over with the Americans during the war and it dominated the glamorous idea of showbusiness here for years. Had Ernie been allowed to stay in the States for more than five minutes, I think he would have caught the same disease that Bruce Forsyth caught briefly and horrendously. Bruce is a great performer; not, for me, on a par with Eric and Ernie, but still a towering light entertainer. But when he pretends to be an American and does song and dance and cabaret, it's ridiculous. The man is an *English* entertainer and there is a cultural difference.

'They all did it, of course, that generation. Dickie Henderson was the worst offender but Monkhouse, Forsyth, Ernie – they were all guilty and even Eric used to do it when he was singing. Now, it worked well enough over here at the time simply because it was everyone's idea of glamour – the performers, the producers and the audiences – and, for the most part, none of them was really aware they were doing it.

'But it never worked for anyone in America, certainly not if they knew they were doing it. So if Eric and Ernie had moved to the States, I think it would have been a mistake and it would have affected Ernie more than it would Eric.

'As it is, I find Ernie's obsession with America rather charming and I think he should be indulged. He's got a lot of friends there, he's got his holiday home there and he just loves America.

'And, anyway, they did have a lovely little American side career with Ed Sullivan. They did loads of shows with him and were well paid. We should all be so lucky.'

In 1968, revolution was in the air as governments and institutions throughout the Western world were challenged by a new order. Draft-dodgers marched on the Pentagon in America; revolutionary students brought France to a virtual standstill; and in the West End, the abolition of the Lord Chamberlain's office ushered in the psychedelic musical, *Hair*, preaching its message of free love with accompanying stage nudity, four-letter words and exhortations to indulge in sodomy and drug-taking.

The times they were indeed a-changing, as Bob Dylan wrote, and though they were not involved directly with the political and social revolution sweeping the world, Eric and Ernie would also look back on 1968 as a milestone year: one which forced them to examine and reassess their lives and careers.

The single most important thing to happen that year was, of course, Eric's heart attack, which came close to killing him and exerted an enormous influence on their working lives from then on. But even before that, 1968 had seen the end of their Rank film career, their last show for American television – and, most relevant of all, the severing of their association with Lew Grade's ATV to join the BBC.

Two of a Kind had been an unimagined smash-hit, firmly establishing Morecambe and Wise as Britain's favourite comedy duo, and that success had manifested itself in awards and adulation as they were named TV Light Entertainers of 1963 and won both the BAFTA and Variety Club awards in 1964. Their 1967 summer season at Great Yarmouth broke all known records; they released a successful LP called 'An Evening With Ernie Wise at Eric Morecambe's Place', and Lew Grade included a series of their shows in a £2,000,000 sale of programmes to North America, bringing them a new following in Canada.

But there were rumblings of discontent in paradise, and the rumblings broke out into open warfare early in 1968, when Eric and Ernie's contract was up for renewal with ATV. There were two principal sources of conflict between the parties: money and the actual production of the shows themselves.

Lew Grade was offering £39,000 for a three-year contract which would tie Eric and Ernie to making thirteen shows a year for ATV. It was a large sum of money – one which Eric, initially at least, was tempted to accept – but Ernie didn't feel it was enough.

Furthermore, Grade proposed to make the new series in black and white. But colour transmissions, which had been officially launched on British screens on 1 July 1967, were the future, and both Eric and Ernie felt that only colour shows could appropriately reflect their new status as the nation's foremost clowns. Whatever the outcome of their financial negotiations, Eric and Ernie were adamant; it was a colour series or nothing.

Grade's position was equally entrenched. *Two of a Kind* would remain in black and white, and his attitude was very much take-it-or-leave-it. To his immense surprise, Morecambe and Wise decided to leave it.

'It was appalling to me to see them leave ATV,' says Philip Jones, who a decade later would be instrumental in luring Eric and Ernie from the BBC to join Thames, but who, in 1968, was a producer/director at ATV. Jones believes there must have been another reason that prompted the move. 'A lot of people theorised in the industry at the time, and the official reason given was because they were offered colour on BBC2. Whether it was that or the money, I don't really know. But I couldn't help feeling at the time that ITV could've made a few contractual concessions to keep them.'

Perhaps because of the heat of the conflict between Morecambe and Wise and Lew Grade – Ernie admits they ended negotiations with a furious row – those contractual concessions were never made and the BBC, in the personage of Bill Cotton, then BBC's Head of Light Entertainment, stepped in to the fray.

Ironically, it was Michael Grade, Lew Grade's nephew, who was working for Billy Marsh at that time, who opened the dialogue between Cotton and Eric and Ernie.

'Billy was on holiday in the States, when it all came to a head,' says Michael Grade. 'We knew a break was coming because the negotiations with ATV had got very heated, but as it happened it fell to me to tell Lew that they wouldn't be signing a new contract.

'Lew thought he had all the trump cards during those negotiations, but Eric and Ernie decided to gamble by going to the BBC.'

'The critical moment came when I received a call from Michael Grade, who was then acting on behalf of Billy Marsh at London Management,' says Cotton. 'He told me that Eric and Ernie hadn't signed a new contract with ATV. They wanted more money, but Lew wouldn't pay. Michael asked if I was interested.

'Like everyone else, I was a great admirer of *Two of a Kind*, because they were just plain bloody funny. So I told Michael that if he could wait for fifteen minutes, I'd be up in his office.'

Cotton dashed to London Management with an immediate offer to secure Morecambe and Wise for the BBC. 'It was an offer for a three-year contract,' says Cotton. 'And I made the financial arrangements on this basis: for the first year, they would receive a ridiculous amount of money; the second would be just about right; and the third year would be a bargain for us – if I was proved right about their potential.'

Furthermore, Cotton accepted that Hills and Green would be hired – indeed, in a unique gesture of loyalty to their writers, Eric and Ernie had Hills and Green's involvement written into their own contract – and the series would be made in colour.

Eric and Ernie accepted the deal, and duly joined the Corporation where their first series for BBC2, was scheduled to be shown in the summer of 1968.

Despite buying the *Two of a Kind* package virtually intact, Cotton wanted to introduce changes to the Morecambe and Wise shows. He didn't just want to consolidate their previous success; he wanted that to be a starting point for even greater success. And he had his own ideas of how to achieve that.

'*Two of a Kind* had been very successful for them in that half-hour format,' says Cotton. 'But by 1968, I knew that they'd outgrown the half-hour. Twenty-five minutes was just too short a programme, especially for Eric. He'd become much more expansive in their routines, supported, of course, by Ernie. I felt that what they needed above everything else was space. So although the first series they did for the BBC was in a half-hour format, I soon got them into fifty-minute slots.'

The first series of Morecambe and Wise shows for the BBC was made without any problems and went down very well with audiences.

Eric's heart attack, and subsequent long recuperation, postponed the second series for a long while, but Cotton was happy to wait until Eric was fully recovered: as far as he was concerned, their contract was valid.

As Eric gradually began to recover his strength and plans for a second BBC series were made, a problem emerged when Bill Cotton had a meeting with Roger Hancock, agent for Hills and Green.

'Roger told me that Hills and Green would only sign a contract to write for Morecambe and Wise if they were also allowed to be executive producers on the show. I told him that wasn't something which was even worth discussing: I didn't think that the writers should also be the producers. Roger then said that under the condition that I wouldn't sign them as executive producers, they would be signing an exclusive contract with ATV instead to write their own show.'

Hills and Green duly signed their contract with ATV, which precluded them ever writing for Eric and Ernie again. A highly successful formula and professional relationship had come to an abrupt and slightly bitter end, and the first Eric or Ernie knew about it was when a steward on a flight to Barbados spoke to Ernie. He asked Ernie if the story he'd just read in the newspaper about their writers leaving them was true.

In fairness to Hills and Green, who can emerge from this sequence of events seeming callous, it should be pointed out that, as professional writers, they had a living to make like anyone else. As Ernie is keen on reiterating, showbusiness is show*business*, and during the months following Eric's illness, when it was uncertain when, or even if, he would return to work, they had to make enquiries about a future without Morecambe and Wise.

Indeed, the shock to Eric and Ernie was caused less by the actual loss of their writers – though that was considerable – than by being the last to learn about it. In public, they remained gracious, saying it had been an unfortunate business and no one was to blame: in private, both felt let down and Eric, in particular, was left with a nasty taste about the whole affair, according to Joan Morecambe.

'Eric was particularly hurt; more so, I think, than Ernie. In fact, I was surprised just how hurt he was, and I believe that was because of the manner in which it was done. I know Sid and Dick didn't mean any harm: they didn't see it as being underhand in any way. But after all those years of working together, Eric and Ernie heard about it third hand. That hurt. And Eric, I know, thought that Sid and Dick didn't think he could ever return to full strength after his heart attack and were writing him off.'

Publicly all parties remained dignified and Morecambe and Wise and Hills and Green were to cross paths at various functions where any bad feeling from the past was all but forgotten. On one such occasion, Dick Hills presented Eric with an award at a Lords Taverners' charity ball, and the two continued to share many a joke together.

The immediate problem back in 1968, however, was finding new writers. 'They were the first people to tell you they were totally script-dependent,' says Glenda Jackson. 'If the scripts weren't good, then they couldn't be good.'

Although the script provided by any of their writers was only a show's starting point on which they themselves could build, Jackson accurately pinpoints their need for a regular supply of good material.

'And when Hills and Green left,' says Bill Cotton, 'we were without a writer. Worse, Eric and Ernie's contract had a clause which said we would book Hills and Green to write the series. So not only, did we have no writers, but Eric and Ernie's own contract with us was severely flawed because it was dependent upon Hills and Green being the writers. And, believe me, I really had to convince Eric and Ernie that we should go ahead and try and find someone else to write the shows.'

'Bill Cotton had to persuade Eric and Ernie that they could no longer allow Hills and Green to run their careers for them,' says Michael Grade. 'And I think that was crucial for them, because Eric and Ernie had begun to believe they couldn't survive without Hills and Green whereas, in practice, the break from Hills and Green proved to be a great release for them. It was the reason why their move to the BBC was very important in allowing them to move in such a different direction.

'In any event, I think their relationship with Hills and Green would have fractured anyway, because I don't think Hills and Green ever gave Eric and Ernie full credit for what they achieved with their material.

'Many was the time I'd go into Eric and Ernie's dressing-room after they'd recorded an ATV show at Elstree, and Eric would be seething because Hills and Green had already been round to snipe at and criticise them. Eric never reacted to that in public, but I know that it used to drive him mad.'

It was not long after Hills and Green parted company with Morecambe and Wise that Cotton heard of the availability of a suitable candidate: Eddie Braben.

'It was within about two or three weeks after Hills and Green departed I heard that Eddie Braben, who had been writing for Ken Dodd, had split from Ken,' recalls Cotton. 'I offered him a three-year contract to write for Morecambe and Wise.'

Eric and Ernie had long admired Braben's work for Dodd, one of Britain's most original acts. Initially, though, Braben was less certain that he was right for Morecambe and Wise. 'I don't do sketches,' he told them. 'I only write jokes.'

It soon became apparent that Braben was entirely suitable, so dispelling early concerns. He provided them not only with excellent material, but also tried successfully to develop the duo's relationship. What transpired was that the distinction between funny man and feed became even more blurred.

'I didn't touch Eric's character at all,' says Braben. 'I concentrated on Ernie, gave him this character of the egotistical writer of the "plays wot I wrote". It was a pompous, almost Victorian character who'd never do anything untoward, and what we ended up with, in effect, was a double act without a straight man: we had two funny men instead.'

Precisely how much of Morecambe and Wise's success can be apportioned to Eric and Ernie themselves and how much to their writers, probably not even they would know. Certainly, writers need no excuse to feel taken for granted and Braben was no exception, allegedly once sending forty blank sheets of paper to Eric and Ernie at TV Centre with a curt note saying, 'Fill these forty pages if you think it's easy!'

On the other hand, Eric and Ernie had had a successful act long before they'd had the luxury of writers and both men were in no doubt about who were the most important contributors to the partnership.

'The makers of Morecambe and Wise were Eric and I,' says Ernie, firmly. 'We were indebted to our writers, Hills and Green and then Eddie Braben. But in the final analysis, we had to shape the scripts to our personalities.'

Braben, himself, once said, 'If I write a good script then they make it a great script, if I write a great script, they make it brilliant.'

'There's no doubt that Eddie was marvellous for Eric and Ernie,' says Joan, 'but – and the same applies equally to Sid and Dick – the secret was in what Eric and Ernie did with the scripts. Unless they had been prepared to go into rehearsal every day with those scripts, to work on them, to add their own little touches and, yes, to make alterations, those Morecambe and Wise shows would never have been the same. For instance, script-writers don't write in movements or any of the visual gags: all that had to come from Eric and Ernie themselves.

'Eric was always very careful to give the accolades for the writing to the writers because he felt that he and Ernie were given the

Penelope Keith enjoys herself in another of Ernie's 'plays wot he wrote', Christmas 1977. (*Syndication International*)

Joanna Lumley found it 'absolutely fabulous' to work with Eric and Ernie at Thames. (*Thames Television*)

Sir Ralph Richardson and Robert Hardy receive the traditional Morecambe and Wise treatment at Thames, Christmas 1981. (*Thames Television*)

Eric and Ernie recreate their famous 1950s vent act for *The Sweeney*. (*Thames Television*)

Following You Around with Max Bygraves, 1981. (*Thames Television*)

Relaxing between takes with long time producer Johnny Ammonds, 1982. *(Thames Television)*

Night Train to Murder, 1983. A disappointing end to a glorious career. *(Thames Television)*

Unquestionably Two of a Kind.

credit for everything else. Eric believed that most viewers didn't even bother to watch the end credits and so didn't read who the script-writers were. So, although he and Ernie always put a great deal into the scripts – and on some shows it was quite a high percentage – for years they never had "additional material by Morecambe and Wise" on the credits. Later on, they did have that credit put on because they felt they had to establish the fact. Otherwise they had no claim on the material that they had produced.'

Ben Elton claims there is always this conflict between writers and performers: 'Eric and Ernie always claimed that the script changed in rehearsals and that they improvised all the time. All performers say that and they're right – to a point. And with forty-odd years together I'm sure that in Eric and Ernie's case it was probably more true than in many other cases.

'But, as a writer, I must leap to Eddie Braben's defence and say they couldn't have done it without him. He was writing for that process of rehearsal. Let me give you an example from *Blackadder* which Richard Curtis and I wrote.

'When we named Rowan Atkinson's girlfriend Bob in the second series, we did so because we knew precisely what Rowan would do with that name. No other comedian in the world could make the name Bob sound funny. And Richard and I pride ourselves on choosing that name.

'Now, people out of the business might think it strange for us to claim credit for the name Bob. And that's fine. I'm not seeking any great recognition from *Blackadder* fans for Richard and myself, and I don't want any Morecambe and Wise fan to think Eddie Braben's the greatest part of the Morecambe and Wise shows.

'But inside the business it's terribly important to keep pointing out the importance of writers in feeding the comic genius. And sometimes it's just a matter of knowing when to say "stop" or "pause" or whatever.'

Eric, like Ernie, was fully aware of Eddie Braben's importance but, ever the perfectionist, he was rarely fully content with any script provided by any writer they used. He frequently resorted to rewriting scripts himself – a habit which led directly to his developing a taste for the written word and a secondary career as a novelist towards the end of his life. He confessed his dissatisfaction with writers in a quiet moment to John Thaw in the mid-1970s.

'Eric told me that their problem for years had been scripts,' says Thaw. 'He told me that the bane of his life was finding the right material, and he said he was fed up with having to regurgitate the material he'd been doing ten years earlier. It was basically the same stuff – even though it was coming from different writers. And he told me it was just wearing him out.

'Don't forget, he used to rewrite everything. He even took away some of the routine stuff they'd been given on that *Sweeney* episode they did with us, and rewrote it. There's no doubt in my mind that the greatest problem in his life was scripts. That's why I believe if someone had come up with a more serious project for them, he'd have grabbed their hands off just to have the chance of working on some fresh material.'

Nonetheless, Eddie Braben made an enormously creative contribution to the new BBC series, which Eric and Ernie seized on greedily to mould into what are now regarded as classic television comedy shows. Rarely leaving his Liverpool home to travel down to London, Braben's style of working was in total contrast to that of Hills and Green. Where Hills and Green and Eric and Ernie would remain locked away in a room, arguing out a list of script ideas which would be finally agreed upon and then turned into proper script form by the two writers, Braben supplied them with a more complete script through the post. Hills and Green, though, did appear in most ATV sketches with Eric and Ernie, which explains why they needed to be in from the beginning of a script right through to filming. The difference with Braben was that he wrote comedy but he didn't act or perform comedy.

Once Braben had supplied the script, the producer of the show (first Johnny Ammonds, then Ernest Maxin) would refine the material accordingly and discuss it with Braben after he had further reworked it.

Braben also laid more emphasis on the importance of their guest stars, pulling them into the shows via Ernie's 'terrible' plays. And the flat routine became a regular feature which ran in most shows like a mini sit-com. For Ben Elton, it was these intimate moments which worked best in the BBC shows: 'The musical numbers were not my favourite and the sketches were sometimes weak. Sometimes, quite obviously, the sketches were brilliant; but I do remember one very long drawn-out World War I sketch which had funny trousers and a funny hat but that was all.

'I loved the acrobatic Michael Aspels and all that, but compared to the dialogue it just wasn't as good. I feel the same thing about *The Young Ones*. Now I'm not suggesting for a moment that *The Young Ones* was anything like as good or as well honed as the Morecambe and Wise show, but it had its moments. Personally, I found all the exploding stuff and the spacemen coming through the roof in *The Young Ones* absolutely awful. What I liked writing and watching was the three or four of them sitting round discussing a game of Monopoly or wondering what they were going to do when the telly was over.'

Although Eddie Braben claims to have left Eric's character alone, it did gradually evolve. 'Eric gradually transformed into a harder figure,' says Joan. 'He was a kind of straight man who was funny as opposed to Ernie, who became the comic who tried to be funny but wasn't.'

Eric himself noted this and told an interviewer: 'Eddie's made me tougher and less gormless. I'm much harder towards Ernie now.'

The result of all of this, according to Kenneth Tynan writing in the *Observer* Magazine in 1973, was that Eric, 'has burgeoned into one of the most richly quirkish and hypnotic performers in the history of the box.' And he went on to say, 'The combination is brilliant, wholly original and irresistible. How much of it is due to Braben and how much to the performers is hard to determine: but we know that the scripts are heavily modified in rehearsal and that most of the changes come from Eric.'

Ironically enough, Eric's first heart attack indirectly contributed to the success of the BBC shows. Concerned that he should not be put under any undue strain, Cotton determined that their new contract should have a lot more time built into it. Instead of having to complete one show a week, as had been the original agreement, the Morecambe and Wise shows were given three weeks in rehearsal and two days recording time in the studio. It was an unheard-of luxury in television production, but one which paid off handsomely. This more leisurely pace of work transferred to more on-screen assurance. The pressure they'd endured up to November 1968 had noticeably eased; and they were better comics for it.

'Their first series for us, written by Hills and Green, was a success,' says Cotton. 'But we really began building with that second series. I think the second Christmas Show they did for us was about the biggest thing that had happened on British television up to that point. At that time, we always used to run really big feature films at Christmas, and films were a huge attraction. But that year, more people were talking about the Morecambe and Wise show than anything else.'

Indeed they were, and from 1970 until 1983 Morecambe and Wise became synonymous with Christmas. Their weekly series throughout the rest of the year were popular to be sure, but their Christmas show was the one you looked forward to and often planned your eating arrangements around.

'I was a fan of those shows, like everyone else,' says Rowan Atkinson. 'I remember sitting down watching the Christmas shows, like the one they did with André Previn. They were at the height of their fame and power in the 1970s, and they had those unbeatable ratings.'

For Glenda Jackson, who appeared on two of their BBC Christmas shows, their relationship with the British viewing public had evolved into nothing less than a love affair.

'The incredible thing about them, certainly then, was not only that they were admired – I certainly admired them – but that they were loved by their audience. I don't think that's too extreme a word. And that's what made it so easy to say yes to their request to appear on the show because you really could have gone on to that show and done anything and it wouldn't have mattered. The response their audience had towards them was such that you, as a guest star, were enveloped in that love as well. That was why I was happy to appear on five Morecambe and Wise shows, but would never appear with any other comedians: it was not only that they were the best in their particular field, but also because there was a particular national identification with their shows.'

Certainly, Morecambe and Wise's achievement was most impressive in the 1970s as, both Rowan Atkinson and Bill Cotton point out.

'The 1970s were a remarkably rich time for British comedy,' says Atkinson. 'Very tolerant and less trendy and media-orientated. In the 1990s, it's entirely possible that the coming of, say, Monty Python, might have killed the likes of Morecambe and Wise. But in the 1970s, the two co-existed quite happily.'

Adds Bill Cotton, 'The 1970s were a remarkable time for Light Entertainment at the BBC. We had a vast repertory of good comedy: *Dad's Army*, *The Good Life*, *Monty Python's Flying Circus*. But I must be honest and say that Morecambe and Wise were at the heart of it all. They were the Head Prefects.'

It had taken them three decades to reach the absolute top, the first decade of which had been nothing less than a desperate struggle.

But Eric and Ernie – Morecambe and Wise – were there at last.

14

*'Eric and Ernie were among the most
consummate professionals I've ever
worked with.'*

Glenda Jackson

With their scripts by Eddie Braben, their dance routines by Ernest Maxin, and some of the most assured performances of their careers, Eric Morecambe and Ernie Wise gave the BBC a succession of shows in the 1970s which became instant classics.

But for many viewers, it was the involvement of big-name guest stars which makes the Morecambe and Wise shows so memorable. No performer was too big a name to be considered to take part in the fun and nonsense and, indeed, some of the biggest stars in the business soon began secretly to long for the coveted invitation. Where else but on the Morecambe and Wise show could one see England's most celebrated living actor, Laurence Olivier, uttering the line, 'Velly solly. Long number. Chinese waundry 'ere,' into a telephone as the pay-off to a running gag about him avoiding a request to appear on their show? Or Alec Guinness standing centre stage and being told by Eric, 'I'm very sorry, we don't allow members of the public up here. If you're Mr Wise's taxi driver, would you mind waiting round the back?'

'When Dennis Waterman and I were invited onto the Morecambe and Wise show, the feedback we got from other colleagues was envy,' says John Thaw. 'The general feeling was "you lucky bastards, being invited on to that." It was a great accolade: the equivalent in those days of being asked to do *Desert Island Discs*.'

'People used to ask us how we managed to get all those big stars on the show,' confesses Ernie, 'but I have to say that we never really had an answer for that. We just used to invite them and somehow they all seemed to have enough courage to come along.

'Peter Cushing was one of the first ones we used and I always remember him because he was such an elegant man. He appeared in the "play wot I wrote" about King Arthur and the Knights of the Round Table, and we started the joke about him not being paid for appearing. The audience reaction to that made us realise the value of it, and it became a running gag throughout the series.

'Another early guest star was Eric Porter. He'd never danced before but Ernest Maxin got him moving. That was the key to the successful guest star appearances, I suppose: we had big stars – really big stars – doing things the audience hadn't seen them doing before.'

In itself, the inclusion of guest stars in television variety shows was a tradition as old as television variety shows themselves; a tradition which Morecambe and Wise had followed during the long run on ATV of their *Two of a Kind* series.

The BBC Morecambe and Wise shows were different, however. Classical actors were jokingly duped into appearing in one of Ernie's 'plays wot I wrote'; internationally famous singers, like Shirley Bassey or Tom Jones, were interrupted by Eric and Ernie mid-performance, and André Previn found himself jumping up and down on his podium to conduct Eric's mangled version of Grieg's Piano Concerto.

'Guest stars had always been used in all the big variety shows,' says Bill Cotton. 'But what really marked out the Morecambe and Wise shows was the different use of the guests. I think that really boiled down to a combination of Eric and Ernie's timing and Eddie Braben's anarchic sense of humour.

'In my opinion, the Shirley Bassey routine where she ended up wearing size ten boots was comic perfection. And the André Previn one was absolutely remarkable as well. In both those cases, I think it was because they played their parts brilliantly that the sequences worked so well. Bassey never expressed anything during the whole sequence while Eric and Ernie were crawling around her feet. She just kept on singing, flat out. And Previn played his sketch perfectly.'

'After Eric and Ernie moved to the BBC, and although I was producing and directing other shows there, Johnny Ammonds used to come and ask me to choreograph Eric and Ernie's shows as well,' says Ernest Maxin. 'I ended up doing all the musical numbers from about 1970 onwards. The first one was with Susan Hampshire, fresh from *The Forsyte Saga*. The Cliff Richard routine with them dressed as three sailors was great fun because it was the first time they had done that type of thing.

'The Shirley Bassey routine is perhaps the best known one. Johnny, then producing the shows, asked me to develop a comedy routine around her, and I thought of the boot idea having already tried it out in the first show I ever did, which was at Earls Court, where they had an annual event called the Earls Court Exhibition. Eric Sykes, I remember, was in it. I used a man for the routine, an Australian singer. And I did the same thing with this man as we did with Bassey in the Morecambe and Wise show. But all I did on this occasion was to make him have his foot caught, then they came on with the shifting scenery either side, and instead of putting on another boot, as Eric did to Shirley Bassey, he ended up with two bare feet.'

'Famous guest stars were never nervous about appearing on the Morecambe and Wise shows,' says Philip Jones, 'because they knew they could put themselves in Eric and Ernie's safe hands. The trick was, you see, that it was really Eric and Ernie who were making fools of themselves, not the guests. The boys built it up against themselves. They'd have filmed sequences with people like Laurence Olivier or Ralph Richardson picking up a telephone and saying, "Appear with Morecambe and Wise? Oh no!" That, of course, was a very clever piece of programming because they could record those short sequences anywhere and it meant they had someone of the calibre of Olivier on the programme without him ever coming into the studio.

'I suppose if a performer was worried about his image, he might think twice about appearing on the show. But the guest stars trusted them and I can't recall one who didn't look forward to appearing with them enormously.'

'Actually, I *did* have to think twice about appearing with Morecambe and Wise,' admits John Thaw. 'Not because I was worried about my image, but because it's a totally different world for me. And I'll be quite honest and admit that I was petrified when we recorded the show. That's not to say I didn't enjoy it – the actual rehearsal period was wonderful – but I was frightened when we came to the recording because the way they worked was totally different from the way I was used to working on a series or a play.

'They were terrific to work with, though. They were always amenable to any suggestions you might have, even though it was their show. And they would go out of their way to fit you in. They weren't "stars" in that sense at all, and as a result one felt very relaxed with them and confident in what they could do.'

Eddie Braben agrees with Thaw that some stars *did* feel nervous on the shows. 'The thing that never failed to astonish me was that no matter how big the stars were, they were terribly nervous. I've seen big stars pacing up and down and chain smoking just a couple of minutes before they were due to go on with Eric and Ernie. Some of them were petrified because although they knew they'd rehearsed, they also knew that something else was bound to happen as well – which it invariably did with Eric and Ernie.'

John Thaw, like Glenda Jackson, agreed to appear on the Morecambe and Wise show, but they both refused similar offers made before and after their appearances with Eric and Ernie. Their reasons for agreeing to guest with Morecambe and Wise went beyond the simple fact of the boys' stature, as Jackson explains.

'Their secret was that they seemed to touch something in their audience which obviously was connected with their performance but also with the way their audience regarded them in a very personal way. That's why, when I always refer to a love between Eric and Ernie and their audience, I don't think it's a misapplication.

'And that was the real reason I agreed to do it when I received the letter asking me to appear on the show. I regarded it as the apotheosis of my career to be asked to work with those two because I had seen their shows and I'd always thought them absolutely remarkable.

'And, believe me, I wasn't disappointed when I did it. I always say working with Morecambe and Wise was like holidays with pay. But it wasn't simply a treat: it was a privilege to be around them and to see the sheer professionalism of their work.'

According to Penelope Keith, Glenda Jackson's first appearance on the Morecambe and Wise show, though hardly the first time a big-name guest star had been used, was the one which really established the show as the place to be seen.

'Glenda had such a lot to do with blazing the way for their really great guest stars,' she says. 'She wasn't known for comedy so it was very daring of her to do it because she could have made a total fool of herself. I think everyone in the business admired her for that.'

For Jackson, herself, the consequence of that first appearance with Eric and Ernie manifested itself more significantly than in admiring murmurs from colleagues: as a direct result she was offered the leading female role in a comedy film, *A Touch of Class*, opposite George Segal, for which she won her second Oscar.

'The producer of the film saw me do the Morecambe and Wise show,' Jackson explains, 'and that's how I got the role. I told Eric and Ernie that story, and when I won the Oscar for *A Touch of Class*, they sent me a telegram which said: "Stick with us, kid, and we'll get you a third." '

Just as it had with Glenda Jackson, the appreciation of Morecambe and Wise's sheer professionalism spread quickly throughout the acting profession. That, allied with a reputation for affability, made an invitation to appear on their show difficult to turn down, though some, notably Michael Caine and Sir John Gielgud, chose to do so.

'Eric and Ernie were always popular with other pros,' says Bill Cotton. 'I always think of them at the BBC Light Entertainment Christmas party, where they were the mainstays. They'd be there with Joan and Doreen, and always mix in well with everyone else.'

Even the late Kenneth Williams who, as mentioned earlier, had remained unimpressed by the double act as comedians, was forced to admit to himself in the early 1980s that they displayed a 'fundamental honesty and goodness which probably accounts for their universal popularity.' What Williams had belatedly discovered was that both Eric and Ernie found it impossible to behave, as John Thaw noted, like prima donna stars.

'That was really underlined when they appeared with Dennis Waterman and me in that last *Sweeney* episode we made,' says Thaw. 'Their agent had insisted they must have a caravan each on location. Thames had agreed to that and asked what kind of caravan they'd like. Eric and Ernie didn't really know, so Eric said they'd have whatever kind Den and I usually used.

'Now, on *The Sweeney*, we didn't have anything! We changed in cars or public lavatories and got made up in the backs of pubs. When he found that out, Eric said, "You can't expect us to come on to a set and have a bloody big caravan each when the two stars are getting made up in a toilet round the back." So he insisted that if they had a caravan, then we had one as well.

'That was the only time in four years on *The Sweeney* that Den and I had a caravan.'

The guest stars didn't just enjoy working with Morecambe and Wise, they joined in the fun of the thing, seeming to understand what it was all about even in advance of the first rehearsal.

Their guests perpetuated running gags as much as Eric and Ernie did themselves. A good example is Peter Cushing returning to chase payment for his role as King Arthur. And this continuing to play along after the initial guest spot was over spilled on to other guests.

Dame Flora Robson wrote, 'I have retired now, but the cheques from faraway places, such as China, Singapore, New Zealand, and so on, are still arriving … ' And Glenda Jackson pointed out that, 'To work with these great talents is enough. To expect money would not only be greedy, but a waste of time.'

The money gag apart, it is perhaps André Previn in a written piece in 1974, who pinpoints the meaning of working with Morecambe and Wise. '…The boys have always been extremely kind and courteous to me. I want to give you an example of that: Eric never fails to apologise both before *and* after he hits me. I have been given to understand that they will ask me back to work with them again, as soon as they can think of further humiliations to put me through. What's more, I look forward to it a great deal.'

According to Ernest Maxin, a minority of viewers failed to understand or appreciate Eric and Ernie's use of guest stars. 'Some viewers used to take those things quite seriously, and they'd take me to one side and ask if Eric and Ernie were like that in real life. I remember the reaction in particular to a running gag we did with Elton John.

'It started with Elton receiving an invitation to appear on the Morecambe and Wise show, and then arriving at Television Centre looking for Eric and Ernie and then being sent deliberately to all the wrong places. It ended with him opening a door, falling out and down into the Thames.

'Believe it or not, we got several phone calls and letters saying what a cruel thing that was to do to Elton John.'

Another aspect of the BBC shows many viewers didn't understand was the appearance of Janet Webb. Just prior to the end credits, she would push the boys aside and take the bows by saying 'Thank you for watching me and my little show here tonight. If you've enjoyed it as much as I have, then it's all been worthwhile. And I love you all!' This routine might be rounded off by her receiving flowers or champagne or even lighting up a cigar.

The joke was a funny one and delighted many viewers. Some, though, found her inclusion baffling and, rather unfairly, Janet Webb's appearances prompted a large proportion of the rare letters of complaint received by the Morecambe and Wise production office.

Not everyone appreciated every guest star routine. Ben Elton, who always preferred the shows when it was Eric and Ernie alone in front of the tabs or in the flat or bedroom, recalls some sequences he didn't like:

'Obviously the André Previn sketch was good – Previn was an absolute gift from heaven – and I liked the boot on Bassey. But I remember one Christmas show with a very boring running gag with a succession of guest stars saying, "I worked with Morecambe and Wise and look what happened to me" before driving a bus away, or doing something similar to that.

'That was just an exercise in showing their pulling power by that time. But they did hundreds of hours of TV and if anyone started picking my small body of work apart they'd soon find some bloody great howling holes.'

One thing Eric and Ernie did not do when considering their guest star lists was simply to think of a big name and issue an invitation. They considered it essential that guest stars had to be included for a reason and any sequence involving a guest required the right scenario tailored for that particular artiste if it was to work properly.

'All right, so there are one or two names you'd say, yes, let's have them on come what may,' Eric admitted in the early 1980s, 'but with the majority, we have to use them with a purpose. There are big names we've toyed with inviting on to the show – people like Paul and Linda McCartney, Roger Moore and Sean Connery. But we couldn't come up with the right idea of how to use them, and there has to be an angle.'

A classic case of the correct use of a guest star was, according to Eric, the 1976 routine with the newscaster Angela Rippon, which began with her emerging from behind a desk to perform an assured dance routine.

With Angela Rippon, the idea had long been mooted before finally jumped upon. It was Ernest Maxin who played a fundamental role in all of this.

'I saw Angela in the canteen at the BBC one day,' says Maxin. 'She was with a friend or relation, and asked me if she could show them around the studio. I said I'd be delighted, then suddenly noticed, having previously seen her only from the waist upwards, that she had lovely legs. And I didn't realise she was so tall. After a moment, I asked her if she'd like to do a Morecambe and Wise show. She was very keen, but doubted her head of department would let her. I mentioned it to Eric and Ernie. They said it would be a nice idea to use Angela, but they'd have to say no, because they had had such huge stars on their show before, which was true. But they reconsidered after meeting Angela at a charity luncheon.'

'Once we knew Angela Rippon could dance a bit,' said Eric at that time, 'the whole routine had virtually written itself.'

'On a purely personal level,' says Angela Rippon, 'being asked to do that show was a milestone for me. And being asked to do something which was fun but also within my capabilities was even better. Dancing was an easy thing for me to do because I'd trained as a dancer until I was seventeen.'

The result was a routine which caught both the public imagination and the attention of the press. 'Rippon Dances!' was as astonishing a concept to TV viewers as 'Garbo Talks!' had been to moviegoers forty-odd years earlier. For Rippon, herself, the impact of that appearance lingers on, nearly twenty years after the event.

'I don't think a week goes by when someone doesn't come up to me and mention that show. And people are always telling me that it was a historic piece of television. If the British public had to pick the top twenty major events in television, I guess my appearance on the Morecambe and Wise show would be one of them. I take that as a huge compliment. I'm not sure it changed my career – though a lot of people thought it did – but it did change other people's perception of me.

'You see, a year before I did that show, Max Bygraves was on the stage of the London Palladium, and told the audience, 'Now we have to go back to the studios of the BBC for the news read by Angela Rippon.' As an afterthought, he ad libbed, 'She hasn't got any legs, you know. She moves around on castors.' And that was how the viewing public thought of newscasters. They'd never seen me from the waist down.

'That was the reason my sequence was introduced on Eric and Ernie's show as a newsflash, and because viewers had never seen me do anything else, it worked brilliantly. You must remember that at that time the BBC wasn't looking for personality newscasters, and that only added to the viewers' disbelief when my desk parted midway through the newsflash and I began doing high kicks across the stage to be joined by Eric and Ernie.'

The show with Rippon was exceptional for another reason. It was one of few during this buoyant era not to have been written by Eddie Braben. The writers of the 1976 show were Barry Cryer, Mike Craig, Lawrie Kinsley and Ron McDonnell.

What the true pros appreciated most about working with Eric and Ernie was their professionalism. And nowhere was that professionalism revealed more clearly to visiting artistes than in the customarily assiduous rehearsal of every Morecambe and Wise show. Regardless of stature, every guest star was expected to rehearse with the rest of the cast at the BBC's rundown premises near Wormwood Scrubs, until each show was as polished as they could make it. And no one was exempt.

'It was our golden rule,' explains Ernie. 'They had to come to rehearsal. It didn't matter who they were or what they were. If they didn't come to rehearsal, they could forget it.'

'There was this popular misconception about Morecambe and Wise that they made the shows up as they went along, and that it was simply a group of people having a good time,' says Glenda Jackson. 'But Eric and Ernie were among the most consummate professionals I've ever worked with. On those shows you rehearsed and you worked and you rehearsed some more: that's just what you were expected to do. They wouldn't have tolerated you not knowing your lines or your moves. Equally, you knew they would never let anything too dreadful happen to you.'

'Eric and Ernie would rehearse and rehearse to ensure they had a solid bedrock which Eric, in particular, could build on,' adds Michael Grade. 'That was the key to their success: those sketches didn't happen by accident. I'll give you a contrast. Around the time that Eric and Ernie were at their peak with the BBC, I was brought in as an agent to help Mike and Bernie Winters. Now, Bernie was a delightful clown – I know for a fact that Eric liked him enormously – and Mike was a good straight man. But Mike and Bernie Winters simply didn't have the same degree of comic intelligence or industry that Eric and Ernie had. And having worked with Morecambe and Wise and then watching Mike and Bernie Winters work, it soon became obvious to me why Morecambe and Wise were Morecambe and Wise, and why Mike and Bernie Winters were – well, Mike and Bernie Winters.'

An exception to their rule of extensive rehearsals was the appearance on their show of André Previn. Previn was fresh back from the States, literally hours before he was due to record the Christmas show with Eric and Ernie. The boys initially expressed deep concern that Previn claimed to have learned the script during the flight and by torchlight in the back of a cab on the way from Heathrow airport.

'And you can see the fear on Eric's face going into that sketch,' claims Grade. 'It's something I love to watch again and again. You can see in his expression that he isn't quite sure whether it's all going to work or not because they are relying on a guest with whom they haven't had the chance to rehearse enough.

'If you watch that tape now – and I always watch for this moment – Eric visibly relaxes when André Previn exquisitely times that line of his: "I'll go and get my baton – it's in Chicago", and it gets a huge belly laugh from the audience. His face changes and you can see him thinking, "Boy, this is going to be good." He obviously relaxes into the sketch and suddenly can't wait to get into it.'

The rehearsal period should not be expressed as a time of Draconian terror for guest stars. No guest star on the Morecambe and Wise show has ever publicly stated that rehearsals were anything other than great fun, if hard work, and an opportunity to study the double act at close quarters – though radio and television presenter Terry Wogan, a one-time guest star, has recently expressed mild surprise at the amount of rehearsal time they insisted upon having.

Some stars – with good reason – did balk at the less than glamorous surroundings of the rehearsal rooms. 'We used to rehearse at premises in Delgano Way,' Eric once recalled. 'It was basically an old folks' home. I remember Robert Morley coming on the show, arriving on the Monday and, at half-past twelve, asking, "Now where do we go for lunch?"

'I told him that they didn't make lunch at the rehearsal rooms, and that what we tended to do was that I brought a flask of pea soup and some sandwiches, and Ernie brought a mug so he could take some of my soup and eat the sandwiches I left. So I told Robert that if he wanted something he could have a bowl of soup and a sandwich. He mumbled something and ate the lot. Afterwards he said, "Leave lunch to me, tomorrow."

'Next morning he arrived with no parcel in his hands – no food, no goodies. Half-past twelve came so we stopped for a break. At twelve forty-five we heard someone hooting on a car horn outside. We looked out and saw a liveried man opening the boot of a Rolls Royce. Out came a Fortnum and Mason's hamper which the man then dragged up the stairs and into this grotty place. And lunch that day was champagne, pâté and roast duck. It was absolutely fabulous.'

On recalling the occasion, Robert Morley went on record as saying how horrified he was by the lack of lunch facilities when he rehearsed with Morecambe and Wise. 'It was also fairly horrifying working near Wormwood Scrubs,' he added. But like his fellow pros who guested on the show, Morley both appreciated the extensive rehearsals and had his own ideas why some actors chose to appear with Eric and Ernie.

'To be with them, to go on that show, was to prove you were a sport. That's why the actors did it; and partly to get in with the BBC. And some of us – though I don't think I did – had dreams of stealing the show. That would have been quite impossible because they both knew so much more about it than we did. A few of us did have illusions we were going to shine: I must admit that I don't think any of us did.'

The extensive rehearsal periods were not solely designed to ensure Eric and Ernie's material was honed to the point where it appeared ad libbed, but also to relax guest stars who, as John Thaw has admitted, were nervous at working in a new medium.

'One of their greatest gifts,' says Penelope Keith, 'was taking actors who are not at home extemporising, and making them feel relaxed and confident.'

'Any changes were made during that rehearsal period before you got into the studio,' says Glenda Jackson. 'Perhaps a line took too long to say or needed an additional word. That was all sorted out in rehearsal. And I'll always remember Eric's practical note of advice when we were rehearsing my first show with them: "Louder and faster!" '

'They absolutely insisted on rigorous rehearsals,' confirms John Thaw. 'And the thing that sticks in my mind about those rehearsals is when Eric added an idea for a joke one day, and then cut it the next. He said, "I'm cutting that laugh because we've got too many." I remember thinking clearly that that was ridiculous because that line had me in stitches. But he was adamant. He felt there were too many laughs in that sequence, which upset the balance, and he was cutting it.'

John Thaw's observation of that incident underlines what most guest stars discerned while working with Morecambe and Wise during the 1970s: that Eric remained the creative force behind the act – but a creative force which needed the support of Ernie acting as midwife to give birth to that creativity.

Says Thaw, 'There's simply no question about that: creatively, he was the man. But when I say that, I'm not taking anything away from Ernie. As half of that act, he served Eric extremely well. And although Ernie appeared to be doing very little, believe me, he was doing a great deal in terms of timing. He was also good at knowing when to let Eric have his head when things were going well and knowing when to clamp down when Eric was going too far.'

'Eric had genius, and that's not too high-flown a word to use,' says their one-time producer, Johnny Ammonds. 'In rehearsals he'd always come out with these extra bits and pieces – visuals – especially – which would go into the script.

'Eric used to work and work, coming out with ideas all the time. At times, I used to think, we've done enough rehearsal, why on earth can't we just go home? But no. He'd go through it all again because he couldn't work less than a hundred per cent. And, you know, it would only take one person in that rehearsal room to laugh and he'd take off. Laughter was his tonic, and he'd work even harder if he heard it.'

'I always felt that Eric was the one doing the driving all the time,' agrees Glenda Jackson. 'Eric had a creative energy which could be switched on and off like a light. That energy, though, was entirely dependent on Ernie, whose own energy came from another direction.

'You see, the essential part of them as people was what you saw on-screen. It might not have been there all the time but that essential fabric of them as individuals was at its best in the work they did together. That was why Eric would reiterate time and time again, "We are a double act!" '

Michael Grade agrees and stresses the importance of Ernie's role in making the 1970s shows so successful. 'I always felt that when Ernie was on form, which was most of the time during their peak at the BBC, the whole act just took off into a new dimension. You could tell on some of their shows that Ernie was really enjoying himself.

'Eric was inventive and lived on his wits and his nerves. Ernie was more studied. That's why they complemented each other. They were a double act, and Ernie was crucial to Eric because he was such a brilliant straight man.'

Both Eric and Ernie's greatest delight from any of their shows was the opportunity to do the big 'Hollywood' number. 'The three of us loved the old movies,' says Ernest Maxin. 'It was that that bonded us together. And I think that's why our shows had that sense of occasion on the screen, more so than a lot of other shows: they had a film look behind them as opposed to a stage look.

'Whenever we went to discuss a new musical number, Eric would ask, "Are we going to have the full Hollywood go this time, Ernest?" I would say, "Yes, yes, Eric. You'll have all the moving cameras and everything." They used to love that; the camera sliding along on tracks, following them as they danced. It follows them back and forth, so there's a constant flow. You don't see that used much in this country. And those numbers, like the one with Diana Rigg shot at a castle near Banbury, were so well rehearsed that they only took about twenty minutes to shoot.'

The *Singin' in the Rain* pastiche is one of Maxin's personal favourites, and developed during rehearsals when he was dancing about with an idea and Eric turned to him and said, 'Sit down, Gene Kelly.'

'After that the three of us immediately started throwing ideas out among ourselves,' says Maxin, 'and Eric came up with the idea of doing the whole *Singin' in the Rain* number without it actually raining.'

Maxin told the set designer to make it look as near to the original as possible. 'Even Ernie's suit had to look as near to Gene Kelly's as possible.

'But the thing that was successful,' he points out, 'was Morecambe and Wise. If I had done these things with anybody else, whether it was *The Stripper* breakfast routine, *Singin' in the Rain* or *Nothing Like a Dame*, it would not have been the same. And I feel because of that I loved their work so much, and if you like someone's work then *you* get inspired – it makes you more creative.

'What's essential when you're putting a show together is that all of you are on the same wave length. You can all be very good at what you do, but still be on a different wave length.'

Other ideas, such as *The Stripper* routine – one of Morecambe and Wise's most popular routines with both audiences and themselves – were more creatively difficult because there was no original for them to use as a blue-print.

It had been Ernie who had had the original idea, many years earlier, of doing something around making breakfast in the kitchen, and when this was discussed at rehearsals, Maxin just couldn't get the idea out of his head. That night he got out of bed and started destroying fruit, catching toast and whisking eggs, the *Stripper* music constantly humming in his head. 'My family came down and saw me and thought I'd gone completely mad.'

A regular yet mostly forgotten aspect of the Morecambe and Wise show, and one integral in creating the whole picture of their work, was the costumes. It is surprising that in a show chiefly remembered for stand-up comedy routines and comic song and dance, just how numerous were the times their sketches and dance routines required various outfits, some more outlandish than others.

It was Ernie who usually played the female – though not always: for instance, they both dragged up to be part of a backing female vocal and dance group in one routine.

And there were times between them when they appeared as old men, char ladies, gardeners, butlers, kings, Romans, sailors, British Legion soldiers, British Army soldiers, Napoleon and Wellington, tennis players, archaeologists, eighteenth-century English gentlemen, pop stars, musicians, flamenco dancers, highwaymen, vicars, nuns, monks, repair men, waiters, fishermen, snooker players, boxers, footballers, pilots, Alaskans, city gents, private detectives, secret agents, police officers, tourists, hillbillies, nurses, a bird, a cat, reindeer and tortoises!

In the decade from 1968 to 1978 Eric and Ernie were clearly at the height of their popularity, confidence and creativity; something which Rowan Atkinson, though he never worked with Eric and Ernie, was able to observe at close range when he had the chance to meet Eric at his home in 1977.

The meeting between established and embryonic comics had

come through a mutual friend. At the
embarked on a career in comedy, but was
the Oxford fringe audiences, to whom he
Two years hence, he would be a star, th
popular, *Not the Nine O'Clock News* se
Mel Smith, Griff Rhys-Jones and Pamela

Always a perceptive and intelligent
meeting in a way that provides one of the best objective accounts of
Eric's character at that time.

'The first thing that struck me was how funny he was in the
house. To me, that was completely alien, because I'm from a
totally different comedy culture: one which was more middle-class,
less music hall tradition and more carefully constructed scripted
television tradition.

'The people I started working with then – and have continued to
work with since – were lawyers and barristers: highly-educated
people. They were relatively fun-loving, but serious-minded
people who weren't cracking jokes all the time. But here was Eric,
who blatantly was. And it was extremely impressive to see how
natural it was with him. But it was also daunting because I knew I
was nowhere near as funny as that in real life, and I wondered if
you really had to be as funny as that around the house in order to
have a successful career in comedy. You know, when you meet
someone oozing such comic confidence from every pore, it doesn't
exactly fill you with great confidence in your own potential when
you consider the contrast with yourself. I remember thinking,
"God, how oppressive to be expected to be this funny all the time."
My other thought was to wonder what it must be like for the family
to live with this man. My family have never had the concern that
I'm going to be relentlessly funny around the house because I'm
exactly the opposite. But Eric's family had to live with this "act" all
the time, which must have been difficult.

'I then started thinking about how difficult Eric must have found
it to live with himself. I thought that if he had this natural ability
and a need to be funny all the time, what must it be like when he
didn't feel he wanted to be funny and the pressure remained on
him to be so?'

For Eddie Braben, though, this was a sign of Eric's comic

hen you go in search of perfection, you rarely find it. Morecambe came as close as anyone. But that constant g for perfection brought with it pressure. And that's where most valuable person in his life deserves her tribute: Joan.

'It can't have been easy living with Eric when he was carrying the worries of his work, but she never let it show. She's a remarkable lady; a lady of great charm, dignity and elegance which never left her, even when the going was severe.

'I honestly believe that because of this wonderful lady, we got a few extra years of Eric Morecambe's magic which we weren't really entitled to.'

15

*'Audiences will not accept us doing
anything different.'*

Ernie Wise

Success usually comes at a price, but at least for Morecambe and
Wise the price was an enviable one.

They became, in a sense, almost too successful at the BBC in the
1970s. That is, too successful for their public to accept them doing
anything other than the style of show for which they have since
become revered.

Even as early as 1973, both Eric and Ernie were publicly stating
in interviews with journalists a desire to move on to do other things
beyond the Morecambe and Wise format, as we had come to know
it. It seems incredible, now, that they could possibly have
contemplated this when one considers what was yet to come in
terms of great shows.

In an astonishingly frank interview for *Titbits* magazine in March
1973, which pre-dated their virtual canonisation by Kenneth
Tynan in the *Observer* magazine by just a few months, Eric and
Ernie told Alan Day just how deeply they yearned to make changes
to their comic style.

'We want to get away from doing the kind of stuff we've been doing for so long,' said Eric. 'We've been kicking ideas around but we haven't worked out a new format yet. There's nothing we'd like to do more than get away from the old routine and make a complete switch. Situation comedy would suit us fine. But the main problem is finding someone who can write a basic situation for us to play.'

Ernie acknowledged the problems they would face should they make changes. 'The trouble is, we've been doing the same thing, sticking to the same kind of comedy, for so long that nobody wants us to do anything else. It doesn't matter what we do or how we switch the show around, we're still Morecambe and Wise. We're too well known and audiences will not accept us doing anything different.'

The fact that a decade later, in 1983, the Morecambe and Wise shows they were making for Thames were still produced largely adhering to the established formula, if with subtle variations, demonstrates they were never truly able to attempt a serious break from the formula that had helped make them stars. But then Eric and Ernie also recognised that abandoning a formula which held nearly half the nation transfixed with each new show invited peril. And neither man, however much he desired change, was willing to risk their status. They'd seen too many comedians, like Sellers, like Hancock, damage their careers by changing track. Hancock, in particular, had cruelly exposed himself as being profoundly sad and not nearly so funny once he'd taken the axe to the props of his early career – Galton and Simpson, and East Cheam – which had provided the basis for him to demonstrate his comic genius.

Like Noël Coward who, when asked by an interviewer if he wished he'd been a significant playwright, answered tartly, 'I don't think I've ever wanted to be "significant",' Morecambe and Wise had no pretensions about the 'significance' of their own work. They let the intellectuals ponder over such imponderables. When they spoke of change in their act, they weren't proposing to perform comedy which dealt with the state of the world or tried to expose mankind's inhumanity. They were talking about a change of style or emphasis but not, essentially, content. This was why, they both felt, a situation comedy would provide them with the ideal departure: one which, as evidenced by the Braben sketches in their fictional apartment, they knew they could carry off. Certainly, their search for a sit-com vehicle was well known and they considered several scripts and ideas.

'Over the years I worked with them, they did both become tired of simply doing the same comedy sketches,' says Glenda Jackson. 'And I know they would both have liked to have done a sit-com. It was something they were always looking out for but never actually found.'

'The trouble is,' says Bryan Forbes, 'audiences always want the mixture as before. There was a formula to what Morecambe and Wise did – such as Ernie writing the terrible play which pulled in some of their greatest guest stars – and that was the formula the audience wanted.'

They experimented briefly with a slightly different format – though it was more an interlude between shows – when they hosted a series called *Child's Play*. Children would submit short dramas which various actors, such as Beryl Reid, would star in. Each programme was wrapped up with Eric and Ernie starring in a submitted comedy sketch, very much along the lines of Ernie's plays. It was fun and refreshing, but hardly heralded a new-style Morecambe and Wise, and nor was it intended to.

It wasn't necessarily that either Eric or Ernie was one of the clichéd clowns yearning to play Hamlet. And they certainly weren't bored with success: having struggled together so hard for so long to achieve their own stardom, they were not going publicly to denounce their fame as some kind of curse. As far as Morecambe and Wise were concerned, recognition – the requests for autographs, the perpetual demands on them to be funny – were the guarantee they were doing all right. And the fans at the stage door were to be cherished, not despised. Even when they had audiences for television of twenty million upwards, they continued to display surprising humility.

'Eric and Ernie were never "stars" like that, at all,' says Michael Grade. 'I regularly used to go to football matches with Eric – he loved his football, and really relaxed at a match. I'd get tickets for Wembley or wherever and we'd go with Harry Worth and Jimmy Tarbuck. And we'd have a good time. Harry would make him laugh, and Jimmy would make him laugh: in fact he was a very generous man like that, because he never minded other comics getting laughs.

'But it was his attitude to fans I remember. He would always respond to recognition, and had half a dozen or so nice stock ad libs he could use in those situations. He was always charming to fans, always gave them a giggle.

'Ernie was the same. They both had great humility. But then they were personalities of their own backgrounds – they'd come up through a very hard school. Eric's humility came from his mum, Sadie. He told me that she used to give him a hard time, and he once told me a great story about her. They'd appeared on an edition of *Sunday Night at the London Palladium* before they hit it really big. Eric had had the flu, and he and Ernie had done a terrible performance. In fact, the whole thing had been a disaster for them. He was feeling awful, and what with the flu and everything, got himself into a depression and convinced himself it was the end of his career.

'When he told Sadie, she said, "It's all right for you, but I've got to go to the butcher's on Monday and face people." He told me that made him laugh so much that it got him out of his depression.'

Although he related that story to Grade as a joke, at the time Eric had not found Sadie's attitude funny. Indeed, as Joan Morecambe points out, although Sadie did not keep criticism of Morecambe and Wise to herself if she felt it justified, her comments were always characterised by fairness. On this occasion, though, Joan feels that Sadie went too far.

'She was absolutely scathing about the whole thing, and particularly about Eric, whom she seemed to be blaming as though it was all his fault. Now, it's true that they hadn't done well; hadn't come across to the audience. But it was also true that Eric was ill and had had an injection before going on stage.

'So Sadie was being very unfair, and I remember Eric, who was a great talker himself and always had a lot to say, going completely quiet. He didn't defend himself – in fact, he didn't say anything at all because he knew that at that moment she wouldn't understand and he couldn't make her understand by retorting, "Well, no one goes on stage and dies on purpose."

'When he really needed her to support him and to boost his

confidence, she was letting him down. But I have to say that that was the one single occasion I can ever remember her doing so.'

While in Florida, Eric and Joan had been invited to one of Liberace's homes for tea. As Eric surveyed the glittering scene – including the piano-shaped swimming pool and the liveried servants – he began seriously to doubt that he and Ernie really could be classed as stars at all. 'I am a star, aren't I, Louis?' he asked Louis Benjamin, chairman of Stoll-Moss theatres, and a long-time family friend. True, the life-styles he and Ernie enjoyed were beyond the wildest possibilities they could have imagined forty years earlier in Liverpool, but they had no servants awaiting their instructions. There were no swimming pools back home in the shape of a pipe or pair of spectacles.

Though Benjamin assured him he was a star, Eric was never fully convinced after that occasion.

'They were quite extraordinary,' says Glenda Jackson, recalling their attitude to their own stardom. 'When I first appeared with them, everyone in the business I knew told me they were envious of me for being invited on to the Morecambe and Wise show. Everybody wanted to work with them: there was no variety-straight theatre divide when it came to Morecambe and Wise. There was such an amazing respect for them. But they, themselves, seemed genuinely surprised by their own success. I confess, I found that very surprising because the respect for them was so widespread.'

'I suppose they did both manage to keep their feet on the ground,' agrees Joan. 'Maybe that's because they'd started so young and came from fairly harsh backgrounds where neither of them had had a lot as children. Certainly, they were both extremely grateful when things went well for them and they never became conceited.

'They got such a great kick out of having people like Glenda Jackson on their shows, and they recognised that it was very generous of these people to come on and be insulted.'

As Roy Castle once put it, 'It was an honour to go on a Morecambe and Wise show and be insulted.'

'Compared to a lot of other comics, Eric and Ernie were different,' says Bryan Forbes. 'I always remember Eric and Joan coming to lunch with Nanette and myself at our house. And we just laughed all the way through the meal because Eric was very seldom off. Some comedians hate being like that. I mean, Peter Sellers couldn't stand being expected to be funny when he wasn't working. Tony Hancock was the same. In Peter's case he suffered because everyone who came up to him did a "Goon" voice. With Hancock they wanted him to be the character from East Cheam, basically his alter ego.

'Frankie Howerd was a sad, sad, somewhat bitter clown. He was a closet homosexual who'd have been better served in coming out because really everyone knew he was one. It was a painful, unnecessary pretence. I remember him crying on my shoulder saying, "What can I do? I'm so lonely. I can't make a relationship."

'And look at Sid Field. He took to drink. Having wandered in the wilderness for twenty years, he came to London and was the biggest star anyone had ever seen. But he was dead within four years.

'Eric and Ernie never took to drink or drugs. It was obvious they enjoyed what they did and enjoyed life. And they didn't mind giving the public what was expected of them.'

John Thaw, who often saw Eric at showbusiness functions, says he never saw Eric on anything less than his top comic form, even when he wasn't performing. 'I don't know if he made himself do it to get through the night, but he was always wise-cracking. It was almost as though he'd come out armed with a bagful of gags to see him through.

'I used to see much more of Eric than of Ernie at these "dos", especially awards ceremonies. I remember sitting next to Eric at one London *Evening News* Film Awards Ceremony. Joan Collins was announcing the nominations for Best Actor, which were Laurence Olivier, Peter Finch, James Mason – and me, for *The Sweeney* movie.

'I'd convinced myself I'd no chance of winning, and just sat there in a dream world waiting for Larry to get up to receive the award. Next thing I knew, Eric was ecstatically digging me in the ribs and hissing, "It's you, it's you – get up – it's you!"

'I suppose I used to see much more of Eric socially than Ernie, because the curious thing was that Eric and Ernie didn't socialise much together. It was certainly rare to see them together socially.'

This aspect of their private lives had been a feature of the Morecambe and Wise partnership more or less since they had been married and, although it would occasionally be seized upon by tabloid hacks during the 1970s as evidence that they didn't really get on, for most pros it was an accepted part of sustaining their working relationship.

'Eric and Ernie worked hard at their professional relationship, but they simply didn't socialise together; didn't live in each other's pockets,' says Michael Grade. 'And the simple reason for that was that they both had good marriages, different interests and different outlooks on life.'

Glenda Jackson qualifies this further. 'If anything, I always felt that they clearly worked at keeping as separate as possible their professional and their private lives. When it came to the actual comedy business, together they were the best there was. But it is quite clear to me that they met to work.'

Joan feels too much shouldn't be read into their conscious decision not to socialise much together. 'What people forget about Eric and Ernie, was that they were actually closer than husband and wife. They did so many shows together and really worked at those shows. This meant that they would see each other every single day except weekends: they really did spend a lot of hours together.

'Now, we'd see Ernie and Doreen at the Variety Club "dos" and things like the BAFTAs, but apart from that we did go our separate ways because, basically, they saw enough of each other and they both had to have some other life away from the act. And of course we didn't live close to each other, and they had their own interests and hobbies.'

Ben Elton agrees. 'It doesn't surprise me they didn't socialise much together,' he says. 'Or that they didn't share the same hotel when they were on tour. Richard Curtis and I are partners when we write the *Blackadder* series and we don't spend more than four days together in the writing of an entire series because we write separately. That doesn't stop us being very good friends.'

When together, at the studio or on location, Eric and Ernie had the ability simply to pick up where they had left off last time. And although the intense rehearsal period, which they both insisted upon, could be extremely tiring, there was still time for both men to enjoy playing practical jokes, as Ernest Maxin, their BBC producer from 1975 to 1978, explains.

'I always look through the viewfinder on the camera to make sure all the shots are exactly right and to finalise when I'm going to pull back and so on. These things are very important and make a difference to the laughter you're going to get when you see it on the screen. If you pull away too early or too late, you can lose the laugh completely. For instance, with Eric, he was funnier when he was doing certain things in different lengths and, sometimes, he was even funnier from the back. So, consequently, I was always looking through the viewfinder at the Morecambe and Wise shows to make sure everything looked just right.

'One particular day, when we were on location with Eric and Ernie and John Thaw and Dennis Waterman, I was taking a hell of a lot of time looking through the camera. Eventually we finished and went back to Television Centre. I got on the Tube, sat down and the guy sitting opposite winked at me. Then I looked across the carriage and there was a woman giggling at me. I thought I'd got into a carriage full of lunatics and didn't feel very comfortable. So I got out at the next stop, got into the next carriage along, and the same thing happened again. And it kept on happening everywhere I went until I got home, where my wife opened the door and gave me a long, bemused look.

'What Eric and Ernie had done was to put black charcoal and chalk around the viewfinder of the camera. Furthermore, Eric had come up to me, saying things like, "I like the way you've had your sideboards done," while tracing his finger round the side of my face and eyes. I remember wondering at the time what the hell he was doing. What he'd done, of course, was to draw a pair of glasses on my face with his finger.'

16

'From that day on, Sadie just lost her drive ...'

Joan Morecambe

The enduring success of Morecambe and Wise during the BBC era, manifested itself in ways beyond huge ratings. To add to the awards they had received as a result of *Two of a Kind*, they were further honoured by the Variety Club of Great Britain and BAFTA.

In total, Eric and Ernie won four awards from the Variety Club (in 1964, 1974, 1976 and 1978) and six from BAFTA (1963, 1969 and 1970 to 1973 consecutively.)

'The BAFTA we won in 1963 was the first big award we got,' says Ernie, 'and we always had reason to remember it because when we were on stage being presented with it, there was a disturbance in the audience as news of President Kennedy's assassination came through.'

In addition to these major, prestigious awards, Eric and Ernie were also the recipients of OBEs and the Freedom of the City of London in 1976, and their alleged wax likenesses were exhibited at Madame Tussaud's.

Their gratitude at Eric's relative wealth was one of the main reasons why he and Joan decided in the mid-1970s to adopt a little boy called Steven.

Steven came to them through Gail, who had been working as a nursery nurse at a childrens' home. On occasion she took some of the children back to Harpenden to give them a day out. Steven became a regular visitor, soon addressing his hosts as Mum and Dad.

Knowing how much Steven had begun to identify himself with the family, the question of formal adoption arose. It was not an easy decision to make but, knowing the alternative was for Steven to spend the rest of his childhood in care, Eric and Joan, after family consultation, realised they had no real choice: through his brief visits, Steven had already become part of the family.

Sadness came in 1977, with the death of Sadie: the indomitable woman whose intelligence, foresight and sheer force of personality had been responsible for the birth of Morecambe and Wise.

Though she had long since ceased to make any direct input into the act – if never failing to pass on her opinion about a sketch or routine – neither Eric nor Ernie could ever forget the importance of her support in the early years.

As Morecambe and Wise became increasingly popular and successful in the 1970s, Sadie watched it all with quiet satisfaction and pride. Her only son, and her virtually adopted son, Ernie, had made it. She knew just how vital a role she had played in that success. Though forced by circumstances into letting go of her boys once the early days of chaperoning were fulfilled – when they had matured into independent young men, and she had returned to be with her husband, George, back in Morecambe – she must have delighted in her own sense of timing. Never did she try to stifle or dominate the double act once it was on a fairly steady course in variety, and even after she allowed Eric and Ernie to take control, the act continued to prosper.

Since then, she had dedicated her life to George whose life, ambitions and career could not have been more removed from Eric and Ernie's, but whom she loved no less because of that.

One night in January 1976, George got up from his armchair, told Sadie it was time they were getting to bed and then collapsed and died instantly.

'From that day on, Sadie just lost her drive,' says Joan. 'It was as though she saw that her life was at an end and all she wanted was to be reunited with George.'

Sadie's decline was not overly prolonged. After a spell staying with Eric and Joan at Harpenden, Sadie moved to live briefly in a bungalow in Morecambe. But she became very ill and after hospitalisation in Lancaster moved back to Harpenden in the spring of 1977 to recuperate.

She fell ill again, requiring further hospitalisation in Harpenden, and then suffered a stroke.

'She battled for days,' says Joan who, due to Eric's working commitments, did most of the nursing of Sadie in those final days. 'Although she sometimes had to struggle to express herself, she'd talk and talk and talk about the old days with Eric and Ernie.

'Towards the end, Eric was away for three days and although I knew she couldn't last much longer, she wouldn't give in and I began to sense she was waiting to see Eric one last time. He arrived back from Manchester and went straight up to see her. As he walked through the door, she turned to look at him and then died.'

Sadie's death was an immense sadness to Eric but, as the oldest showbusiness cliché of all has it, the show had to go on. Though he had to mourn Sadie in his own way, Eric still had to go about his business of making people laugh.

Much the same had happened to Ernie eleven years earlier, in 1966, when Harry, his beloved father, had died after a long illness. Though he didn't play as pivotal a role in the development of Morecambe and Wise as did Sadie, Harry was essential in their story in the way he had nurtured and encouraged Ernie's very earliest aspirations.

Even today, that very special bond between Ernie and his father makes it difficult for Ernie to talk about him without becoming emotional. But at the time of Harry's death, Ernie was so deep in rehearsals for a forthcoming show that grief simply couldn't take hold of him. Indeed, such was the pressure they were working under, Ernie managed to get only one day off to travel home to Leeds for the funeral.

'Dad would've understood though,' Ernie says. 'He'd have known the pressures we were under and been proud we were so much in demand.'

Sadie's death came just a few months before Eric and Ernie did finally make the change in their working pattern they'd been talking about publicly since 1973. Then they had talked about a change of style; of format. In practice, the format remained more or less intact, with variations on a theme introduced, but, for the BBC at least, Eric and Ernie made the biggest change it was possible to make: they changed channels and signed an exclusive deal with Thames Television.

'They had begun thinking that they couldn't go on for ever doing the same format,' Joan says. 'You've got to have a change eventually and that was one of the attractions of switching to Thames from the BBC. They felt it was a change in all senses: the people they worked with, the directors, even the camera crew. What they needed were new challenges.'

And the greatest challenge of all was to prove that they could be just as successful, just as popular, divorced from the organisation with whom they had enjoyed the most successful decade of their careers.

17

'I'm tired of being funny ...'

Eric Morecambe

The headline said it all.

On 27 January 1978, in the extra large print usually reserved for a death of a member of the Royal Family, or a change of government, the *Evening Standard* led with: 'Morecambe and Wise Switch to ITV.' After a decade of being the most glittering jewel in the BBC's comedy crown, Eric and Ernie had signed an exclusive two-year deal with Thames which guaranteed they would make four Morecambe and Wise shows a year, plus a major film.

'We serenaded them,' admits Philip Jones, then Head of Light Entertainment at Thames, who'd known Ernie socially for years through their mutual friend, the writer Vince Powell.

'I'd often thought how great it would be if Eric and Ernie would join us at Thames. But I never mentioned anything because it would have been wrong to let that intrude on our social lives.

'However, there came a point when I sensed they might be willing to listen to an offer of some sort. I was very fortunate in that the managing director of programmes at that time was Bryan Cowgill who, like me, was a great fan of the boys. And Bryan wasn't just supportive in the negotiations, he was also active in helping me persuade them to join us.'

Jones arranged a lunch at Thames, hosted by Cowgill, and invited Eric and Ernie and their agent, Billy Marsh. 'During the course of lunch,' Jones recalls, 'the conversation turned more and more seriously to the idea of Eric and Ernie joining us. Bryan and I asked if there was any chance and, if there was, what they would be looking for. In the end it wasn't just money which was the deciding factor. They were looking for new opportunities; mainly, of course, the films.'

'Two things happened,' says Bill Cotton. 'I left Light Entertainment to become Controller of BBC1, and they went to Thames the next day. Someone once told me that Eric had said, "Well, Bill Cotton's looked after himself so I think it's about time we looked after ourselves." '

Their move affected Cotton deeply, as he readily admits, 'It was like a divorce, actually. I first heard about it in America, where I was buying programmes. I was ill with Asian flu, and it was pouring with rain and my secretary called from London and told me they'd gone to Thames. For the rest of the day I just felt completely and utterly empty.

'I think I felt it more acutely because I was in the position of having supplied the Controller of BBC1 with all those great shows for ten years and then just when it became my turn to run BBC1, they'd pushed off.'

Cotton is aware that it was the promise of a film rather than the money that seduced Morecambe and Wise. But Cotton also claims that it wasn't as difficult as he'd anticipated to fill the void they had left. 'It wasn't difficult because the Two Ronnies had come up very strongly and, anyway, to a degree Eric and Ernie had slowed down their output. Of course, The Two Ronnies weren't a double act at all. They were two fine comedy actors who, at the same time as performing together, did other things separately. But they did fill the double act hole left by Morecambe and Wise.'

Ever since the disappointment of their three films for Rank back in the 1960s, Eric and Ernie had craved another shot at starring in a hit film. In 1978, the BBC did not have its own film company. Thames did: Euston Films, which was responsible for making *The*

Sweeney and *Minder* – and this was the ace up Thames' sleeve in negotiations. The importance Eric and Ernie put on the prospective film deal cannot be overstated.

They'd always been vaguely disappointed with the BBC's inability to sell their shows successfully in the States, in the way that *Monty Python* had been sold.

Their appearances on the Ed Sullivan shows had not been an enjoyable experience for Eric, and he didn't share Ernie's driving ambition to get to Hollywood. This doesn't mean that he was devoid of all desire to find success in the States; just that he would have preferred it to be achieved away from the vaudeville tradition in which he and Ernie had made their names in Britain.

So the prospect of a film which might relaunch them in America satisfied both halves of the partnership: Ernie would, so to speak, get his crack at Hollywood, while Eric could make his name out there without having to appear live in front of American audiences. And, as stated earlier, both men loved the movies anyway.

'There was always this thing with Eric to do a film,' says Joan. 'He really loved films, and not just comedy films. You see, Eric was a very intelligent man and he loved good material, good films. He was also terribly knowledgeable about showbusiness – the American side as well – so he knew how important a good film could be to them.

'One of the problems of being a partnership like Morecambe and Wise compared to, say, the Two Ronnies, who came together as a team but also did things apart, is that every offer of work had to be suitable to the two of them. Eric did have two or three offers to do film parts by himself, but he just wouldn't do them. 'It wouldn't be fair to Ernie,' he told me. He also felt it could jeopardise their partnership, so he wasn't interested.

'The only things he did do were a couple of short films for Anglia in the 1980s, and only because he felt they were harmless and fun.'

Despite its determination to keep Morecambe and Wise on its books, the BBC soon came to accept that their wish to make films meant that it was unable to compete. James Gilbert, then Head of Light Entertainment, while wishing his two stars well, was frank with journalists about why the BBC had failed to hold on to Morecambe and Wise: 'The BBC is not a film company and cannot compete with an offer which links a feature film to a TV contract.'

Although the BBC tried to put a brave face on it, Eric and Ernie's switch hurt, and it was a massive blow to BBC1 in its ratings battle with ITV. Their 1977 Christmas show for the BBC had pulled in a record twenty-eight million viewers and taken them into *The Guinness Book of Records*. (A matter hotly contested by ITV, who claimed Mike Yarwood's Christmas show had topped that figure.) Now the 1978 Christmas show was to be made for Thames.

There were dark mutterings from Shepherd's Bush about 'desertion' and 'defection'; words not heard a decade earlier when Eric and Ernie, as relative newcomers, were on their way from ATV to the BBC.

Then came BBC1's strategic scheduling of Morecambe and Wise highlights to compete directly with Thames Television's new offerings. BBC programme announcers were even instructed to introduce the repeats as 'The *best* years of Morecambe and Wise,' knowing exactly where to place the emphasis.

Such sabre-rattling after the event masked a rather obvious fact. While no one, least of all the boys themselves, would deny that the BBC had provided them with ten years of excellent production, towards the end of their decade there the Corporation had taken the loyalty of its two stars for granted. Eric and Ernie had always maintained a policy of signing only contracts of a year long, which allowed them to retain their freedom. This had always been understood by the BBC and accepted by them. So any suggestion of disloyalty was absurd.

Moreover, as Ernie is always fast to point out, showbusiness is show*business*. Morecambe and Wise, like every other act working in the country, had to take a business decision with every contract they signed. And, when it comes to toughness, there's certainly 'no business like showbusiness'.

Ernie would remember for ever Max Miller's advice, imparted at Watford in 1948: 'When one door shuts, they all bloody shut.' When things were going well, performers had to take any advantages at once in case, come tomorrow, no one was remotely interested in what they were selling.

This continuous struggle to strive forward is shown in Eric's long-running concern for the future of Morecambe and Wise. It wasn't until as late as the mid-1970s that he was able to accept that not only had they truly achieved what they set out to achieve – and a good deal more – but that they were now safe; that they could ease off the frantic pace just a little. Yet the niggling doubt that they could fail and become unwanted did, in lesser form, remain with him until the day he died.

In the early days of television stardom, with ATV in the early 1960s, both the boys honestly believed they might well be no more than a flash in the pan; that within a couple of years it would all be over and they would be back treading what was left of the variety boards.

'As long as you keep producing the goods,' points out Ernie, 'everyone wants you. The moment you stop, no one wants to know. It's inconceivable that BBC managers would have been "loyal" to us if we'd stopped providing first-rate shows. All this talk about disloyalty was very unfair. The simple fact is that Eric and I were unique, and uniqueness can set its own price.'

So when Philip Jones approached them in 1977 with an offer which included not only a film deal, but three times the money the BBC was currently paying them, it was the proverbial offer they couldn't refuse.

In retrospect it is clear they had to accept, but words like 'defection' and 'desertion' struck a nerve as many Morecambe and Wise fans wrote to the BBC, complaining bitterly of their move. Some industry insiders, as well as viewers, considered their move to a commercial channel a retrograde step as a kind of cultural snobbery came into play. Now, in the 1990s, it is the commercial channels which are regarded as producing programmes of higher quality, and the BBC has suffered several years of lacklustre programming and a series of embarrassing flops. But in the late 1970s, the BBC was, justly or not, still considered to be the vanguard of broadcasting excellence in Britain. This was coupled with the sentimental, almost inexplicable, loyalty of audiences who could not contemplate change – Auntie Beeb was well able to demonstrate a mesmeric hold over its viewers.

Just as die-hard film fans cling to the belief that Sean Connery was the only James Bond, while ignoring the fact that Roger Moore's films made more money at the box office, so some

Morecambe and Wise fans resented their move to Thames – believing they weren't as funny as they had been at the BBC, even though their audience figures stood up extremely well.

Nevertheless, changes of style did evolve between Eric and Ernie's last show for the BBC and their Thames era. On the day the news broke about Eric and Ernie joining Thames, the *Evening Standard* quoted Philip Jones as saying his intention was to make the new Morecambe and Wise shows as different as possible from the BBC's format.

Today, Philip Jones says he was misquoted and had, in fact, said the opposite. 'When the news broke it was a very big story and the question everyone asked me was how the show was going to change. That was the easiest question to answer. I told them it wasn't going to change one bit.

'We wanted Morecambe and Wise because they were the most popular and classiest act available. And when you buy a Rolls-Royce you don't try to convert it into an Austin Seven.'

Their shows did change, however, though not as radically as had been feared when Jones's misquoted answers were published. Certainly the change of channels did more than just put commercial breaks into the show – something which Ernie now believes worked against them. The Thames era, the last in the development of Morecambe and Wise, saw shows with a different texture from all those that had gone before.

On the road from Shepherd's Bush to Teddington the Morecambe and Wise show evolved and mellowed. Although musical routines still featured, the quality of the sets was rarely comparable to those designed by the BBC. Indeed, the production of the shows seemed deliberately to shy away from the lavishness of what had gone before and to seek a more confined, confidential feel, returning, in essence, to the main core of what Morecambe and Wise were and always had been about. The jokes and gibes at Ernie's expense, which had been a hallmark of their BBC shows but which, of course, had long pre-dated their association with the Corporation, continued with even more vigour because they served more than anything else to expose best the workings of their relationship.

At Thames, Eric and Ernie were surrounded by new people with new ideas, and one of the obvious changes was that they became gentler and more laid-back than at any time in their careers.

Famous guest stars still graced their shows – their elimination would have been too radical a departure from an established formula that had begun in the ATV days – and the first outing for Thames featured Dame Judi Dench and Donald Sinden. And yet, even in this department, there were subtle changes.

On the Thames shows, less emphasis was placed on the ritualistic, good-natured humiliation of guests, and they came across, as a result, as less harried and more relaxed. The feeling was almost as though everyone connected with the shows, not least Eric and Ernie, were aware that these were the autumn years of a wonderful career, and the focus was on celebrating the double act *with* the double act. A party atmosphere developed.

One noticeable absentee was Eddie Braben, who had not wanted to join Thames. 'Eddie Braben didn't want, at that time, to join the ITV club,' says Jones, 'though he did join us later.' Braben returned to write the 1981 and 1982 Christmas shows. Producer Johnny Ammonds would also return for a spell during their final years at Thames.

Braben's initial absence wasn't as big a hurdle as perhaps first perceived, both Eric and Ernie having wanted a fresh slant to the material they would use at Thames. It was generally felt that maybe they had gone as far down the line with Braben as was advisable. Consequently other writers were drafted in, with John Junkin and Barry Cryer featuring as the regular ones.

Philip Jones, while accepting that the change of writers inevitably meant a change in material, disputes the notion that the Morecambe and Wise shows changed noticeably. He says that any changes which did occur were not intentional. 'Don't forget that the pattern of the shows was a bit different anyway,' he points out. 'The BBC had been doing a series a year, plus a Christmas show. We only did three specials a year, although later that changed to a series of half-hour shows plus a Christmas show. But as to the style, I don't know that it changed at all. If it did, then it certainly wasn't our intention when we set out.'

Another reason why there might have been a change was in the guest stars themselves. 'The BBC had had the tremendous

advantage of having used up all the spectacular guests,' remarks
Jones. 'They'd had André Previn, they'd had Shirley Bassey, and
they'd had Angela Rippon showing her legs for the first time in that
dance routine. They'd used every guest you could think of from
straight actors to variety performers to singers. Now there are only
a certain number of famous people available. And we found it very
difficult to top what had gone before.'

Jones gives a third reason to account for a possible difference in
style, and that was the change of producers and directors. 'Let's get
one thing absolutely clear: the Morecambe and Wise show was
essentially their show. In terms of laughter quotient, those guys
knew what they were doing and in my view the producers of the
show were very lucky to be assigned to do it. As a
producer/director in the old days, I'd have loved to have had the
opportunity of having the Morecambe and Wise show to produce
because you were in safe hands. And only a fool wouldn't have
listened to them.

'Nevertheless, all producers and directors bring their own stamp
to anything they do and they're very important in the final product.
So if you look at their producers over the years – Johnny Ammonds
and then Ernest Maxin at the BBC, Keith Beckett and Mark Stuart
at Thames – you'll see that they're all excellent practitioners, but
with different strengths. That's particularly true in Ernest Maxin's
case: Ernest's background was in song and dance and
choreography which meant he could bring that full Hollywood
dream to the Morecambe and Wise shows.'

Other changes were purely physical. On their first Thames
outing, Ernie's hair had begun to whiten and Eric's had further
receded and greyed at the sides. Another physical change, and
possibly a mistake, was Eric's change of glasses. Gone were the
characteristic black, and sometimes brown, oblong pairs he'd worn
at the BBC, and that had stood out as prop and persona-extension
for over a decade. According to Kenneth Tynan, the black
horn-rimmed frames were an essential part of Eric's comic persona.
But at Thames they were jettisoned in favour of a mottled
tortoise-shell frame which were remarkable only for being
completely unremarkable. For true fans, it was like Tommy
Cooper swopping his fez for a top hat and carrying on as though

nothing had changed.

Despite the changes, at Thames Eric and Ernie found a remarkably professional production team whose intelligence was matched only by their consideration of their new stars.

Their inspirational heroes, Laurel and Hardy, had found in their tragic last films that Stan Laurel's comic genius was ignored by new producers, to the detriment of the act's reputation; Thames, howver, consulted Eric and Ernie at every possible stage of development.

This was the most obvious manifestation of their power. By 1978, Morecambe and Wise had reached that very rare pinnacle in showbusiness when they could say and do almost anything they wished and remain critic-proof. They had been taken to the nation's heart and as such had become a national institution. Ironically, both men were beginning to feel the need to inject some freshness into their work.

'By the time we'd reached the 1980s, we were into our fifth decade of partnership,' says Ernie. 'We'd got a solid body of work behind us and were looking for new challenges.'

In a sense, the record-breaking audience for their 1977 BBC Christmas Show was as much a catalyst for change as their move to Thames. When a mountaineer has conquered Everest, there is no higher peak to climb, so achievements are a virtual series of repeats.

The grand BBC productions with those large budgets had done them proud, and they were the first to acknowledge the fact. Harry Secombe focuses on the André Previn routine. 'The large production routines played an ever-increasing part in their comedy,' he explains. 'You have André Previn with a full orchestra behind him on stage, and Eric's there tapping out a few wrong notes on the piano. It's building up this false grandeur to then knock it down that makes it so funny. It was done in America quite a lot, but you didn't see it in Britain before Eric and Ernie. The BBC played their part – they spent money.'

Both men felt some change was necessary to stave off any danger of staleness. Their other major concern was the one they could do nothing about: ageing.

Eric and Ernie, particularly Eric, were wary of old comics, but if, in their younger days, they had considered the creative peak of a comic to lie between the ages of thirty and fifty, turning fifty had been of little actual relevance to either man. It had just been another birthday. 'I didn't feel any different then or now,' said Ernie on the occasion of that birthday which took place in 1975.

But by the time they reached Thames, both were midway to sixty. And being sixty was a different prospect altogether. Eric, who was to die at fifty-eight, said, 'I do worry about being sixty. After that age I don't think it matters any more. Anything after sixty-five is a bonus career-wise.'

They knew the next few years would see an inevitable slowing down of their act. Even before the recurrence of his heart trouble, Eric was looking to the old comics who had successfully carried on into old age – Arthur Askey, Jack Benny, George Burns, Bob Hope and others – and trying to ascertain just how they'd done it. He concluded that the secret of remaining funny while ageing was to do it subtly.

'We must let the audience grow old with us,' he explained. 'If they don't like us, we must stop at once. But if they still enjoy the shows and don't mind us getting older, then we'll feel confident about continuing. We'd have to revise things as time went by. For instance, the dance routines would eventually have to stop.'

What certainly didn't alter in the Thames shows was the superb timing between Eric and Ernie. Whatever else could be tampered with, that essential relationship, the magic that was the basis of their success, had to be preserved.

Fundamentally, that was what Thames had bought. In Philip Jones' own words, 'the Rolls-Royce' of comedy acts. Indeed, Thames's desire to lay emphasis on the relationship between the two men was evidenced by the manner in which they presented the shows as 'Eric and Ernie'; little reference was made to 'Morecambe and Wise'.

Rowan Atkinson felt they would have been better served by staying off screen completely for two years. 'They could have let their heritage speak for itself,' he says, 'just kind of rarefied themselves so viewers didn't have the chance to say, "Oh God, not them again." But they tended to have a formula, and of course Thames only wanted the formula. I'm not sure how interested any commercial TV company, or at least a TV company with as commercial an angle on Morecambe and Wise as Thames had, are in new areas. I'm sure they offered the film just in the hope that, as exactly happened, they would clinch the deal. But I'm sure they wanted them to do exactly what they had done for years. They didn't want them to explore new areas or do anything different.'

Despite Philip Jones' assertion that he had no desire to see the shows change, moving to Thames did mark another change in the style of Morecambe and Wise which had been evolving since Liverpool in 1941. This was probably a natural phenomenon which would have happened anyway, had they remained with the Corporation, in an attempt to ensure their perpetuation.

Whatever the reason, the BBC-style Morecambe and Wise, which is how the nation had come to perceive them for over a decade, had gone for ever.

Did the changes, particularly the noticeable easing off of mock-Hollywood glitz and big production numbers, really matter? For a small number of their fans the answer has to be yes. However, general comments passed and sizeable viewing figures indicated that the vast majority continued to enjoy them as much as they had before.

Rowan Atkinson confesses he is unconvinced Morecambe and Wise would have maintained their peak had Eric lived. 'I didn't feel that once Eric and Ernie got to Thames, subtle marketing or infrequency of appearance was what they were going for,' says Atkinson. 'They were under contract to make a certain number of shows, and were presumably making a lot more money. But if I was at their stage in my career,' he adds, 'I would do exactly the same thing.'

According to Ben Elton, there was a definite decline after their move to ITV. 'I wasn't a particular fan of the work they did at Thames. Eddie Braben wasn't with them at that time and I don't think you can talk at too great a length about the brilliance of Morecambe and Wise without sooner or later mentioning Eddie Braben. By producing that Ernie character of the frustrated playwright, he showed such an understanding of the Morecambe and Wise act that, in a sense, he was like the third member of the double act.

'The absence of Eddie Braben was part of the problem. And they were a lot older, which is difficult because the amount of energy and commitment required for their kind of comedic honesty is immense.

'It's easy to forget now just how high the audience expectations were. People actually relished a Morecambe and Wise show; they came to represent Christmas, for Christ's sake. I can quite honestly say they were my favourite act of all time and I can remember Christmas Days when I was just waiting all day for their show to start. Can you imagine the problems they faced living up to that? Morecambe and Wise were a very tough act to follow: but it was they, themselves, who had to do the following and they had to do it for so many years.

'By anybody else's standards, their work at Thames was very honourable. But it was very middle of the road and less challenging. There was more reliance on costumes and routines whereas, for me, the brilliance of their act was the two of them in front of the tabs or in the flat. Those were the great moments of Morecambe and Wise and there seemed fewer of them at Thames.'

'The audience figures at Thames never quite achieved that ridiculous twenty-eight million figure they'd had for the 1977 Christmas Show,' Philip Jones admits. 'But from the early 1980s onwards, TV audiences became increasingly fragmented, and those huge audience figures were simply unattainable.'

Certainly their appreciation figures, a more accurate guide to how audiences receive a programme, remained as high as ever, proof that the public was not really bothered which channel they appeared on.

'I don't think they would have advanced themselves in that particular relationship with Thames,' says Atkinson. 'I think it would have wandered along being perfectly adequate, which should be fine. I'm not aware they ever did a bad show at Thames. But somehow, from my perspective, they were just doing the same thing and they were past their best. That's the trouble: if you do the same thing over and over again, audiences' perception of it is that you're getting worse.

'I remember John Cleese saying this about *Fawlty Towers*. The first series was sceptically received at first because it was so different from anything he'd done. But it very rapidly acquired a high reputation. Then a couple of years passed and they made another series which was just as good. But of course everyone was saying, "Oh, this isn't as good as the first series." Today that second series is probably considered slightly better than the first series. It's all to do with expectation, and if you do the same thing people get bored, even if it's of the same quality.'

The press, however, became more critical after the move. Some critics claimed the shows had declined in quality. According to Jones, this was something which worried Eric. 'I think he was worried more than anything else that they weren't getting a good press or, at least, not the press they'd been used to.

'But of course for the press there's no future in writing good things about anyone for too long. It's far easier to build a piece around an opinion that things aren't what they were. I think it was inevitable that critics would write the show had gone downhill. There's no way the critics were ever going to say Eric and Ernie were better at Thames than at the BBC.'

And as Eric used to often say, 'Once you get to the top there's only one way to go, and I assure you it ain't up.'

'I personally wouldn't have been very optimistic about the 1980s for Eric and Ernie,' says Atkinson. 'But I think in many ways they had done their bit; they were past their creative peak, and were in a kind of repetition mode more than anything else. I don't think that situation would necessarily have improved unless they had gone and done something quite different – really gone back to their roots. Maybe started doing more theatre shows, or going to the end of a pier for a few weeks, or really been brave about what they were going to do next. But people tend not to get braver as they get older, and they were getting older.

'It would have been difficult to persuade someone to go along with it, but I think a sit-com is the next step they should have taken. I'm not totally convinced they were suited for it, but you never know. Something like that depends so much on the material and the writing.

'But I don't blame them at all for what they did at Thames. I think they did perfectly well and they did it for good reasons.'

Some people, though, actually thought the shows better than

ever at Thames, and claimed they evoked refreshing memories of their variety days: something which was new to younger audiences and warmly nostalgic to older ones. With the excesses of some of the later BBC shows left behind, Thames presented the essential Eric and Ernie, and for those like J B Priestley, who believed their double act was never better than when it was the two of them alone in front of the tabs scoring points off each other in fast and furious cross-talk, and that the razzle-dazzle asides with prominent guest stars were no more than elaborate interludes, then the Thames shows could be seriously considered an improvement.

Eric and Ernie were naturally proud of their achievements, but they had also been around long enough to be acutely aware of just how fragile success can be in showbusiness. In variety they had seen acts who were once top of the bill slump to embarrassing depths. At the same time, each year the BBC put greater pressure upon them. Each show – especially the Christmas specials – had somehow to top the last, or at very least equal it. The law of diminishing returns can be very cruel in comedy. Comedians have to run to stand still in terms of audience appreciation: the attempt to be funnier than you were last time, year in year out, is ludicrously hard, and the strain on Eric and Ernie in 1976 and 1977, cannot be underestimated.

The move to Thames, and the changes in the format that followed, marked a significant lessening of that pressure they'd been carrying. Simply by switching channels the public perception of them had subtly altered. Whereas they had been the powerful, national court jesters of whom the impossible was expected, they were now the dignified elder statesmen of British comedy accepted come what might.

It quickly became apparent that by parting company with the BBC after such a long and fruitful association, they had created a reason for the television industry to reflect on their talent and achievements. The outcome of this was that by the time Morecambe and Wise were being aired on commercial television, they were more than a national institution: they were legends in their own lifetime.

Like most business, showbusiness is intensely competitive and, naturally enough, Eric and Ernie were always aware that, just as they had successfully fought their way to the top while seeing their contemporaries remain static or slide, so other comics were queuing behind them, hoping to replace them as the top box office draw and television attraction.

But both Eric and Ernie had never been averse to competition. They were at all times highly respectful of talent, particularly comic talent. But if anything truly surprised them then it was the lack of talent coming through.

Both men had, of course, been great admirers of Abbott and Costello and Laurel and Hardy. But there were other favourites including names from their own contemporaries.

As a child, Eric's favourite had been George Formby – 'He's from Lancashire, too,' he had solemnly informed a Morecambe newspaper when they interviewed him after his win in a talent competition – and he also hugely admired Buster Keaton and Groucho Marx. He rated Keaton far above Chaplin, whose comic genius he confessed was entirely lost on him. 'The only thing that to me makes him funny,' he once remarked, 'is that everything is speeded up. Slow his work to normal pace, and do the falls and the gestures honestly still mean anything?' Curiously enough, he was also immune to the appeal of Tony Hancock, finding him for the most part unfunny.

Phil Silvers he could watch for ever, consciously aware that by the 1970s, Sergeant Bilko had manifested himself in diluted form in the screen presence of Eric Morecambe. A great favourite of both Eric and Ernie's was Tommy Cooper, with whom they had enjoyed a long friendship, and they admired the Two Ronnies.

Of the genuine challengers to their throne, Cannon and Ball had long appeared the most promising, and Eric had warmed to them as people several years before they finally took off. Initially acclaimed as an inventive act, though described by some (a little unjustly perhaps) as being an intensely irritating and crude act, Cannon and Ball had been performing together since the early 1960s. Through years of desperate struggle they had fought their way to a level of stardom few achieve, and in the early 1980s were declared ready to inherit Morecambe and Wise's crown. Indeed, they made a highly successful thirteen-week tour of the country in 1983, playing one hundred and thirty-four shows in forty-five theatres and breaking the all-time box-office record at London's Dominion Theatre.

Not unsurprisingly, professional curiosity drove Eric and Ernie to examine the standard of this newly-acclaimed comedy duo. 'Bobby Ball's very funny, and Tommy Cannon's an excellent straight man,' acknowledged Eric in 1982. 'But they've got to progress. Bobby can't forever pull on his braces to get laughs.' Professional though they were, Cannon and Ball were not going to pose a direct threat to anything Morecambe and Wise had done or would go on to do during the next couple of years.

But it was very difficult for Eric to pass any sort of judgement on them, for not only had he come into contact with them socially, liking them and being able to relate wholeheartedly with their work and their struggle to the top, but they also made it very plain, as recently stated in Bobby Ball's biography (1993), that he was their hero. Shortly before his death, Eric did refer to Cannon and Ball as the best double act since Morecambe and Wise, which is a wonderful compliment however guarded it may appear.

Little and Large pre-empted Cannon and Ball's challenge but they were an act which did not overly impress either Eric or Ernie. 'If that's all we've got to worry about,' Eric told Ernie over the phone after seeing them for the first time, 'you and I'll be around for a few years yet.'

One double act which Eric did find interesting was Hinge and Bracket. It was an act which developed and peaked in the 1970s and early 1980s on television – though the act is still very popular and successful in theatres – and has aspects of traditional music hall; not least the fact they are middle-aged men dragging up as elderly, upper-class spinsters. This year – 1994 – sees that act touring the country in celebration of twenty-one years together.

'To my way of thinking, though I'm just a middle-aged actress, the double acts of today don't have the same kind of warmth as Morecambe and Wise,' remarks Penelope Keith. 'Okay, Fry and Laurie and French and Saunders are laughed at by the chattering classes, but they don't span the range of Morecambe and Wise. I don't believe you'll see the like of them again.'

As the 1970s gave way to the 1980s, so the whole nature of comedy began to change and established acts, even those at the very top, began to find themselves frozen out by TV executives. The cause was the rise of what became known as the alternative comedians.

So called because it supposedly barred sexist and racist jokes and turned its back on middle-class, self-satisfied humour, alternative comedy found its greatest supporter in Channel 4. Britain's newest TV channel, launched in 1982, had initially gone out of its way to court a new TV audience by deliberately shocking the established one. And nowhere was this more obvious than in terms of comedy.

Everyone fell in love with the alternative comedians – everyone but the audience, that is. Producers raided the alternative comedy clubs in London's West End, where performers would regularly trip out a barrage of politically correct filth to drunken audiences. Twenty-two-year-old graduates just down from Cambridge would be signed up by balding middle-aged TV executives sporting pony-tails who were trying failingly to give the impression they, too, were in their twenties. The result was that TV audiences of three million for the alternative comedians were hailed as some kind of triumph while performers like Benny Hill, whose shows still go out world-wide and could bring in twenty million viewers in Britain alone, were eventually not commissioned to make new shows at all.

'Alternative comedy is sometimes about as funny as a baby's open grave,' says Bryan Forbes. 'And it's particularly offensive at its worst when a woman gets up and does a stand-up routine. Not just here, but in America, where it's the mainstay of late night talk shows. It's cruel humour, and cruel humour has to be really very witty. *Spitting Image* has gone down the drain in my opinion because it no longer has any wit but is merely cruel. Cruelty without wit is pathetic. All you are doing is slagging off somebody. Eric used to slag off Ernie, but in the most extraordinary way. You sensed it was never ill-meant.

'Morecambe and Wise didn't rely on any sort of sexual jokes. They relied quite often on innuendo. If there was a sexual connotation in the "feed", Eric's reaction was always of shocked amazement, so it never gave offence.'

Says Rowan Atkinson, 'The comedy of the 1980s, the so-called alternative comedy, was more stand-up. More people with microphones being funny in front of an audience in a very singular way. Mainly solo performers rather than double acts, but nevertheless in the more old-fashioned, theatrical, live tradition, rather than television, which is why, I suppose, relatively few of those people have successful television shows as such.'

Atkinson spotlights comedian Billy Connolly as a prime example. 'Other than the odd play on British television he hasn't done much, and he's still seen as a live act, and quite rightly because he's an absolute genius.

'Not many performers have moved into a more comic acting tradition; they've stayed more in the stand-up tradition. Therefore, I suppose they were more sympathetic with the Morecambe and Wise school of comedy than the Benny Hill one. Or with Python, even. So Morecambe and Wise must have inspired.'

Ben Elton, though, firmly rejects the alternative debate as ludicrous and says he always finds Morecambe and Wise the quickest and easiest means of debunking the whole alternative comedy concept:

'I suppose there are points to be made about the political nature of some comedy but basically the whole argument is absurd. Take Rik Mayall and Ade Edmondson for instance and compare them to Morecambe and Wise.

'Rik and Ade, whose work I know and love, are labelled alternative comedians whereas Eric and Ernie are labelled as the greatest mainstream comedians of all time. But the point is, Rik and Ade are successful in the mainstream and Eric and Ernie, in my opinion, are the greatest alternative comedians of all time.

'Look at their work. It was complete nonsense at all times and it was based on great swathes of cruelty and pathos, exploitation of each other, the puncturing of each other's ego. It was all mad and surreal.

'I always think of those sketches of the two of them in bed together, bickering. They'd lie there, without any hint of anything sexual (which would have been totally contrary to the joke), and worry about disputes they'd had fifty years ago; who the teacher had liked best, which of them had had shoes and which of them hadn't. That, to me, is Beckett.

'Balding, middle-aged men in pyjamas worrying about shoes

from half a century before. It's so surreal. If I gave you that description and you didn't know we were talking about Morecambe and Wise, you'd think we were discussing a Samuel Beckett play.

'Now I'm not suggesting Morecambe and Wise should be discussed in some high-faluting intellectual manner because I think they would find that horrifying. But, put in those terms, you can see why I think they were the greatest alternative comedians of all.'

Despite Elton's well thought out argument, the popular concept of what the term 'alternative comedy' means ensures it is not a label many others would readily apply to Morecambe and Wise. Rightly or wrongly, alternative comedy is thought of by a majority to be associated with comics who deliver a stream of bodily-function related jokes – the type of which most mature people have grown out of prior to secondary school. It is material which would have been totally alien to Morecambe and Wise.

Whichever label one wishes to apply to the brave new world of comedy, by the end of the 1980s audiences finally rebelled against this type of comedy and the old guard found themselves welcomed back after ten years in the cold. Both Frankie Howerd and Benny Hill enjoyed a brief renaissance before their sudden deaths, within hours of each other, in 1992.

That same year also saw so-called alternative comedy finally sell out to the system it had railed against for a decade when many of its exponents fell over themselves to sign up for the new Carry On film, *Carry On Columbus*.

As a comedy team, Eric and Ernie were untouched by the new trends in comedy and rarely became a target for the politically correct thought police. This was partly due to Eric's death coming in the mid-1980s; the public shock was so genuine and overwhelming that they could hardly have become a target for alternative comedians' scorn. More importantly, Eric and Ernie's act had never been racist or sexist. They, like Tommy Cooper, were the last of the great all-round family entertainers. For the new wave comics, who targeted politically-incorrect comics with all the fervour of Mary Whitehouse scanning television's output for a bared breast, Morecambe and Wise passed the PC test, and their legendary status among the general TV audience curiously did not grate with the new wave.

Only once, some years after Eric's death, were Morecambe and Wise attacked by 'alternative comedians'. In a television sketch, a skeleton was brought on with a performer impersonating Ernie. The skeleton, speaking in a voice clearly intended to be Eric's, said: 'I'm not funny any more – I'm dead.' Nobody laughed and the sketch merely ended up proving the creative desperation of its perpetrators, and resulted in an apology to the Morecambe family from Channel 4 boss, Michael Grade.

'What is comedy now?' asks Rowan Atkinson. 'It's hard to know. It seems to be only who is the latest thing. I feel that most of those comedians who worked in the 1980s were more admiring of Morecambe and Wise than they were of any other. Therefore, you've got to presume they were more in that tradition.'

Clearly the 1980s did bring in some real new comic talent, and Morecambe and Wise became a touchstone for the likes of such newcomers as Dawn French, Lenny Henry, Rik Mayall, Stephen Fry, Hugh Laurie, Ben Elton, Vic Reeves and many more, including Atkinson himself, though his comedy is clearly far removed from that of Morecambe and Wise.

'I didn't really follow that line,' explains Atkinson. 'I'm not, and never have been, a stand-up comic who could stand in front of a curtain and banter with the audience. My inspirations were Peter Cook and Dudley Moore, and *Beyond the Fringe* and all that. That was the start of my particular line in entertainment. I was in the Python tradition, I suppose, though we have a very contrasting style of comedy at the end of the day.'

Morecambe and Wise were widely accepted as the kings of comedy – a double act to be put on a pedestal alongside Eric and Ernie's own heroes and true predecessors, Laurel and Hardy.

As always with Morecambe and Wise, it wasn't the quality of the material that won them such admiration, but the way in which it was delivered, and the almost tangible magic that existed between Eric and Ernie. With Ernie setting up his punch-lines with his usual understated brilliance, Eric could have even made a shopping list sound hysterical.

Atkinson feels that the Morecambe and Wise tradition of music hall comedy is still with us, in a sense. 'Even Smith and Jones have that "and now this is us and we're going to have some slightly barbed, light-hearted banter between us" sort of thing.

'But it was the great visual of the curtain that Morecambe and Wise used so well. I loved that. Peeping around it – it's such a great yet simple device. And it's remarkable how viewers accepted that there was a curtain across the screen, and we didn't particularly need to see the edges of it. Presumably it was just hanging there in the studio. But television framing was proscenium arch framing, so we just accepted that there was a curtain.'

With nothing left to prove, and an overflow of respect and acclaim wherever they turned, the early 1980s should have been a buoyant period for the duo; a time when they could have dictated their pace of work while gently basking in the adoration they'd spent a working lifetime achieving. Indeed, in 1981, they were voted into the TV Hall of Fame, an award administered by the *TV Times*, and a singular honour.

Sadly, the promised glorious Indian summer of their career was to turn to unexpected showers. Eric's health problems were to re-occur. Eleven years had passed since his first heart attack, and the second one, striking him down one morning while he was opening the fridge door at his Harpenden home, came out of the blue. Only two of the Thames shows had been completed, with an agreed series ready to go into production.

For Eric it was back to hospitals and news updates on his physical condition: for Ernie, it was a case of back to waiting in the wings – though not in the theatrical sense he would have much preferred – patiently awaiting news on his partner's health and future prospects.

But this second attack was much more than just another setback. Though by no means an old man, Eric was in his mid-fifties. Moreover, he had achieved success on a scale far greater than anticipated. As he recuperated from his second coronary, he was given the chance to reappraise his future, using his past as a sounding-board. This forced opportunity for introspection was not only to alter the whole direction of Morecambe and Wise, but to push Eric into a whole new career as a novelist, which he would later confidently claim he found more rewarding than anything he had achieved as a comedian.

Eric's first novel, *Mr Lonely*, written during the summer of 1980,

was published by Eyre Methuen in 1981 and elicited some surprise
from his many fans. For them it was an unexpected diversion by
the great comic, but to Eric it was a natural progressive step. And
he was no novice writer. Eric and Ernie had together written scores
of scripts in their early days, and contributed much to the scripts of
Green, Hills, and then Braben. Also, Eric had made several
half-hearted attempts to write a novel, usually during quiet
moments at his holiday home in Portugal. In the early 1970s he
wrote a full outline to a comedy western, and on holiday completed
one third of a rough draft. On reading it back, he found it too Eric
Morecambe-sounding for his own liking, so binned it. It had some
interesting lines: here is where the villain makes his first
appearance. 'He surveyed the scene through narrowed eyes.
Vultures were circling above so something was clearly dead –
probably the town!'

To his surprise, Eric found *Mr Lonely* incredibly easy to write.
'Eric had held himself back for a long time,' says Joan, who
witnessed the creation of the novel. 'He thought books could only
be written by people who'd had a good education and were good
spellers. Once he gave it a go, he was surprised that he could
achieve the results he did.'

Mr Lonely tells the story of a struggling club comic called Sid
Lewis who finally hits the big time, but ends up accidentally
stabbing himself to death on a silver star he has just won at an
awards ceremony. The idea had been floating somewhere in Eric's
mind for a long time – a tragi-comedy – but it was the enforced
lay-off from performing which gave him the opportunity to get it
down on paper.

The novel was launched in a blaze of publicity at Hammicks
bookshop in Covent Garden, and was followed by a long publicity
and book-signing tour which went from London into a dozen
different provincial towns. To his delight, he found the book
favourably reviewed in serious newspapers and this, like the
Kenneth Tynan appreciation published a decade earlier, brought
home to him again just how highly the media literati thought of
Morecambe and Wise.

Two vampire novels for children quickly followed, and at the
time of his death he was working on a second adult novel, *Stella*,

which was finished by his son and published by Severn House in 1985.

From the time he started on *Mr Lonely* until his death, writing was a source of increasing pleasure for Eric. At the same time, after forty years the pleasures of the partnership were finally beginning to pall. A certain tiredness crept into his soul which became noticeable in the Thames shows to the attuned eye. The timing, the professionalism, remained; but a vital spark had been extinguished. Going through the motions of commanding the show rather than actually doing so is, perhaps, an apt way of considering what was happening. He was tiring of the supreme effort needed to keep Morecambe and Wise at their peak. Motivated by his horror of declining as Laurel and Hardy had declined, he also knew, as Ernie knew, that the effort to stave off that decline and stay ahead would increase as the years passed. There would have to be less song and dance; less hectic repartee.

He was also tired of being ill. Having recovered from the second heart attack, Eric visited Harefield hospital for tests which led to the triple by-pass operation. At the end of all this Eric acknowledged to his family that he was exhausted. 'I've still got it all up here,' he told them, tapping his head frustratedly, 'but it's here,' now tapping his chest, 'that makes it all too much.'

Although working with Ernie on the partnership had always been hard work, it had also been enormous fun. But now, somehow, the fun was beginning to fade.

As he and Ernie returned to work on a new series of Thames shows in February 1980, for the first time ever Eric began trying to justify the effort. Repeatedly he asked himself the same thing: Do I need it? It was a fair question considering the spectre of ill health that now seemed ever present.

The calls and letters from the public indicated that the shows came second to their concerns about Eric's welfare. If he and Ernie performed a hectic dance routine, they wrote or rang in to ask whether he should have been doing it and not to say whether they had actually enjoyed the routine itself.

Ernie sensed the change at once. 'He started coming along to rehearsals drained of real enthusiasm,' he recalls. 'And even when it was time to record the show, he'd lost the drive to perform.

Writing was giving him increasing satisfaction. He was tired of doing the same TV shows. And tired, too, of being the funny man.'

Eric admitted this as much himself, confessing that he no longer wanted to carry the show. He'd reached a crucial moment in his life when he needed to shed the hassle and stress that went with it all. He had reached that time in his life, spelt out by his several near misses with death, when he had to do what he wanted, not just what he was capable of and used to doing. Time was running out – though not as quickly as he realised – and he wanted fulfilment in a way that stretched beyond the Morecambe and Wise package.

'He came into the dressing-room once,' recalls Ernie of this time, 'and said he wasn't enjoying it any more. He had had enough. He felt he ought to stop. "What do you think I should do?" he asked me. "That," I said, "is only something you can decide." '

However, forty years working together is a long time whatever the profession, and Eric felt a deep sense of responsibility for his partner's future. He knew that ending his own performing career would probably sound the death knell for Ernie's – or at least of the envied position they had both grown accustomed to.

That sense of responsibility, matched by the fact that once at the studios Eric would find enough enthusiasm somewhere within that would make him agree to more work, would keep the Morecambe and Wise machine rolling right up to his death in 1984.

18

'How could he do this to me?'

Ernie Wise

Although Eric was disillusioned with comedy at this time, he couldn't bring himself to make the decision to end Morecambe and Wise. The idea had been mooted over a glass of port during the Christmas festivities of 1983. 'What do *you* reckon?' he was asking his family; but a decision that concerned perhaps the most famous double act the country had ever seen could not be lightly answered with a mere 'Yes, you should', or 'No, you shouldn't.'

He understood that he'd reached a time in his life when carrying the stress of the Morecambe and Wise show was too much, and his weariness with the shows was enhanced by his desire to pursue other activities. But it was not to be a simple decision for him, either. And as Eric himself often said, 'Ernie and I always had to fight to prove we were good from the beginning to the end. It was never easy. Never a case of suddenly making it so big we could switch off or go into automatic. It was always a struggle, but one that we won because we knew what we were capable of. We believed in ourselves.' And how do you casually put to sleep what you've spent your working life creating?

Had he fallen out with Ernie it would, ironically, have been much easier. But it was with the Morecambe and Wise act that, in a manner of speaking, he had fallen out – or at least had become disenchanted – after over four long decades.

Not that Eric was drifting around like a lost spirit with a morose expression. Far from it. He was quite looking forward to future challenges and enjoying more time with his wife, Joan. A bit of travelling appealed to him: he had for years nurtured a desire to drive the length of America's east coast, and future novels were in the pipeline.

But the Morecambe and Wise question was left floating; never really answered despite minor hints that perhaps, soon, he would announce his retirement, quickly contradicted by, 'But we could sti'l do the Christmas shows and one or two specials.'

'I'm half a star,' both Eric and Ernie would independently joke. It *was* a joke – but one which masked the stark downside of being one half of a successful double act. Although Eric and Ernie had started to make solo appearances – such as guest spots on TV panel games like *What's My Line* – the thought of either of them attempting to make comedy appearances separately had so far been unthinkable to themselves and their viewing public.

Nevertheless, appearances by both men in a solo capacity, away from comedy, though still rare, were becoming more regular. For instance, Eric appeared in a couple of short films for Anglia Television, based on poems by Sir John Betjeman. He made one in 1979 and a second in 1980. His reasons for adding to his already punishing schedule baffled Joan. 'Why did he do those films? He didn't need to. Why did he take on that extra work?'

Eric's answer was simple: he enjoyed doing them. It was something different from the usual grind. They only required a couple of days away filming on location and he was back home again. He started work on a third Betjeman film in the summer of 1982. It ran into problems and was rescheduled for production in 1984. Sadly, Eric died the week before he should have filmed his scenes.

Ernie could see that Eric was torn between his need to wind down and his natural compulsion to perform. Relaxation had not always come easy to him in the past – though after under-going heart surgery he found it easier – but wherever there was an audience he found it desperately difficult *not* to perform.

Fishing was a genuine passion for Eric and, so long as he was left to wallow in the gentle sights and sounds, he would always return uplifted and refreshed. David Fynsong, a fellow-fisher who had made up some flies for Eric, spent a day on the riverbank with him in the early 1980s. One comment made to Fynsong reveals the dilemma that was facing him:

'It's important to keep in the public eye,' he told him. 'Ernie and I don't do as much television as before so we have to make enough appearances to be recognised. If I walk down the street and no one recognises me, I'm no longer a star. You have to be a star.'

It is more the comment made by someone teetering on the brink of stardom than one who had enjoyed stardom for over two decades. Maybe this illustrates Eric failing to comprehend just how big an institution Morecambe and Wise had become. If he had never made another television appearance again, he would still have been recognised; their act would still have been a cornerstone of British comedy. And should continued stardom and recognition have meant so much? Clearly in his mind it did, even though he could have continued to enjoy it on past merit if nothing else. But he always seemed to fear Morecambe and Wise being forgotten, stemming from over two decades of hard struggle to be noticed. After recovering from his first heart attack in 1968, he wasn't even sure people would be remotely interested in their staging a comeback. That they were given a five-minute standing ovation in Bournemouth when they made their first live comeback appearance touched him deeply, but he still held that their position was always a tenuous one.

'There's a basic insecurity in all comics,' remarks Harry Secombe. 'You can't frame a round of applause: you can't put a standing ovation on your mantelpiece.'

Like Ernie, Eric had been performing in front of live audiences most of his life, and it was terribly difficult to contemplate a future without it. If his love for being an entertainer had diminished, he appeared to find it exceedingly difficult to discard being one.

Typical of the indecision he was feeling was the turn-about he had when their Thames contract came up for renewal. After much soul-searching, Eric told Joan that he would cut right back on Morecambe and Wise. Not total retirement, he insisted, but a year off from everything – what he was quick to term his sabbatical. He left home one morning to attend a meeting with Ernie and Thames executives, determined not to sign a new contract.

'That evening Eric came home,' says Joan, 'and I asked him how the meeting had gone. "Great, great," said Eric. "We've signed a marvellous contract for the next three years. We'll do a series plus a Christmas special and we're going to do some chat shows as well." '

It was a doubling of their existing commitments.

In a short time the initial euphoria of an exciting meeting waned, and the disenchantment and seemingly unanswerable question returned.

But what might have brought the double act to an end, though no one will ever know for sure, was the final result of the promised TV movie that had been such a major part of the Thames deal in 1978. It was dismal.

The opportunity to make the film had been postponed for a handful of reasons – not least, Eric's health problems. This had served only to add excitement and expectation to the final product. Called *Night Train to Murder*, it was to be the big chance to score where they had failed with Rank back in the 1960s.

Speaking of the Rank efforts, Ernie frankly admits, 'Those three films weren't much good. But we had always half hoped to do more.'

In addition to poor scripts and low budgets, the Rank films had primarily failed because the writers had not tailored the material to Eric and Ernie's individual styles. Instead, they had supplied chaotic situations bordering on cliché, which came over as mild slapstick, strung together in unlikely plots.

Night Train to Murder was intended to eradicate all memories of the disappointment of *The Intelligence Men*, *That Riviera Touch* and *The Magnificent Two*. Instead it was a major let-down that came as low as, if not lower than, their previous three outings.

Had it been made at any other time in their careers, *Night Train to Murder* might have just been another low point. But this was 1983, and it was a calamitous reminder for Eric of his recent disillusionment with the whole Morecambe and Wise business.

Sadly, it was to prove the last project they were to work on together and it remains a limp coda to their glorious career. Happily, few can even recall the film, and their tremendous track record remains undamaged by this further disappointment in the world of film.

In the story of *Night Train to Murder*, the boys basically play themselves: a double act treading the music hall boards. It is set just after the Second World War. They become embroiled in a murder mystery loosely wrapped in a Hammer House of Horror package.

Mixing horror and comedy can work: as far back as 1939, Bob Hope had scored with his first starring vehicle, *The Cat and the Canary*, which was the archetypal comedy horror movie. Abbott and Costello had achieved big success in their seemingly endless film series of the 1940s and 1950s during the course of which they comically encountered Frankenstein, the Mummy and several more horror characters.

However, *Night Train to Murder* was no *Cat and the Canary* and, for most of its running length, didn't even match *Abbott and Costello Meet Dr Jekyll and Mr Hyde*. It also lacked the great camaraderie that Hope and Crosby carried through all their *Road* movies.

Fatally, for a film intended as a comedy-thriller, what tense moments exist are diluted by the rather obvious laughs. Some of the laughs are admittedly good, but there is a lack of them to carry the film. What humour there is derives naturally from Eric and Ernie, but even here the script is not different enough from their normal comic personas to dovetail neatly into the plot, and the direction is so sluggish the viewer realises each gag long before it has been delivered.

Some of the better moments derive from clips of Eric and Ernie's variety patter, but this material was never written to be used as part of a film, and does little to improve a poor product.

What finally kills the film, though, is its pace. The Morecambe and Wise act had always been dependent on pace, on sheer speed of delivery and a quickness of thought from both partners which allowed them to react to each other instantly. But *Night Train to Murder* crawls at such a leaden pace as to leave the viewer at least two steps ahead of the plot. Consequently, after a few minutes into the story – following a ludicrous introduction with Morecambe and Wise using American accents to do an irrelevant voice-over, plus a funeral sequence for someone in the film who died during its making (but didn't really, of course) – a curiously lethargic mood sets in. And the viewer, if not making gallons of tea during the film and returning to catch the adverts, is left pondering on why on earth Eric and Ernie are in it at all. Significantly, it is only the music hall scenes depicting Eric and Ernie as a performing double act that offer any satisfaction; hardly surprising as that is what they did best. But as soon as they come out of the act and drop into their film roles, they merely become wooden impressions of how the general public would perhaps perceive Morecambe and Wise should they be spied together outside working hours.

Eric and Ernie immediately disliked the final product. 'It's not what we set out to do,' complained a miserable Eric. Ernie shrugged off the disappointment. He had always been able to leave any problems at the studio, and this was no exception. In any case, there were other matters, more important ones, concerning the attention of Morecambe and Wise. So the film they had wanted to score a triumphant hit with hadn't come off, but it was over with and, as far as Ernie was concerned, it was time to turn to those other decisions and plans.

Eric could not be so sanguine and found it near impossible to hide his extreme disappointment. Indeed, his initial reaction after a private showing was not dissimilar from when he and Ernie had been pilloried by the critics for their first TV series, *Running Wild*, back in 1954.

Eric wanted the film to be stored away for all time – though knowing that not to be a realistic proposition – or shown early evening in the children's programmes slot. Thames, who always went beyond the call of duty when it came to Morecambe and Wise, did just that, despite the not inconsiderable budget it had been allocated. The film would eventually be scheduled for afternoon transmission, though by the time it was shown then Eric would no longer be alive to face that particular ordeal.

Curiously enough, the film did all right in its unexpected time-slot. It got away from being reviewed as adult programming. Furthermore, it sold well in Europe – territories not familiar with

Eric and Ernie's TV work – with the dark action and humour, and Gothic-style settings, appealing to the Europeans.

Although a severe disappointment, this success in Europe ironically mirrored Eric's success there with his Vampire stories which were translated into German, Dutch and Spanish.

Eric did begin to cheer up, especially when he became embroiled in writing his second adult novel, *Stella* – the life story of a girl brought up in Lancaster, a town that had been very much a part of Eric's own childhood.

Stella and her sister, Sadie (a tribute to his mother), are obsessed with showbusiness. It's a dramatic rags-to-riches story that seems exceedingly similar to his own, though he always denied this, saying the similarities were few and far between. It was certainly a clever move to make the lead character a heroine rather than a hero, making it difficult for the press and reading public to draw too many parallels.

'He was getting better and better as a writer all the time,' says Joan. 'He was, let's face it, a novice to begin with, but he gradually built on that. I think he would have carried on writing for all time once he'd got into it because he just loved it.

'You know, he only did it at first out of boredom because he wasn't allowed to do much else when he was ill. But he found it came so easily. I suppose that comes from all those years of writing and working with scripts.'

In the final months of Eric's life, Ernie gradually came to accept that they had begun to pull in different directions. But, unlike Eric, who could no longer share his partner's enthusiasm or ambition, Ernie's drive remained undiminished.

'Many people have told me Eric couldn't have retired, couldn't have given up the business,' says Joan. 'But that wasn't true in 1984. I knew him better than anyone else, and although he had loved showbusiness, he'd worked in it all his life. He was getting older and had much more anxiety over his health.

'At the start of 1984, he wanted to give it all up. I certainly believe he would never have made another series of the Morecambe and Wise shows, although it's possible they would have come together to do a Christmas show.

'No one enjoyed life more than Eric. By 1984 he was yearning to continue living in good health and not jeopardise his chances for the future.'

Eric was aware that if he suffered another heart attack it would kill him. 'And if I do another Morecambe and Wise series, I'll have a heart attack,' he told Joan.

Thus Eric was convinced that life offered him a stark choice: retire or risk death. 'I was aware of his concern,' says Philip Jones. 'But even more than most pros, Eric wouldn't permit that to show to anyone other than, I suspect, his family and Ernie. He certainly wouldn't bare his soul in that way. But yes, I did know he was worried.

'There certainly wasn't any question of their contract not being renewed. We supported them through thick and thin, even to the extent of converting the contract a couple of times when he was ill, so that they had just a chat show to do.'

An accident while filming the 1983 Christmas show had seriously worried him. During a Keystone Kops sequence, Eric and Ernie were required to run at a wall. Putting rather too much effort into it, Eric had collided with the wall with such force that it had knocked his heart out of rhythm.

'It wasn't a heart attack as such,' explains Joan. 'But nobody knew that at the time and he was rushed to hospital by ambulance, which really affected his confidence.'

Eric's heart began to dominate his thoughts and in melancholic moments he could be pessimistic about his future. In July 1983, when discussing David Niven's death with Joan and a friend, Eric shocked them by saying, 'Of course, I won't be here this time next year.'

Tommy Cooper's death in 1984, in front of millions of TV viewers during the course of a live broadcast from Her Majesty's Theatre, shocked him enormously. Cooper had been friends with Eric and Ernie for more years than any of them cared to remember, and they had shared many a variety bill during the 1950s. It further underlined the risks facing Eric if he carried on.

'I was in Portugal at the time,' says Joan. 'I telephoned Eric and he was desperately sad about Tommy. He told me he thought it was awful that Tommy should have died like that: doing the jokes and then collapsing in front of everyone.'

'I've no intention of taking that sort of risk any longer,' Eric told her.

In optimistic moods, though, Eric was apt to doubt even his own mortality, and in the months of his sabbatical following completion of the 1983 Christmas show, he actively relished the prospects of retirement – travel plans, fishing and more writing. All it required was to make the decision to retire.

'Eric was a mass of contradictions,' says Ernie. 'At the start of his career he'd had Sadie to make all the decisions. Later on, I did it all. Towards the end of his life he was torn between his lack of enthusiasm to carry on and his compulsion to perform. I doubt he would have given up if he hadn't had that fatal heart attack, because not to carry on would have required a decision he was happier to let others make.'

Eric thought he had found the perfect compromise in the guest appearances he made as a panellist on *What's My Line*, which he referred to as 'fun shows'. As well as being enjoyable to do, more relevantly, they involved no effort at all. 'I go on, be myself and twelve million people see me every week,' he said. 'All I have to do is turn up.' Again there was the undertone of concern that the public would forget him should they fail to see him regularly.

Ultimately, it was death which finally robbed Eric of the opportunity of deciding upon his future. 'I've really enjoyed this year, you know,' he remarked to Joan one morning shortly before he died. 'I can see I won't have any trouble retiring because I've got the writing and the fun shows.'

The last weeks of Eric's life in 1984 were marked by contentment, an extraordinary sense of tidying up loose ends – as though he had a vague idea of what was coming – and a return to his roots in the North of England.

To the end, Eric remained a man of contradictions. So many of his actions in the spring of 1984 suggest, to Ernie and Joan and all those closest to him, that he really did have some kind of premonition.

'Eric suddenly started tidying his drawers,' recalls Joan. 'Something he hadn't done for a long time. And he did other things which might be described as putting his affairs in order.'

And while tidying up Eric found a letter he had written to Joan back in 1979 at the time of his by-pass surgery. He'd given the strictest instructions that it was only to be opened if he didn't survive the operation. The letter had remained sealed in a drawer ever since. Just one week before he died, Eric found the letter and tore it up. It was a gesture of defiance; a determination to show he was still capable of being confident about the future.

In early May, Eric went to Lancaster with Joan to attend a service to commemorate the opening of a home run by Methodist Homes for the Aged; a new building constructed behind the facade of a church. While there, Eric deliberately took time out to revisit Morecambe and relive pleasurable memories from his past.

He tried looking up a few relatives but found most were away; took Joan down to the sea-front and bought his favourite Morecambe Bay shrimps from the Trawl Shop; and visited the graves of Sadie and George.

In Lancaster itself, he went to the market – where his father had once worked – to buy black puddings and strong Lancashire cheese.

'These things he did were all very special to him,' explains Joan. 'It may just be coincidence that he did them when he had only a matter of days to live. But I find it very strange.'

Eric also behaved out of character on several occasions around this time, most notably when he lost his temper with the press – something he had never done before.

Morecambe and Wise had from the beginning enjoyed a marvellous relationship with the press. They took enormous pains, always giving good value in interviews and providing reporters with quotable lines. Both men regarded it as an essential part of their careers and had long tolerated the inevitable misquotes that arise whenever a journalist interviews a celebrity. Eric's attitude to misquotes and misrepresentations had always been shrugged off with his customary remark: 'The hardest thing to find is yesterday's newspaper.'

Inevitably, because it is in the very nature of journalism, there had been the occasional article speculating about just how friendly the two men really were off stage, and even the so-called 'exclusive' during the 1970s suggesting they were going to split up.

Both men had characteristically taken all these reports in good humour and on one occasion, during a memorable sketch with Diana Rigg, Eric had turned the wildly inaccurate speculation into an ad libbed quip to Ernie: 'Go and read the newspapers. See if we've split up again.'

But an article in a tabloid paper in 1984 inexplicably upset Eric. In retrospect a rather innocuous though mildly provocative piece of journalism, it contained some critical quotes which were supposed to have been made by Ernie.

The piece sent Eric into a rage, though Joan and the rest of his family could not see why he was so upset. He rang Ernie, who assured him that he had not said the things quoted, and Eric gradually calmed down. But his anger returned a few days later at a film première.

With their wives, they'd been invited to the function. Eric and Joan were first to arrive and happened to chat to a young journalist who, by coincidence, came from the same paper that had published the piece. The journalist asked Eric about the article and, once again, Eric flew into a rage.

On this occasion, Joan had to restrain him physically as Eric lambasted the journalist and his profession. When Ernie and Doreen arrived, Eric rushed over to his partner to tell him of his encounter with the journalist. This was witnessed by several people and wrongly interpreted later by at least one newspaper as evidence of some huge row between Eric and Ernie.

Despite this upset, Eric was looking fitter than he had done in years. He had lost weight through a strict diet, and had given up his moderate vices, like alcohol and his cigars and pipe. More than ever he was looking forward to the late spring spent near the riverbank.

But suddenly his health took a turn for the worse as he began to suffer from a stomach and chest disorder with symptoms not dissimilar to chronic indigestion. At first he was reluctant to visit the doctor, but the discomfort grew steadily worse. When he did finally see a doctor, it was thought he could possibly have a hiatus hernia.

Tests revealed this not to be the case, and an ECG examination by a heart specialist revealed nothing too sinister. But there was a slight enlargement of the heart which perturbed the specialist enough to cause him to recommend Eric re-admit himself to Harefield, so as to make absolutely sure there was nothing seriously awry. Eric at once agreed; as soon as the Spring Bank Holiday weekend was over, he said he intended to phone Harefield to make the necessary arrangements.

Privately, Eric's family were relieved as this familiar downward trend in his health had caused them concern. Though still in trim from dieting, he had developed a grey and drawn appearance as well as a hoarse voice, apparently brought about by the enlarged heart.

Nevertheless, Eric felt well enough to attend a friend's wedding on 26 May, joking in front of the video camera: 'Oh look, Thames Television have shown up.' And he was mentally preparing himself for his trip to the Rose Theatre at Tewkesbury on the following day, to appear with his friend and one-time colleague from the variety years, Stan Stennett.

In his mind, Eric had decided this kind of simple question-and-answer format in small theatres and universities was the way he could satisfy his desire to perform while enjoying the less hectic life of a full-time writer. If the show with Stennett went well in Tewkesbury, and his health sorted itself out, he would look into the possibilities of making occasional public outings.

'This is different,' he told Joan, who questioned the wisdom of going to Tewkesbury to work in front of an audience. 'It's not like television. There's no strain with this. I'll enjoy it.'

Question-and-answer sessions were not unfamiliar to Eric. He had done a couple in the seventies; one at Haberdasher's Aske's School in Elstree, and one later at the St Alban's College for Further Education. And, of course, he and Ernie had always ended their live shows with questions from the audience.

With Joan, Betty Stennett (Stan's wife) and members of Tewkesbury Town Council joining the sell-out audience, Eric and Stan took the stage for Eric to reminisce about his early life. 'Eric talked about all sorts of things,' says Joan. 'Even things he rarely mentioned, like his time as a Bevin Boy. He spoke about his early days with Ernie, and even talked about Tommy Cooper and the way he had died.'

As the performance wore on, Eric's voice became increasingly hoarse and he began drinking endless glasses of water to compensate. It was a warning of the imminent end which, when it came, was as sudden as it was unexpected.

'At the end of the show, the musicians came back onto the stage to pick up their instruments,' says Joan. 'Eric joined them and in no time developed it into a bit of nonsense with him playing the vibraphone and the sticks flying off into the audience. Suddenly the act had gone from a calm chat show into a slice of pure music hall. It was wild, noisy and energetic.'

Finally, Eric told the audience they'd had their lot and walked off stage. As he approached the people watching from the wings, he suddenly pitched forward, hit his head and lay still.

The audience, including Joan, were still clapping when someone dashed on to the stage and asked, 'Is there a doctor in the house?' – an old variety cliché, the irony of which Eric would surely have appreciated.

Miraculously, the Mayor of Tewkesbury was a doctor and his wife was a nurse, and they dashed from their seats to the wings and managed to keep Eric alive until the ambulance arrived.

Eric was unconscious but still alive during the ride to nearby Cheltenham. Once he was established in Intensive Care, Joan was allowed to sit with him and, with a nurse, made attempts to bring him round. When they asked if he could hear them, Eric clenched both their hands tightly. Then, in the early hours, his condition rapidly deteriorated; Joan was ushered promptly from the room as the medical team fought to save him. But Eric's prediction that a third attack would prove fatal was tragically realised. The heart muscle just couldn't take it.

John Eric Bartholomew – Eric Morecambe, the nation's favourite clown – was dead at the age of fifty-eight.

Joan called Ernie immediately. He was only half-awake when he took in the drastic information. Obviously Ernie, who had partnered Eric even longer than Joan had, was totally stunned. 'Forty-six years of sharing had come to an abrupt and distressing end,' he says. 'I never saw him again.'

As grief shook the very foundations of his reasoning, Ernie recalls thinking an appalling thought. 'How could he do this to me? After all we had gone through together, how could he abandon his partner?'

That sense of anger is common among spouses in the first moments of bereavement. And that is just what Ernie was: bereaved.

Together they had struggled to reach the top of their profession. Morecambe and Wise were the yardstick against which all other comedians would be measured, and found wanting. That the act would live on for ever through television repeats and video meant little to Ernie. In one phonecall he had lost his partner, his friend and his job.

And a way of life for nearly half a century had been brought to a cruel and an abrupt end.

19

*'When you're dead you probably end up
on a star, each person having his own.'*

Eric Morecambe

Everyone had known about the heart attacks and the recurring bouts of ill health and yet, if Eric Morecambe himself had seemed frail at times, somehow in the nation's consciousness there seemed to be an acceptance that Morecambe and Wise were indestructible.

The shock, therefore, when the unthinkable happened was overwhelming. Eric's death was the principal story in all news bulletins and the lead story in all newspapers. It overshadowed the Bank Holiday, as everyone realised they had lost not only a comic genius but also a man they felt was a friend.

It was decided to hold the funeral in Harpenden, since Eric had for so many years been closely associated with the town. The service itself was held at the Church of St Nicholas, with a private cremation at Garston. Eric's ashes were later buried at the church in Harpenden.

The crowds at the church for the funeral were enormous, lining the two-mile route from Eric's house to the church itself. 'They turned out in their thousands to make a public farewell to the man who'd brought so much laughter into their lives,' says Ernie, who was the focus of as much sympathy as Eric's family.

Ernie and Roy Castle both made speeches at the funeral as did Dickie Henderson, who had given a well-received address at Arthur Askey's memorial service some years earlier. So impressed had Eric been by Henderson's address on that occasion that he wrote to him: 'Your tribute to Arthur reminded us all of what a great comedian he was. I should like to book you for my funeral just to remind everyone what a great comic *I* was. P.S. I'll pay you when I see you – down there.'

In the weeks that followed Eric Morecambe's death, there was a period of readjustment for both his family and Ernie as they all had to try to accept that this remarkable man had gone and that it wasn't some kind of elaborate, nightmarish gag. For months those closest to him truly felt he might suddenly come lumbering along in cloth cap and raincoat, a carrier-bag in one hand and a gormless expression on his face, and say, 'Evenin' all ...' and ask what was going on.

Thames Television organised their own tribute, called *Bring Me Sunshine*, which was held at the London Palladium in aid of the British Heart Foundation. It raised a considerable sum for the charity, had Prince Philip as the main guest and saw some of the biggest names in British entertainment queuing up to appear. Hosted by Ernie, they included Bruce Forsyth, Mike Yarwood, Elaine Paige, Roy Castle, Cannon and Ball, Jim Davidson, Jimmy Tarbuck and, of course, Des O'Connor. 'Before singing, I made some remark about there being one less light on the Christmas tree that year,' remembers O'Connor, 'and I was so choked up I could hardly get through the song that I was leading into.'

For Ernie, the years following Eric's death were not always easy. Still remarkably eager and ambitious, inevitably he had problems. Despite having developed way beyond the standard funny man feed format of traditional double acts, Ernie was still essentially the 'feed' part of Morecambe and Wise. People outside showbusiness rarely understand the intricacies of the two roles, and wrongly assume that one was funny and the other less so.

'I've a feeling that the audience put me slightly lower than Eric in the pecking order,' admitted Ernie in a TV interview in 1993. But if he was hurt by that, he never let it show and, for the most part, accepted it for what it was: an inescapable fact of life.

Nevertheless, he had only been a star as part of the team of Morecambe and Wise. Ernie had not been known as a solo performer since the 1940s and so, in 1984, he found himself in an unusual and wholly unenviable position. He was fit, still comparatively young at fifty-eight, full of zest and talent and still irresistibly drawn to the business he'd lived in since childhood. But this was a desperate position with a bizarre twist, for now he was a wealthy, successful and respected performer with nowhere to go to sell his wares. All the gags and the routines worked at for over forty years were now useless to him. If he was to survive in the professional world he would have to develop a whole new act, and accept that his standing must inevitably be lower than he had grown accustomed to.

The need to re-establish some kind of performing career was all the more telling in Ernie's case because he'd been performing since the age of three. But while he was still coming to terms with his new status as a solo act, the feeling of being alone and of having to strike out in a new direction in life was emphasised just months after Eric's death when his mother, Connie, died at the age of eighty-five. Suddenly Ernie found great chunks of his life breaking away from him, forcing him to question and reassess the whole pattern of security in his life.

Security in showbusiness is, at best, ephemeral; for the first time since he and Eric had struggled to get their foothold in variety, Ernie's future was uncertain. The uncertainty was tempered by the rewards and success he had encountered as half of Morecambe and Wise, but Ernie did not want to sit at home reflecting on past achievements. Repeated bouts of ill health had led Eric to consider retiring, but Ernie had always been thinking of new challenges – first for the double act, and now for himself.

'The simple truth is that without an act I lost all clout in the profession,' admits Ernie candidly. 'I've got the respect and the reputation, but no longer the power. Once the sympathy after Eric's death had worn off, I was back among the harsh realities of showbusiness. And the bitter truth is that though Eric and I left a wonderful legacy, people in the business don't think you can do anything on your own.'

Philip Jones believes Ernie was in a very difficult position at the time. 'Indeed, I think he always has been. Eric was the laughter-maker and, as such, obviously the part of the act which scored most heavily with audiences. Everybody loves a funny man: men and women.'

There were suggestions that Ernie might team up with another performer in a new double act. Bernie Winters was one suggestion; Eric Sykes – with whom Ernie could once again be in a double act called Eric and Ernie – was another.

Sensibly, Ernie laughed off the suggestions, concluding rightly that the public would not accept him in a double act with any other performer. And Ernie was also aware that anything he did must not risk damage to the magic that had gone before – the work of Morecambe and Wise had to remain unblemished.

The clout may have gone, but the ambition was still burning as fiercely as ever. 'I'm still waiting for a Hollywood mogul to come up and say, "I'm going to make you a star",' Ernie told the *Radio Times* in 1993. 'I've had that thought ever since I was nine and watched Mickey Rooney on film. He was surrounded by lovely girls, wore nice suits and borrowed his dad's car. "That's the life, I thought." Most people accept what they have. I don't. I'm an optimist with the aspirations of a teenager, always looking over to the other side of the fence.'

As the years wore on, some commentators found Ernie's naked ambition rather sad. It suited editors to portray this man as forlorn; a rather pathetic figure, lost after the death of his partner. And Ernie's oft-repeated saying that he was still on his way to Hollywood – which he used as the title of his 1990 autobiography – in their view fitted that pigeonholing perfectly.

Ernie Wise, though, is far from being a sad, pathetic little man, whatever anyone may say. 'Still on my way to Hollywood' is a phrase which perfectly encapsulates his life and his work. 'I know it's all fantasy,' he says, 'that it's just a bit of fun. But sometimes you're taken too seriously when really you're being light-hearted.'

After the *Bring Me Sunshine* tribute at the Palladium, Ernie sensibly kept a low profile for several months before embarking on a solo project in Australia.

Morecambe and Wise had always been extremely popular with Australian audiences, and in 1985 Ernie was approached by the Australian agent Lionel Abrahams to appear in a three-month one-man tour of theatres, clubs and hotels. For Ernie it was a chance to return to the very roots of his showbusiness life as a song-and-dance man.

By chance, Rowan Atkinson was on the same flight as Ernie. 'I was also on my way to Perth to do a one-man show,' says Atkinson. 'I remember thinking with some interest, "What is an Ernie Wise one-man show going to be like?" And I recall wishing him the best of luck with it more sincerely than I've ever wished anyone the best of luck with anything. I hope it worked out all right for him. I think the idea was for him to try it out over there and if it went well to then do it over here.'

Ernie opened the show with a medley of songs he and Eric had performed, such as *Bring Me Sunshine* and *Following You Around*, and these were then followed up with a few gags, more songs and then requests from the audience. He also incorporated a nostalgia spot during which slides of Eric and Ernie's lives and careers were projected on to a screen while Ernie casually commented on the pictures. It was not very dissimilar in format from Eric's own intentions, had he lived.

The show, combining a gentle evening of memories with a showcase from Ernie's song and dance repertoire, was a big success with audiences on a tour that took him from Perth to Adelaide and on to Sydney.

For whatever reason, Ernie decided not to take the show on tour in Britain, despite offers to do so, but didn't totally discard the idea. He performed a similar show on the *QE2* liner, talking about his life accompanied by videos, and he received a standing ovation. 'Mind you,' he quipped at the time, 'they hadn't paid to see me. That makes a difference. Maybe that's what I should do from now on, give free shows.' He worked aboard the *QE2* again just before Christmas 1993.

But the real departure for Ernie came with the 1987 musical, *The Mystery of Edwin Drood* at the Savoy Theatre in London's West End.

The musical was based on Dickens' last unfinished novel and had been a smash hit on Broadway, groaning under the weight of its own Emmy awards. 'I was knocked out when I read the script and heard the score for the first time,' says Ernie. Here at last was a truly thrilling prospect for the man who had always dreamed of Hollywood. He wasn't Hollywood-bound, but at least Broadway was coming to him – something he'd longed for.

The Mystery of Edwin Drood came to London with guaranteed success written all over it, and not only because it looked set to repeat its glittering dollar-raking Broadway sell-out run in the West End. In the mid-to-late 1980s, the West End musical was approaching the zenith of its blockbusting popularity with the inexorable rise of composer Andrew Lloyd Webber and impresario Cameron Mackintosh.

Between them, sometimes together though more often apart, these two men were already responsible for the smash hits *Cats*, *The Phantom of the Opera* and *Les Misérables*, all of them playing to sell-out crowds at every performance. *Aspects of Love* and *Miss Saigon* were on the horizon, and audiences had suddenly developed musical mania.

Critics were already beginning to complain about the dominance of musicals in the West End, to the detriment of the straight play: but audiences didn't care. With ticket prices constantly on the increase and a theatre visit to London often requiring an overnight stay, a night out in the West End was becoming more than ever a major financial investment for audiences, and a spectacular musical offered the best chance of getting value for money. Those unable to see an unrecognisable Michael Crawford beneath the Phantom's mask, or to watch the brave revolutionaries perish nightly on the barricades in *Les Misérables*, looked around for the next best alternative. Other shows, therefore, benefited.

Since *Oliver*, a previous musical adaptation of a Dickens novel, had proved one of the most popular and enduring musicals of all time, the omens were pretty good for *The Mystery of Edwin Drood*. It even came with the added attractive theatrical gimmick of an alternative ending. The novel having been left unfinished, the writers for the show decided to let the audience decide which ending they wanted. Ernie was very impressed by the quality of the script and the score, and he accepted the offer immediately. He knew, however, that it was a huge challenge and would be both physically and mentally daunting.

A major West End or Broadway musical is the theatrical equivalent of the D-Day landings, every performer carefully choreographed. Although he and Eric had worked very hard at their shows, they had had the freedom and ability to ad lib and occasionally depart from the script. *Edwin Drood* would not allow Ernie the luxury of such freedom: he had to stick to the script in both movement and spoken word.

Always the professional, Ernie knew that even though he was a veteran he was a novice in the arena he was stepping into and he was determined to learn the immense and complicated script before rehearsals. He was word-perfect on the day of the first read-through; a gargantuan effort from a man who, by his own admission, doesn't find it easy to learn his lines.

Ernie was cast in the role of William Cartwright, a kind of chairman for the piece, and he was on stage throughout the entire proceedings. Thus Ernie was responsible for maintaining the pace of the show by moving the story on from sequence to sequence. Joining him in the cast were Lulu and Julia Harris, and as rehearsals progressed and opening night approached, Ernie became increasingly convinced that the show would be the smash hit in London that it had been on Broadway. Sadly, the critics thought otherwise.

After staggering along for a ten-week run, *The Mystery of Edwin Drood* closed on 4 July 1987. For Ernie it was a body-blow, Independence Day proving to be the end, not the beginning, of his first attempt to live independently of Morecambe and Wise.

It wasn't, though, the end of Ernie's West End career. A few months later he was asked to play the part of Detective Sergeant Porterhouse in Ray Cooney's long-running farce, *Run For Your Wife*. He took over the part from Eric Sykes, and enjoyed a successful run lasting several months.

After *Run For Your Wife*, Ernie was less in the public eye for several years. The problem of establishing himself away from Morecambe and Wise seemed, curiously, more acute now than it had done in the couple of years immediately following Eric's death.

The roles he was being offered reflected this. There were, for instance, many offers of pantomime – in which he would be acting as feed to another comic. But Ernie had only ever appeared in panto with Eric, and did not, initially at least, relish playing straight man to other, inevitably lesser, comics.

Ernie did not, however, disappear totally in the late 1980s and early 1990s. He continued to make guest appearances on television panel and games shows like Channel 4's *Countdown*, and he devoted some of his time to charity.

In 1989, fifty years after he had first met John Eric Bartholomew in Manchester, he raised money for the heart charity Corda by flying around the world, dressed as Phileas Fogg, in eighty hours. Marty Christian of the New Seekers accompanied him, dressed as his manservant.

The drive to reach Hollywood in some form remains floating, half-seriously, in Ernie's mind. As he approached then passed, the statutory retirement age of sixty-five, he found his enthusiasm and ambition for working to be as strong as ever. This emerged as a major theme in his autobiography. Dedicated to 'Eric – the best partner a man could have,' in it he wrote candidly of his feelings about being out of the spotlight at that time. 'The fact is I'm not happy out of showbusiness. I enjoy the company of pros, enjoy talking to them, swapping stories, reliving old times.'

Finally, the allure of performing proved too strong, and Ernie was back in the spotlight within three years of writing that sentence. Throughout 1992 there had been a resurgence of interest in Morecambe and Wise with many more videos of their work released – including material from their *Two of a Kind* ATV series – and a reflection through the pages of the press that revealed the British public's immense dissatisfaction with the state of TV comedy. The names of Morecambe and Wise cropped up frequently as an example of all that used to be good about British comedy.

The alternative wave had waned and although the real talents, such as Fry and Laurie, French and Saunders, Ben Elton and Rowan Atkinson, had emerged and endured, the new comedy culture was not to everybody's taste. Audiences – and not just older ones – acquired a taste for nostalgic samples of earlier comedy shows.

Old comics such as Norman Wisdom, Frankie Howerd and Ernie himself, began to be cherished by viewers who'd seen them first time round, but also by those who were seeing them, often in grainy black-and-white repeats, for the very first time.

Once again, new double acts were being labelled as, 'The new Morecambe and Wise'. French and Saunders and Vic Reeves and Bob Mortimer in particular were thus tagged, the latter duo once being described as 'Morecambe and Wise on speed'.

But the label 'The new Morecambe and Wise' remained the last refuge of lazy hacks, a fact acknowledged by everyone who knew, had worked with or admired the work Eric and Ernie had done.

'There can't be another Eric and Ernie,' explains Philip Jones. 'It's a funny thing, but although the Morecambe and Wise shows are still as funny as ever, they are quite definitely of their time. Comedy has moved into such different areas. It's raunchy, more cruel and Eric and Ernie could never have been cruel in the way TV comics are now. Besides, how could there be another Morecambe and Wise? How could there be another Tommy Cooper? Or Frankie Howerd?'

The resurgence of interest in Morecambe and Wise was a direct consequence of the nostalgia boom, and this was the principal reason that the producers of BBC2's prestigious documentary programme *40 Minutes*, approached Ernie to make a film about him which eventually went out in March 1993, under the suspiciously defensive title, 'The Importance Of Being Ernie'. It followed Ernie returning to his roots in Leeds and Blackpool, preparing for panto in Windsor, and included excerpts from classic Morecambe and Wise shows.

Like many other people, the programme's makers chose to regard Ernie's role as King in *Sleeping Beauty* at Windsor in 1992 as some kind of comeback. This, of course, was incorrect. Ernie hadn't actually been away.

He was older, maybe even semi-retired, but he had not fully retired. And a short panto season was in theory a good tonic for an old pro wanting to keep his hand in.

After years of resisting offers of pantomime, he agreed to appear in this production aware, perhaps, that as he was now in his late sixties it was going to get tougher to find motivation with each passing year, however ambitious he clearly was deep inside.

'It was one of those things where you try to recapture your youth,' he gaily admits. 'My doctor was amazed that I'd agreed to do pantomime, which is exhausting, at sixty-seven. But why not? I was as physically and mentally fit as ever, and I thoroughly enjoyed it.

'I'm still young in mind and spirit,' he says. 'Although I have to be careful what I eat and take half an aspirin a day to keep my cholesterol levels down. My legs still move and I can dance. And every so often the urge to perform comes over me strongly.'

Physically and mentally fit he may have been, but Ernie found that the dust and the heat of the theatre – something that had always been a minor problem for him – had become a major problem after several years away. Nevertheless, he was popular with audiences, and performed a kind of double act on stage with his co-star, Bryan Burdon, with whom he enjoyed a tremendous rapport.

A year later, at the end of 1993, Ernie's health and future would need greater consideration. Suffering a minor stroke that left him in hospital over Christmas, not materialising from hospital until early 1994, he would spend the winter months recovering at his Florida home.

Rehearsals for the pantomime of 1992, with Bryan Burdon, were filmed by the *40 Minutes* documentary team, but by that time Ernie was already having doubts about just how the programme would choose to portray him. Even before transmission he was expressing those doubts to the *Radio Times*.

'It's almost too probing,' he commented. 'About the only thing not asked is how much I have in the bank. I don't like being psychoanalysed. I'm getting to the age where I need that old seventh veil, a little privacy.'

Just a week before the transmission date, Ernie confessed to the authors of this book that he thought he'd made a mistake in agreeing to do it. Sadly, his misgivings proved to be well founded when 'The Importance Of Being Ernie' brought him the most hostile press he'd endured since *Running Wild*.

Basically, 'The Importance Of Being Ernie' was a send-up of Ernie Wise. The mockery wasn't overt but it permeated the whole programme. With the twin themes of 'still on my way to Hollywood' and the forlorn partner left behind without an act, it was blended together with carefully chosen clips from Ernie's glory days with Eric. These clips – routines such as Eric asking Ernie what he actually did in their act – were deliberately lifted out of their original context and inserted into the documentary as some kind of question mark over Ernie's ability and general contribution to the Morecambe and Wise partnership.

Those who knew Ernie well could not equate the rather sad, pathetic figure portrayed through the selective editing of the programme to the man they really knew. But those who knew him not at all, most significantly the press, seized venomously on it as a weapon with which to launch attacks.

His contribution to the Morecambe and Wise partnership was derided. More than one reviewer suggested Eric would have been successful without Ernie, but Ernie would have achieved nothing without Eric. One of the most hurtful comments came from a journalist who asked: 'If the roles had been reversed and Eric had survived, would anyone bother to make a programme about life after Ernie?'

Fortunately, those people in the industry who understood anything about comedy knew that such comments could come only from journalists who knew little of what they were writing about, and they went out of their way to defend him.

'I hope Ernie took no notice of those comments,' says Bill Cotton. 'He knows perfectly well that the part he played in the act was bound to make people say that. That was his value. He played his part so well that he appeared to be contributing nothing. It was just like when Dean Martin and Jerry Lewis split up. When that happened, everyone thought Lewis would emerge as the big comedian. But, as we all know, Dean Martin ended up coming out of the split best because he was a great straight man as well.'

As Eric himself once wrote of his partner, 'He's part of an act called Morecambe and Wise and not Eric Morecambe and That Fellow He Works With.'

'Ernie got a very unfair press out of that programme,' says Philip Jones, who talked to him the night the documentary had been screened. 'He didn't deserve the slating he got for it. People misunderstood him. He wasn't saying that he thought he was star material for Hollywood. He was saying that he'd like to be serenaded by Hollywood. There's a big difference. When you know Ernie well, you know that he jokes about it and we all pull his leg. That's fine. Sadly, in that documentary it came over to the press that he was serious.'

'Their relationship was the essence of the two of them,' says Rowan Atkinson. 'When Eric died a lot of people said, "Well, that's the end of that act because the funny one's gone." But I never really saw it that way. I kept trying to imagine what Eric would have been like without Ernie. I always thought that all those people who said Ernie would be a bit of a sad act now Eric's gone should have thought what a sad act Eric would have been without Ernie, because it was their relationship which mattered, as is always the case in a double act.

'Though one appears to be blatantly more talented than the other, and talent is important and the jokes are important, and that Eric was clearly the more funny of the two, it was actually the chemistry that people tended to identify with.'

For Ben Elton, the 40 Minutes documentary was clearly a mistake for Ernie. 'The trouble is, I don't think Ernie is his own best advocate,' he says. 'But then why should he be? He likes to work, he likes to be on TV and he likes to talk about his extraordinary career. And rightly so.

'But he's not a great analyst or theorist, so he can't be illuminating about what was an instinctive partnership. Come to think about it, I don't think Eric could ever be illuminating about it either.

'But then why is there any need to be illuminating about Morecambe and Wise? It's all up there on screen – that which the bloody BBC have still got and haven't wiped. You can't judge Morecambe and Wise by what Ernie or anybody else says about them: the only way to judge Morecambe and Wise is to watch Morecambe and Wise. And anyone who does that can have no doubts about their extraordinary partnership.

'The reason why all other double acts have paled into insignificance was because of the quality of the Morecambe and Wise act and because of Eric and Ernie's unique individual characters within that act.'

There is no doubt that the ill-informed critical reaction to 'The

Importance Of Being Ernie' hurt but, after the initial wounds had begun to heal, Ernie could console himself with the truth of his achievements with Eric.

No matter what he has done since Eric's death – and no matter what he chooses and is able to do in the future – no one can take away from Ernie that he was exactly one half of the finest, the most popular and celebrated, of British double acts. For just as Stan Laurel is unthinkable without Oliver Hardy, so Eric Morecambe is unthinkable without Ernie Wise.

Michael Parkinson once said that while we continue to have a sense of humour we'll laugh at Morecambe and Wise. And he's right. Morecambe and Wise are legends of comedy and like all icons of entertainment, they are so because they are both timeless and of their time. They are of their time in the sense that there never will or can be another Morecambe and Wise. In evolving the male double act to its most perfectly developed level, they drew a line under it in the process and effectively ended the tradition.

But they are timeless in the way Hancock, Cooper and Sellers are timeless: audiences who appreciate fine comedy will always laugh at them. And for Morecambe and Wise, their timelessness has nothing to do with the quality of their gags, the lavishness of their shows, the fame of their guest stars, nor even their own unassailable reputation.

The reason is something far simpler than all that.

It is because for forty-three years, John Eric Bartholomew and Ernest Wiseman enjoyed being Eric and Ernie.

And for forty-three years audiences enjoyed watching them enjoy being Eric and Ernie.

Epilogue

1994 saw an unprecedented renaissance of Morecambe and Wise: one which stunned television executives and finally established Eric and Ernie's place in history as the British public's all-time favourite comedy team.

Although Morecambe and Wise repeats had been popular on TV and video compilations of their shows – from ATV's *Two of a Kind*, through the classic BBC era, to the Thames years – had sold extremely well, as the tenth anniversary of Eric's death approached the public profile of Morecambe and Wise was elevated to a new level.

The renaissance began in earnest at Christmas 1993 when an hour-long video compilation of some of the most memorable moments from Eric and Ernie's BBC Christmas Shows, *Eric and Ernie's Christmas Cracker*, became one of the bestselling videos of the year. It was so successful, in fact, that it was repackaged for Christmas 1994 and a new compilation of Eric and Ernie's musical numbers released as a companion volume.

That same year – Christmas 1993 – the prestigious London store Liberty's highlighted two of Eric and Ernie's best-loved dance routines in their Christmas window display: the classic *Stripper* and *Singin' In The Rain*. Both routines, choreographed to comic perfection by Ernest Maxin, were broadcast to Christmas shoppers on continuous video loops through Liberty's windows and huge crowds gathered in Regent Street outside to watch.

On Christmas night, BBC1 Controller Alan Yentob scheduled a repeat screening of Eric and Ernie's BAFTA-winning 1977 *Christmas Show*: their last ever for the BBC and the one which earned them a place in television history with twenty-eight million viewers. The repeat did not begin until nearly midnight and finished long after. Nevertheless, it still managed to attract nearly twelve million viewers. This encouraged Alan Yentob to commission three tribute shows to Morecambe and Wise which would commemorate the tenth anniversary of Eric's death in May 1994. Ernest Maxin, Eric and Ernie's long-time choreographer who was also their producer/director between 1974 and 1978, was drafted in to oversee the production of the tribute shows. It was an astute decision since Maxin, like Eddie Braben, understands Morecambe and Wise better than most.

The shows were scheduled across three Saturdays in May 1994: the first to coincide with what would have been Eric's sixty-eighth birthday on 14 May, the last to coincide with the tenth anniversary of his death.

Ben Elton was a controversial choice to host the programmes and many critics thought his involvement was out of place. But there was no mistaking his genuine enthusiasm for and appreciation of Eric and Ernie, and Elton's presence, plus the contributions of contemporary acts like Fry and Laurie and Hale and Pace, merely reinforced the obvious conclusion that Eric and Ernie really were 'The Masters'. Hale and Pace stated unequivocally that 'Morecambe and Wise were the best and the greatest double-act there's ever been'. And Stephen Fry commented that their *Stripper* routine was 'a classic piece of showbusiness history performed with panache and élan'.

The tribute shows also featured contributions from guest stars like Glenda Jackson, John Thaw and the late Roy Castle and they were accompanied by scores of articles in tabloid and broadsheet alike – each one deifying Morecambe and Wise.

When the ratings came in for the first tribute show screened on Saturday 14 May, 1994, it became apparent that Morecambe and Wise had lost none of their appeal. The tribute shows became the entertainment hit of the summer and were second only to *EastEnders* in BBC1's ratings. Furthermore, audience appreciation figures – always a more accurate guide to what audiences have enjoyed – were phenomenal and when the audience profiles were examined they revealed that children who had not been born when Eric died had enjoyed the shows as much as anyone else. A new generation of Morecambe and Wise fans had been created.

Stunned by the success of the first tribute shows, Alan Yentob immediately ordered that another three compilation shows be rushed into production so that what he had envisaged as a three-

part series could be extended to six. The last three appeared without
the presence of Ben Elton or any other contributors but, even if the
hastiness of their production was occasionally apparent, the second
batch of three shows perpetuated the astonishing ratings of the first
three. Not surprisingly, Alan Yentob scheduled a repeat of Eric and
Ernie's 1971 *Christmas Show* – considered by many their finest hour
with the classic Shirley Bassey and André Previn routines – for
Christmas Night 1994. Again, it proved the highlight of Christmas
television for millions of viewers.

Once rekindled, the interest in Eric and Ernie did not abate,
although Ernie's recurring bouts of poor health throughout 1994
sadly prevented him playing as active a part in the commemorations
as had been hoped.

Indeed, as 1994 gave way to 1995, Eric and Ernie's legion of fans
were delighted by news that the lives of Morecambe and Wise were
to be celebrated in a major West End show which would trace their
story from 1939 to 1984.

Called *Behind The Sunshine: The Morecambe and Wise Story*, the
script is by Gary Morecambe and Martin Sterling – authors of this
book, on which the show is based. Ernest Maxin has joined the
production as director and Eddie Braben has supplied additional
material. Thus, the stage show reunites essential elements of the
original team which made the Morecambe and Wise shows everlast-
ing classics.

The Sunshine is back.

Index